The problems of evil and suffering have been extensively discussed in Jewish philosophy, and much of the discussion has centred on the Book of Job. In this new study Oliver Leaman poses two questions: how can a powerful and caring deity allow terrible things to happen to obviously innocent people, and why has the Jewish people been so harshly treated throughout history, given its status as the chosen people? He explores these issues through an analysis of the views of Philo, Saadya, Maimonides, Gersonides, Spinoza, Mendelssohn, Hermann Cohen, Buber, Rosenzweig, and post-Holocaust thinkers, and suggests that a discussion of evil and suffering is really a discussion about our relationship with God. The Book of Job is thus both the point of departure and the point of return.

The
Wiesel, Nobel lecture

nobelprize.org/nobel prizes/
peace/laureates/1986/
wiesel-lecture.html

A Jew Today

CAMBRIDGE STUDIES IN RELIGIOUS TRADITIONS 6

EVIL AND SUFFERING
IN JEWISH PHILOSOPHY

CAMBRIDGE STUDIES IN RELIGIOUS TRADITIONS

Edited by John Clayton (University of Lancaster), Steven Collins (University of Chicago) and Nicholas de Lange (University of Cambridge)

1. *Religion and the individual: A Jewish perspective*
   Louis Jacobs
2. *The body divine: the symbol of the body in the works of Teilhard de Chardin and Rāmānuja*
   Anne-Hunt Overzee
3. *The feminine principle in the Sikh vision of the Transcendent*
   Nikky-Guninder Kaur Singh
4. *The religious culture of India: Power, love and wisdom*
   Friedhelm Hardy
5. *Women under the Bō tree: Buddhist nuns in Sri Lanka*
   Tessa Bartholomeusz
6. *Evil and suffering in Jewish philosophy*
   Oliver Leaman

EVIL AND SUFFERING IN JEWISH PHILOSOPHY

OLIVER LEAMAN

Reader in Philosophy
Liverpool John Moores University

CAMBRIDGE
UNIVERSITY PRESS

PUBLISHED BY THE PRESS SYNDICATE OF THE UNIVERSITY OF CAMBRIDGE
The Pitt Building, Trumpington Street, Cambridge CB2 1RP, United Kingdom

CAMBRIDGE UNIVERSITY PRESS
The Edinburgh Building, Cambridge CB2 2RU, United Kingdom
40 West 20th Street, New York, NY 10011-4211, USA
10 Stamford Road, Oakleigh, Melbourne 3166, Australia

First published 1995
First paperback edition 1997

Typeset in 11/13 Monotype Baskerville

A catalogue record for this book is available from the British Library

Library of Congress cataloguing in publication data

Leaman, Oliver.
Evil and suffering in Jewish philosophy / Oliver Leaman.
p.   cm. – (Cambridge studies in religious traditions; 6)
Includes bibliographical references and index.
ISBN 0 521 41724 4 (hardback)
1. Good and evil (Judaism). 2. Suffering – Religious aspects –
Judaism. 3. Judaism – Doctrines. 4. Philosophy, Jewish. 5. Bible.
O.T. Job – Criticism, interpretation, etc., Jewish. I. Title.
II. Series.
BJ1401.L35   1995
296.3´.11 – dc20   94-33186   CIP

ISBN 0 521 41724 4 hardback
ISBN 0 521 42722 3 paperback

Transferred to digital printing 2003

תּוֹרַת חָכָם מְקוֹר חַיִּים
לָסוּר מִמֹּקְשֵׁי מָוֶת

The teaching of the wise is a fountain of life
To depart from the snares of death. (Proverbs 13:14)

In fond and respectful memory of Dr Erwin Rosenthal

Contents

Preface	*page* xi	
List of abbreviations	xii	
	Introduction	1
1	Job	19
2	Philo	33
3	Saadya	48
4	Maimonides	64
5	Gersonides	102
6	Spinoza	121
7	Mendelssohn	146
8	Cohen	157
9	Buber	165
10	The Holocaust	185
11	Back to the Bible	220
Bibliography	251	
Further reading	253	
Index	255	

Preface

It seems to me to be surprising that more has not been written on the ways in which the Jewish philosophical tradition dealt with the topics of evil and suffering. These topics have been discussed extensively right up to the present time, and more recent disasters such as the Holocaust have renewed the search for a satisfactory resolution of the apparent contradiction between a good and omnipotent God and the suffering of the innocent. It is argued in this book that there is a tradition of dealing with these topics within Jewish philosophy, and it is my intention to outline it for readers. The text presupposes no knowledge whatsoever of either philosophy or Judaism.

I should like to thank a number of people and institutions for their help in writing this book. My college library has been very helpful in getting books and articles for me. I have had interesting discussions with John Clayton and Paul Morris about the topic. An anonymous reader for Cambridge University Press made interesting suggestions. The main debt I have is to the undergraduates whom I have taught, and also to the students at St Francis Xavier College during my term working there. I presented some of the ideas in this book at conferences in Paris, Cambridge, Newcastle upon Tyne, London, and Wolfenbüttel. I am grateful to the participants for their comments and advice. Christine Lyall Grant and Alex Wright made many useful suggestions for improving the style of the text. None of the above is to be blamed for anything in the book, which represents only my views and arguments.

This is the first time that I am unable to thank Dr Erwin Rosenthal for his advice, since sadly he died when I had just started writing this book. He has in the past been a formidable critic and a very encouraging commentator on what I have written, and I missed his advice very keenly in preparing this work. I am sure that there is much in it with which he would have disagreed, but I should like in any case to dedicate it to him. I hope that he would have felt that the book is not entirely unworthy of being associated with him in this way.

xi

Abbreviations

Philo
Abr. — *De Abrahamo*
Decal. — *De decalogo*
Op. — *De opificio mundi*
Spec. leg. — *De specialibus legibus*

Saadya
BBO — *Book of Beliefs and Opinions*
BT — *Book of Theodicy*

Maimonides
GP — *Guide of the Perplexed*

Gersonides
J — *Commentary of the Book of Job*

Spinoza
E — *Ethics*, in *Collected Works*, vol. I.
Short Treatise — *Short Treatise on God, Man and his Wellbeing*

Mendelssohn
Jerusalem — *Jerusalem or on Religious Power and Judaism*
MM — *Moses Mendelssohn: A Biographical Study*, by Alexander Altmann

Cohen
Religion of Reason — *Religion of Reason out of the Sources of Judaism*

Rosenzweig
GS — *Gesammelte Schriften*

Leaman
Averroes — *Averroes and his Philosophy*
Introduction — *An Introduction to Medieval Islamic Philosophy*

Translations are taken from the references in the bibliography, occasionally modified by me. Passages from Maimonides are normally adapted from the translations found in either Pines or Leibowitz. Passages from the Bible are modified versions of the translation found in *The Holy Scriptures* (Philadelphia, Jewish Publications Society of America, 1917).

Introduction

At one level it is easy to see why the topics of evil and suffering have been so much discussed in Jewish philosophy. The Jewish people have had a bumpy ride along the historical road and the question of why the innocent suffer arises for most Jews at most times. There have not been many periods during which there has been no persecution of Jews at least somewhere, and it is natural for the objects of the persecution to wonder why they are being subjected to such treatment. This is certainly not to suggest that this is an issue which only occurs in the thinking of Jews. Ever since human beings were able to stand back from the immediate exigencies of their lives and consider why the world is arranged as it is they have asked the questions 'Why is there evil in the world?'. 'Why do apparently good people suffer?' 'What is the point of suffering?' Not only do these questions take place on a personal level, but they also occur for groups, and many groups in history have been persecuted for the sole reason that they differed from more powerful or numerous groups, so that it is possible to differentiate at least two versions of the problem of suffering. One problem is to explain why individuals suffer although they are innocent. The other problem is to explain why individuals suffer as result of their membership of particular groups. Neither of these questions is in any way limited to Jews.

Jews have, however, asked themselves these questions frequently for a number of reasons. In the first place, Israel is supposed to be the chosen people of God through whom God's work of redemption will take place in the world. Israel made a covenant with God, and as a result of that agreement might expect preferential treatment by the deity, provided that it kept its side of the contract. Israel is the nation to which God has attached his name, and anyone who attacks Israel attacks God. It might seem rather surprising, then, that the Jewish people have had such a difficult time, since there has been plenty of scope for God to intervene on behalf of his people. There are frequent references in the Bible, especially in the Psalms, to God's assistance and the dramatic effect it had on Israel's enemies, yet not a great deal of evidence from history that much of this went on. As we shall see, there is a variety of explanations for this state of affairs, and the explanations involve a particular interpretation of Jewish history. But in addition to the specifically Jewish aspect of the problem there is the entirely general question as to why the innocent suffer in a world created by a God. These topics are often intertwined in the literature, and we will show that Jewish philosophers had some very interesting comments to make about them.

A whole range of philosophical questions arise here, and in this book we will not be considering directly some of them. How can an omnipotent God be omniscient and immutable at the same time? If God can do anything, can he know what is going to happen in the future and affect what the future is going to be, so that the apparently contingent events in the world are really necessitated by his decisions? If he knows what goes on in the world, then his thoughts must change, and so he cannot be unchanging. How can we reconcile a God without sensory equipment with knowledge of the ordinary world? Can a God who concentrates upon abstract and universal matters know what takes place in the contingent realm? Are there any limitations on God's power? I have discussed some of these issues in my previous books, and the central concern here is not with these logical problems about how to reconcile God with his putative attributes. The central issue of the book is this. Let us take it that according to the Jewish religion God is omnipotent, omniscient and good. Let us also accept that he has a particular interest in the fate of Jews, both individually and as a group. How is it, then, that so many individual Jews, either as individuals or as members of a group, have suffered in the world although they appear to be innocent of any wrongdoing? This is part of a question which certainly has broader scope, namely, why would a good God allow evil in the world? If God could prevent evil from occurring, which we might expect him to be able to do given his power, why does he not prevent it from affecting our lives? This issue will also be discussed in the book, since it is vital for an understanding of the problem in so far as it applies specifically to Jews. Although the examples of the thinkers we are going to consider are often based upon Jewish topics and individuals, it will be found that they have much broader interest than one might expect. If we refer again to the suggestion that the Jewish people are often represented theologically as symbolic of the human race as a whole, we can see that we are not dealing here with only a parochial topic. We are looking at an important issue in the philosophy of religion which has entirely general consequences.

The starting-point for the discussion is in the Bible and the Book of Job is the most concentrated treatment of the issue. There are many other parts of the Bible which refer to the topic, and some of these will be mentioned, but it is in the Book of Job that it most dramatically arises and that work forms a continuing thread of commentary and exposition throughout Jewish civilisation. An extraordinarily large number of works have been written to explain the Book of Job, and it is a work to which Jewish (and not only Jewish) philosophers return again and again. It would have been interesting to consider in some depth the discussions of evil and suffering in the rabbinic literature, in popular Jewish literature and in Jewish theology as a whole, and there are references here to aspects of these works, but the emphasis in this book is on the treatment of the topic by philosophers, and specifically by Jewish philosophers. There are a variety of ways of tackling such a topic. One might look at its development in Jewish philosophy as a whole, thus including aspects of every Jewish philosopher's thoughts on it. This has not been the approach followed here. I have concentrated upon a few leading Jewish thinkers, those whom I felt had considered the issue in an important and creative manner. I hope that most readers will find that the majority of the thinkers whom I discuss find an uncontroversial place in this sort of discussion. There are certainly others who could easily have been included, and who are by no means lesser thinkers than the ones we deal with here. There are many twentieth-century philosophers who have very interesting things to say on our topic and whose views in general are very important. Soloveitchik comes to mind here, as do many other modern authors who wrote on the Holocaust. Also, there are many earlier philosophers such as Halevi and Hasdai Crescas whom it would have been intriguing to bring into the discussion. However, I think it preferable to give the topic a sharper focus by limiting the discussion to a number of thinkers who in some way embody a particular cultural and philosophical context. The aim has been to produce a survey of a religious tradition from a philosophical perspective and so it was considered acceptable to restrict the survey to some of the major figures who developed the original concepts.

Can we really talk about a tradition of Jewish philosophy? This is itself a controversial issue, and some of the thinkers we are considering here had quite stormy relationships with the religious establishment of their time. There are clearly many Jewish philosophers who have no professional interest in specifically Jewish formulations of issues such as those of evil and suffering, and it would be facile to introduce them into the discussion. On the other hand, there are thinkers who are ethnically Jewish and who are interested in the discussion, but who do not really take part in the continuing debate from Job onwards. The thinkers who have been included here represent a broad series of views of the topic of evil and suffering, and they actually constitute a group in the sense that they are all concerned with a similar formulation of the topic. Does this not imply that they left the topic in much the same state as they found it? This certainly is not the case, since, as one would expect, later commentators commented on the work of their predecessors and as we shall see the result is something of a progressive conceptual development of the topic. That is, over time the topic has become more refined and the kinds of argument which can be applied to it are better understood. The thinkers we discuss are clearly members of the same tradition, whether they appreciated it or not, and we have here sustained intellectual work on a range of issues extending over a very long period and reaching right up to our own time. Indeed, the Holocaust and the creation of the State of Israel has given the whole topic an enormous boost today, leading many Jewish intellectuals to look with renewed interest at what their forebears had to say about evil.

It is interesting to compare the way in which the philosophical tradition has developed as compared with the religious tradition. The latter is much more wedded to specifically religious texts, of course, and relies on the development of new and extended readings of those texts. Some of these readings continue to use the same exegetical approaches to interpreting scripture and history as obtained in the past, while more radical developments of Judaism involve quite distinct readings which, over time, become themselves the structure within which new readings can take place. It is not always easy to differentiate between the philosophical tradition and the religious tradition. There is no doubt that much of the latter is affected by the former, but the influence is certainly not all one way. As we shall see, there is a continual interplay of philosophical and religious arguments in the content of the philosophical tradition. This interplay is capable of being rather problematic, since philosophy and religion are based upon distinct methodologies for much of their work, and it is always confusing if one has to assess reasoning which strays from one universe of discourse to another. But it will be very much the theme of this book that it is not possible to draw a clear distinction between philosophy and religion in discussing our topic. This is because the topic is itself so embedded in a variety of theoretical perspectives that it is not possible to extract it and cleanse it, as it were, of its non-philosophical accretions before subjecting it to logical analysis. As we shall see, the topic of evil is not only part of a variety of theoretical discourses, but it also has a vital practical and experiential side to it, and any philosophical account which is going to be worth establishing must pay due respect to that side. We are not dealing here with an abstract concept only; rather, it is an essential part of our experience of human existence, and its philosophical elucidation must pay attention to that experience. Any results which we derive should be in line with that experience, and help us to understand it.

It is important to put the thinkers we are going to discuss here within some sort of cultural context. Although they were concerned with aspects of the same problem, they came from different backgrounds and there often seems to be as much to distinguish them as to bring them together. They were all part of a Gentile culture and often represented that culture in their work. What is the point, then, of calling them Jewish philosophers? The justification is that they took aspects of the general culture in which they lived and used it to transform Jewish philosophy. This set up an interesting dialectic between the Jewish and the general culture which persists to this day, and has to persist as long as the Jewish community is not completely assimilated into the general community. Jewish philosophers were impressed by the contributions which non-Jewish culture made to thought, and so were happy to employ new ways of thinking, but at the same time they sought to protect the distinctiveness of Judaism as a faith and Jewish philosophy as a possibility. But the clash between the two cultures of Judaism on the one hand, and philosophy on the other, will be evident in much of their work.

Two important theoretical issues about methodology have arisen in writing this book. The first relates to the distinctness of the issue we are considering here, why innocent people suffer, from other related issues. There will be a good deal of discussion in this book on how God relates to events in this world, but not much on the logical status of future contingent events, given that God may know how they are going to turn out before they happen. We will not be saying much here about the puzzles which arise in trying to reconcile God's various attributes – these have been discussed in my previous work – but it may be that the answers to such questions have an important bearing upon our main concerns here which does not come out in the present treatment. We are just going to have to assume for the sake of this discussion that it is possible for God to be good, omnipotent, omniscient and so on without any logical problems which cannot be settled in a way acceptable to religion. If this assumption is false, or only partially true, then any results we obtain here may be suspect. What we shall have shown, though, is what can be derived from the ordinary conception of God, the notion of God and what he can do and know, which is accepted by most believers, and there is some value in exploring the implications of that notion with respect to responsibility for evil and suffering in the world. If our notion of what God can do and know is in need of refinement at a later stage as a result of logical problems with that combination of attributes, then our conclusions about evil and suffering may need to be modified. We are assuming here that the ordinary conception of the deity is more-or-less workable as a concept, although we shall certainly look at ways of altering it to make it more intellectually respectable, given the theories we shall consider.

The other theoretical difficulty is a more serious one, and this concerns the very process of Jewish philosophy itself. What is Jewish philosophy? One might be tempted to reply that it is philosophy applied to Jewish cultural objects and ideas. When one looks at the literature of Jewish philosophy it has a certain fairly constant form. First of all there is the philosophy, the precise nature of which depends upon the school of philosophy from which the philosopher operates. Then there are the Jewish parts of the text, the quotations from the Bible, parts of the Talmud and Midrash, legal judgments and items from Jewish history. Many other specifically Jewish texts can be included also, such as relevant novels and poems, and aspects of Jewish ritual life, and so on. What tends to happen is that there is a mixture of content, so that there is a bit of philosophy and a bit of Jewish material, and one works on the others until we get a conclusion which is designed to throw philosophical light upon a Jewish topic. Much of this sort of writing is very interesting, and authors blend together the philosophy and the Judaism in perceptive and attractive

ways. It can be done well and it can be done poorly, and there does not
seem to be anything wrong with this way of doing philosophy in itself.
It is the norm when we look at philosophy of religion to combine the
application of philosophical methods with aspects of religious life and
tradition.

Is it as simple as that, though? If we look at the sort of non-
philosophical literature produced by a religion we should notice how
varied it is and how different are the techniques for dealing with it.
The Jewish novelist produces material which operates on entirely
different principles compared with the Talmudist or the rabbi. The
cabbalist and the historian might both be dealing with Jewish topics,
but they deal with them in very different ways. The philosopher looks
at this confusion of methodologies and adds to them her own. One
way of representing what happens is to say that the philosopher uses
the most general demonstrative methods and is capable of subsuming
all the other approaches to the topic under the one philosophical
approach. Complex religious issues have aspects which are capable of
being analysed philosophically, although there are also, no doubt,
aspects of religion which are not so amenable to philosophical
attention. After all, a religion satisfies many human demands and not
all of these are usefully explored by the techniques of the philosopher.
The philosopher is primarily concerned with the rational aspects of
religion, and the rest of the form of life can be better explored using
other more appropriate methods.

One thing we rarely notice when we look at an example of Jewish
philosophy is how mixed are the systems of thought we are confronting. There is a tendency to think of the variety as all part of the same
organic unity, since they are all aspects of Jewish culture. And they
are, but this should not be allowed to hide from us the fact that Jewish
culture incorporates a large plurality of theoretical and practical
perspectives, and we should be careful about taking an instance of
such a plurality and being confident that we know what is going on.
Within the system of the Talmud we do know what is going on.
Within the cabbala, within the writings of Isaac Bashevis Singer,
within Maimonides we know what is happening, or at least the sort of
thing which is happening, but it is important to note that whatever is
going on is distinct from what goes on within a different area.
Novelists and jurisprudents are not engaged on the same activity,
although they might both be acting within a Jewish context. The rules
of religious law and the rules of artistic expression are different from

each other. When the philosopher introduces examples from the very varied corpus of literature available from Jewish writing, what is being done is to establish a general way of thinking which is then subjected to philosophical analysis of one type or another. Since philosophy is often regarded as the most general approach to a topic, this seems highly appropriate. The philosopher subsumes the other forms of looking at an issue under the particular philosophical methodology which is being employed, and as a result we get another and even more abstract approach to the topic.

So when we come to the topic of this book we shall find that philosophers consider a whole variety of sources when they discuss evil and suffering. Some of these sources are biblical, legal, artistic, historical and ritual, while others, of course, are clearly philosophical. The medieval thinkers had a neat way of describing all these different approaches to a topic by using Aristotle's division of areas of discourse in terms of different logical methods. The poet uses a different form of reasoning as compared with the politician, and the theologian a distinct way of arguing as compared with the philosopher. These different forms of argument work within their own sphere of operation, but if they are extended to a different universe of discourse they no longer make sense. For example, the politician and the prophet use figurative language incorporating vivid examples in their discourse, since the aim is to move an audience in a particular practical direction; Aristotle's account of rhetorical reasoning can be used to characterise this method. There is nothing wrong with such an approach, but it would be entirely out of place were it to be employed by someone else: the theologian, for example. His or her techniques are different from those of the prophet, although the same subject-matter may be discussed. The theologian seeks to get to a conclusion by working dialectically from premises within a religion to conclusions which display the implications of those premises, and yet which are limited in generality by the nature of where they start. Provided everyone sticks to his or her own area of thought there is no conceptual confusion. The philosopher works at the highest level of generality and certainty, and philosophical analysis can encompass everything else of a lower logical order.

When we consider the issue of evil and suffering there does seem to be a set of problems which are specifically philosophical, and we might expect the philosopher to concentrate upon those problems. If God is able to prevent suffering, and does not, then the philosopher has to show how this can be explained, if it can be, in terms of the concepts in which the problem is expressed. Those concepts can be developed into other concepts, of course, but we have to start with the way in which the problem is expressed in the religion. That is why we need to look at formulations of the problem from a variety of different perspectives in the religion to give as broad an understanding as possible of how that religion sees the issue. I used to think that it was possible to make a clear distinction between those aspects of a topic which are philosophical and those aspects which are not, but now I am not so sure. The idea that the philosophical analysis of a topic can encapsulate all the other approaches to it may have to be abandoned. The problem here is that so much of the essential core of the topic necessarily escapes the philosopher's gaze, since it consists of material which is not amenable to philosophical treatment. We shall see towards the end of the book how far this limits the strength of any conclusions which we can derive. Perhaps we shall have to see philosophy as just one way of approaching an issue, rather than the very best way.

It is worth pointing out that the individuals we discuss in this book are rarely professional philosophers in a contemporary sense. Most of them were involved in a whole range of activities, and often philosophy was quite tangential to their main interests. Nonetheless, they produced an important and extended debate on a central issue, that of the justification of evil and suffering in a world created by God. Often their discussion of this topic is part of a much wider discussion, and I hope that I have managed to convey enough about their general approach to philosophy to make their treatment of the topic comprehensible. Since they were rarely simply philosophers, they brought in a wide range of arguments in their discussion of the topic. I have tried to concentrate upon the more philosophical features of that range, but the reader should be aware that the texts being considered are part of a long and rich tradition of writing which is only occasionally directly concerned with philosophical issues. The chief concern of such writing is often the continuation of the tradition itself with all its complexity, and by concentrating upon the philosophy there is no attempt at presenting an accurate version of the whole tradition as it has developed. On the other hand, by following up a particular issue along its philosophical development over a long period we might get a glimpse of how a tradition grows and changes in response to a number of different factors. There have been few issues in Jewish cultural life with the omnipresence and poignancy of evil and suffering, and the history of their philosophical treatment should throw light upon the tradition of Jewish intellectual life itself.

It is worth adding, though, that the main concentration here will be on the philosophical implications of the discussions concerning evil and suffering, and no attempt will be made at encompassing the broader aspects of these issues in any more detail than is required for their philosophical understanding. This is not because it is thought that the extra-philosophical aspects of the discussion are unimportant, nor because they are unrelated to the philosophical argument, but a history of the culture of the topic is far beyond the scope of this enquiry. Yet it is not easy to distinguish between the philosophical and the non-philosophical aspects of the topic. We have to beware of the common practice of allowing an easy interplay of philosophical and non-philosophical ideas, which tends to establish a conclusion in a rhetorically attractive manner, but which really has very little logical force. The sorts of language which sound impressive from the ministerial pulpit in a synagogue are designed to move the congregation to action, and they work if the speaker is able to understand the kind of points which will move his audience. It depends also on the nature of the audience. Some audiences are amenable to a more technical and logical discussion than are others, and the skilful speaker will adapt his text to the requirements of the situation. This is even more true of religious writings. These are many-faceted works, with a whole variety of feasible interpretations which are designed to appeal to a diversity of readers and potential worshippers.

Let us see how this point relates to the Book of Job, which is at issue in this discussion. The text starts with Job complaining about the injustice of his fate, and he is taken to be seeking an explanation for the apparent existence of innocent suffering. Job is himself virtuous and certainly does not deserve what is happening to him. He then wonders why the sort of God in whom he believes, an omniscient, omnipotent and benevolent God, allows these things to happen to him, or actually makes them happen. Job's friends take a variety of lines on his troubles, often arguing that he cannot be as innocent as he thinks he is, and so deserves his suffering. God does respond to Job, but not directly. He shows Job how powerless and ignorant he is by comparison with the deity, and this does the trick of persuading Job to accept his suffering, and as a result by the end of the Book he is rewarded by the return, and even increase, of his possessions. God does not criticise

Job for demanding an answer from God for the latter's apparent mismanagement of the world. On the contrary, God is critical of Job's friends for having blindly upheld the existence and pervasiveness of divine justice.

It has often been wondered by commentators why Job is satisfied with the response he gets from God. Why should the demonstration of divine power bring Job round to the acceptance of his sufferings, given that those sufferings are not caused by Job's guilt? We wonder why Job is satisfied with God's answer, which does not even seem to be an answer to Job's question. If we look at the context more carefully we can see that Job is not brought around by the demonstration of divine power so much as by the argument that the difference between God's point of view and his own is so great. Our grasp of reality is very limited, since we are finite creatures and there is clearly a relatively near horizon with respect to the extent of our knowledge. God, on the other hand, is infinite and understands exactly why everything is as it is. We are obliged to find out what the nature of his creation is, whereas he has maker's knowledge, he knows precisely the reasons for things being as they are. Were the world to be based upon an open principle of fairness, which balanced deserts with rewards and punishments, it would represent the sort of moral organisation which comes closest to our ways of thinking that things should be arranged, and yet we should then have no need for a supernatural mechanism which is assumed to lie behind the world. Job is impressed by what God says because Job comes to understand that the nature of divine action is based on mystery, and that mystery represents the religious aspect of the world.

Now, Job could have rejected this explanation. He could have insisted on receiving an answer to his original question, which was why God allowed the innocent to suffer. Job comes to see that the question which he originally posed is in fact the wrong question. The right question which should replace it concerns our relationship with God. God does not really respond to this question either, but the important development in the Book is that Job comes to see that his original question requires alteration. Through his experiences Job grows into a different sort of person, and the material rewards which he eventually receives are symbolic of the ways in which he has changed. This explains why God criticises Job's friends. They do not change at all, they remain the same throughout and do not cease repeating the same tired religious banalities, while Job does not allow his sufferings to sink him into either a cowed submission to God or a strident opposition to God. This brings out something which is worth noticing about religious language. It is designed to help its readers and hearers work out for themselves how they are to behave and what they are to think. If it was immediately obvious what the language meant, then it would be easy to know what is intended by it. We could just follow the instructions and directions, and so arrive efficiently at the end to which the language points. This is what Job's friends try to do, and as a result they are rebuked by God. One might think that God would approve of their apparent orthodoxy and willingness to accept the pervasiveness of divine justice, but this is not so. What God values is the ability to work through one's problems, or at least to make the effort to come to terms with one's experiences. Job's friends never do this, they are not affected by Job's experiences at all. This has important implications for our understanding of the sort of religious language which both Job and his friends employ. It has to be flexible enough for different users to be able to decide how they are going to work it. The language has to be able both to guide its users on where they wish to go and also advise them as to where they ought to go, and it must be open enough to allow for a wide variety of feasible interpretations, since otherwise it would not give its users the opportunity to decide for themselves how they were going to use it.

This is certainly not the place to get involved in the analysis of how religious language differs from other types of language, but it is certainly relevant to say something about how it is possible to use philosophy to make relevant points about non-philosophical, and here religious, texts. It is of the nature of philosophical language to be closed, in the sense that it operates via deductive reasoning to try to establish a conclusion which follows logically from premises, and the process is a necessary one. The philosopher tries to refine the concepts which are used to such an extent that they inevitably point in a particular direction, since any subsequent looseness in expression will invalidate the argument, or at the very least restrict its general value. It follows that there is going to be a big problem in combining religious statements which stem from a religious tradition and philosophical analysis. The former are going to be useful only if they provide adherents of the religion with enough room for interpretation for them to grow and develop with the user. Religious statements will be suggestive, and they can only be suggestive if they are open. It follows that we have to be very careful about combining such statements with a philosophical treatment, since it is much too easy to select religious examples which can be made to fit a whole variety of philosophical theories.

We have seen that it could be argued that the problem which Job sets up in his Book is not so much about the rationale for the suffering of the innocent, but is rather about our relationship with God. This is perhaps hardly surprising, since the question about innocent suffering is only a question if the assumption is made that there is a being available who could undo the evil if he thought it desirable to act in this way. Quite naturally, we might move from raising the question of innocent suffering in a world potentially controlled by a being who could do something to relieve that suffering, who knows about its existence and who is full of good intentions towards his creation, to an enquiry into the nature of the being concerned. There must, after all, be something about him which explains his apparent inactivity when one might otherwise expect him to act, and so the discussion would move on to the nature of God and his relationship with us. It is very much on this form of the discussion that this book is based. This does not mean that we will not really be investigating the issues of evil and suffering, though, since, as Job discovered, these issues go hand in hand with an enquiry into the nature of God's relationship with us. While the approach which is being followed here is very different from that of the great twentieth-century Jewish philosopher Franz Rosenzweig, we can make use of his technique of *erfahrende Philosophie*, a philosophy of experience which seeks to understand what is behind the way in which people feel problems affect them, how the structure of our experience gives rise to and necessitates a metaphysical investigation into the presuppositions of that experience. It is of the nature of philosophy to be able to cope with only an aspect of the total historical experience of the Jewish people. Different and more expressive forms of representation are more appropriate for other aspects of that experience, but there is definitely an important role for rational enquiry into that experience too, and it is the intention of the discussion in this book to establish the value of such an approach.

The notion of an *erfahrende Philosophie* inevitably raises the question yet again of the link between philosophy and religion. There is no problem in understanding how philosophy can be expected to deal with the formal aspects of any system of thought, including religion. The sorts of concept which occur in religion can be abstracted and subjected to philosophical treatment, and the form of that treatment will depend upon the philosophical commitments of the particular writer. When we are dealing with the links between an omniscient and benevolent deity on the one hand, and the suffering of the innocent on the other, a problem clearly arises which is logical in nature. The problem consists of an apparent incompatibility, and much effort has been expended to try to show that indeed this incompatibility cannot be resolved, or that it can be if we understand the concepts in the formulation of the problem correctly. Some discussions of the issue deal exclusively with logical aspects of the problem which can be discussed without any specific religious reference. One thinks here of the protracted debate which has followed Aristotle's analysis of the status of the future sea battle, whether its existence even before it takes place is determined, or whether it is free to happen or not. Clearly, the approach which one takes to this sort of problem will be important for the understanding of God's knowledge of the future, and by implication for his understanding of how far that future is available to him to change. If future events are already laid out in a predetermined manner, then neither God nor his creatures can do anything to affect them, and so it is facile to expect divine intervention to improve our situation. If the analysis of future events leads to the conclusion that we can do nothing now to affect them, then this will have implications for our understanding of God's participation in the world and our freedom to change the future. In this sense, then, philosophical views clearly contribute to the nature of religious views which rest on shared concepts.

But the link is more complex than that. Religion is more than just a set of formal beliefs, expressible as propositions. It also consists of experiences, and those experiences cannot often be tidily filed under the appropriate concepts. The experiences give rise to questions about the concepts, and they lead to the believer thinking about how the concept might be changed, or whether it should be abandoned entirely, or indeed reaffirms her faith in the concept. This might appear to be a dubious process to those who are unsympathetic to religion and its claims. After all, it will be said, a concept has instances coming under it, and there should be clear instances which at least on some occasions exemplify the concept. There certainly may be many times when it is difficult to be sure whether the concept applies to a situation, and the vagueness of a particular ascription does not in any way invalidate a concept. We expect there to be problematic situations in which we cannot be sure how far a concept applies, or whether it applies at all. Yet there are also quite firm applications of the concept, when one feels like saying that if it does not apply in *this* case, then one does not know when it does apply. This is a reflection of the fact that there are paradigmatic examples of the concept, and to refuse to acknowledge these is to display a disinclination to use the concept at all. While one might argue about how far the concept applies to difficult cases, there must be a body of unproblematic cases which demonstrate the main use of the concept, and which show that the speaker understands its meaning.

Religious concepts often seem to behave differently. For example, a pious woman may acknowledge both the existence of a benign, omniscient and omnipotent God, and evil affecting the innocent. She may be willing to point to examples of events which provide evidence of those divine qualities while at the same time refusing to consider that contrary events disprove those qualities. This is something which Job criticises when he is told by his companions that there are plenty of examples of God's goodness, and that Job's sufferings may be for the best in the end. Job cannot see how one can look at evidence of God's goodness and reconcile it with apparently quite different evidence as all coming under the same concept, namely, that of divine goodness. If it is reasonable to treat events in the world which go well as examples of such goodness, then it is *prima facie* unreasonable to treat entirely dissimilar events as also being examples of such goodness. Of course, one might have a theory according to which everything that happens is for the best and has been arranged by God to fit into our lives in the optimum manner for us, but that we are unable to understand how, probably because of our limited grasp of the plan which lies behind our experience of the world. Job is dubious about this sort of explanation, not because it is impossible, but mainly because it is too easy a solution to the problem. It is rather like saying that a concept has quite general application even when we cannot observe such application, because we are not in a position to carry out such an observation. It is certainly feasible to make such a claim, yet one might worry that it allowed far too much to come under the concept, since there is no clear criterion of what comes under it and what is excluded. Any event which occurs can be regarded as evidence of divine beneficence, since were we to understand it completely, we should see how it falls under that description. We certainly can talk in this way, but it stretches the notion of *evidence* rather far if we see everything which happens as evidence of divine providence, since it seems that the evidence will only ever be allowed to point in one direction.

It might be thought that this is a rather misleading way of looking at this particular aspect of religious language, since it suggests that the believer is uncritically employing our normal language to make the sorts of distinctions which we ordinarily make, while at the same time widening the scope of that language to allow in far more than we should normally accept. When we come to look at the comments of some of Job's companions, it will become clear that this is precisely what they do, and Job quite rightly is not convinced by their arguments. But the religious attitude is not necessarily as simple as this, and the religious use of ordinary language can be quite different. The believer has a different attitude to the world than does the non-believer, and this attitude is as much emotional as it is rational. The believer may look at the world and see it as the product of God's love, and she may feel that love as imbued in the most mundane and prosaic objects in her world. The whole world is suffused with the spirit of God, and that meaning which is ascribed to the world is the most important thing which we can know about it. It is certainly true that some of the events in the world are difficult to reconcile with that love, but, in a sense, that is besides the point. The world is seen *as* a particular kind of world, and while it is seen in that way it cannot be seen in any other way. A religious attitude implies a certain view of the world, a view which takes account of the facts, but a view which takes account of those facts in a particular way. In religion, just as in science, the facts under-determine the theory which accounts for those facts.

Religion does more than just assert that the world is to be seen in a certain way. It can also insist that the meaning of the world is beyond the world, that there is more to explaining what there is than can be experienced by us. When comparing religion with philosophy there is a tendency to make them too similar, since otherwise it seems that they will have little in common, but there is an important potential aspect of distinction, and that lies in the sense of mystery which is so often part of the religious attitude. This resides not so much in the idea that the explanation of our common-sense world lies outside of that world, but rather in the sense that however much we grasp of reality, there is yet more which we cannot grasp. The sense of wonder which one may have when contemplating the world is more than just an acknowledgment that there are features of the world which one cannot grasp, given the limitations of our finitude. It is not so much that we are missing a part of the jigsaw, but more that the jigsaw can be put together in different ways, and only one pattern is available to us. When we come to look at Job we shall see that this is an important aspect of his approach to God. Job's friends suggest that Job is just unaware of the ways in which divine providence operate, and they present a picture of the world according to which there is a rational structure in the sense that there is a balance between pleasures and sufferings. A moral calculus exists which we could in principle observe, were we able to know enough of that structure. What Job comes finally to understand, by contrast with his companions, is that the religious essence of reality lies in its mystery, in the mystery of there being something rather than nothing, and it is for arriving at this understanding that Job is eventually rewarded by God, while his friends are roundly condemned. This brings out nicely an aspect of the contrast between a religious and an philosophical understanding of reality. That latter will seek to show that we can produce a variety of categories which are capable of summarising the main features of that reality. Religion, on the other hand, may suggest that the rationale of reality is far beyond our capacity to think and experience, and it is something of which we may attain only a glimpse or a hint.

But it would be wrong to think of religion and philosophy as essentially trying to do different things. They are often engaged on very much the same activity, and there are clear links between them. They both set out to provide a framework for an understanding of the world, and sometimes they may give very similar answers, albeit expressed in different ways. As we shall see, this was something of a theme of writers in the Middle Ages. One of the features of religion which will be emphasised in the discussion of Job and his philosophical interpreters is the way in which it seeks to enforce demands on the personality of the individual. The believer is not concerned only in attaining an intellectual awareness of her position in the world, she is also interested in working out how that awareness effects her own development as a person. The believer uses her philosophical and religious understanding to change herself, to become a different sort of person. This brings us back to the notion of an *erfahrende Philosophie*, of an intellectual system which, at the same time as it establishes a conceptual framework, also sets out to reorganise our experience. It might be said that this is what makes a particular sort of philosophy a religious philosophy; that it has direct implications for the practice of the individual and the community. This was a point made frequently in the Middle Ages, where the distinction between philosophy and religion was often articulated as the difference between theoretical and practical knowledge. The epistemic content of both philosophy and religion were taken to be identical, and the only difference between them lay in the form of delivery of that content. We do not have to go along with this medieval form of analysis, but it does reinforce a highly significant feature of religion, namely, its practical aspect. The ways in which this aspect is going to influence our behaviour will determine how far our lives are religious.

It is important to realise, though, that the influence of religion on the lives of believers is not a simple event. It is not just the translation of theoretical ideas into practical action. Religion also enters into the way in which the individual develops over a period of time, since the believer is obliged to work out for herself how the truths of religion are to be applied in her life. Of course, there is no lack of advice from religious authorities as to how to interpret the principles of religion, yet it is up to the individual to work out for herself how those principles are to have meaning in her life. We can see this when we look at the situation of Job. He knows what the religious answer to his predicament is, but he has difficulty in reconciling that answer with what he is feeling at the time. His task is to redefine the notion of divine providence in a way which makes sense of his experience, and the way in which this is done is obviously, to a certain extent, going to be personal. What satisfies one individual may not satisfy another. What is so important about Job's task is precisely that it is a task, that he makes an effort to reconcile his understanding of the world with his understanding of himself. His companions are not up to this task, they are satisfied with the tired clichés of religion, and the implication is that they do not really apply those formulations to their experience. They just repeat them without working out for themselves how they affect their lives, how they require to be incorporated in those lives in a real rather than just a nominal manner. They are operating with a *Philosophie* without an *Erfahrung*. Yet what gives philosophy its importance in this sort of situation is precisely its ability to be cashed in in terms of experience, since if it is not it is empty. Acceptance of divine providence is only meaningful in a religious sense if it can be made part of the living experience of the individual who accepts it. It is not just an idea with an internal logic. It has powerful implications for the lives of believers, and for that idea to have meaning from a religious point of view it must be capable of becoming part of those lives.

CHAPTER I

Job

Much of the Jewish Bible is concerned with evil and suffering, but perhaps the area in which the most concentrated discussion of these topics arises is in the Book of Job. There has been a great deal of argument over the exact origins of the text, its relationship to Babylonian folk-tales and the nature of its structure, and there can be no doubt that the Book of Job is a very attractive and accessible piece of literary construction. It consists initially of a dialogue between Job, his three friends Eliphaz, Bildad and Zophar, and God. Job is a righteous individual who in the past enjoyed good health, wealth and a high reputation. Suddenly, for no apparent reason, everything goes wrong. He loses his money, his children die, he is wracked with illness and misfortune, and quite understandably wonders why things have turned out so poorly for him. After all, he was an upright individual in the past and feels that he does not deserve such rough treatment in the present. This is very much the theme of the text, and Job's friends do not help much in the way of providing arguments which explain how to reconcile Job's sufferings with a notion of moral balance in the world.

Eliphaz informs the miserable Job that the righteous do not finally lose their material wealth in this life while the evil do not in the end gain materially in their temporal existence. He also suggests that no one really suffers for no reason, and implies that Job must have done something iniquitous in the past to account for his present troubles. Job is prepared to accept that he may have inadvertently sinned, but he is not prepared to conclude that since he is suffering now he must have sinned in a big way in the past. He wants some explanation from the deity for his present suffering, and not just for his situation, but really for the position in which people find themselves as a whole. There exists a great deal of apparently innocent suffering in the world, and Job wants God to provide some justification for it all. It is really no use at all for Bildad to claim that those who suffer must have sinned, because it is just patently false. It is a familiar and undeniable experience that on occasions the guilty flourish and the virtuous decline, and Job's friends never manage to produce a convincing argument to reject this experience. In fact, the scope of Job's discussion rises to a different plane. While his friends keep on trying to discover reasons for the suffering of the evidently innocent, Job is probing the nature of the relationship between human beings and God. He seems to be working on the assumption that either God has power to affect events in the world and chooses to punish the innocent on occasion, or, God does not have much in the way of contact with the world, and what happens here is independent of his interest and concern. This emerges as the real focus of Job's concern throughout the text, and is accompanied throughout by a steadfast belief in the importance and power of God. The worry is that despite the existence of a powerful and well-informed deity, he has no interest in what goes on in the world, and that the relationship which we assume we have with such a deity is profoundly mistaken.

Zophar returns to the general theme that Job must have sinned in the past, with no greater success than his colleagues in teasing out of Job an admission of prior ill-doing. What Job does is go on at great length about the vagaries of the world and the apparently random way in which favours and punishments are distributed, and he produces a far more convincing view of the world than that of his friends, with their simplistic identification of misfortune with sin. Of course, a neat solution would be to point to the next life as the arena in which rewards and punishments are balanced with desert, and this is a solution which was eagerly grasped by some Jewish thinkers. Job, to his credit, rejects it outright, and puts his reliance throughout upon an approach based upon empiricism. He is arguing that we should base ourselves upon what we have evidence for, at least in so far as human events are concerned. Eliphaz disparages this approach, arguing that there is a close connection between the possibility of religious commitment and the prospect of reward and punishment as a result of one's behaviour. What is the point of behaving oneself if it makes no difference to how things will turn out from a personal point of view? So Eliphaz has to argue that the successes of the wicked are really only temporary and that they would really have been much better off had they behaved virtuously. Job quite rightly ignores these suggestions, complaining at length that God seems to have gone out of his way to make life impossible for him. Zophar takes a similar line to Eliphaz, but Bildad at least addresses the problem in something like the way in which Job is now going, in terms of the sort of relationship which we can expect to have with the deity, although Bildad rejects the demand which Job makes of God for a response to his query about the reason for his apparently innocent sufferings.

Job's response to Zophar's long account of the misfortunes of the wicked is to produce a detailed account of their continuing wellbeing. It has to be said here that Job has a very sound objection to the notion that God punishes the wicked through their children, a particularly nauseating suggestion with which he will have no truck. Job's basic observation, yet again, is not that God controls the world unjustly but that he does not control it at all. It just runs on with no divine influence. Eliphaz is unconvinced by this possibility, and returns to his guiding principle that Job must have sinned in some way to deserve what is happening to him now. Although Job is quite prepared to admit that he is not perfect, he is not prepared to conclude that he must have sinned just because he is now being punished. On the other hand, he is also reluctant to let go of the idea that what is happening to him is indeed a punishment, something which occurs because of God's desire that he suffer. How can he discover what it is that has brought about this present attitude of God? This issue is directly confronted by the intervention of Elihu. He argues that one way in which God communicates with people is through their experience of misfortune. This is done through the mediation of the angels. Elihu bitterly criticises Job for his claim that there is no just distribution of rewards and punishments in this life, and Job is taken to have challenged the notion of retribution which is so important a part of much religious faith. But Elihu does not really take the discussion much further. When he suggests that God's greatness is such that it is impossible to hold him accountable to anyone else, he is making an emotional rather than a rational point. We may be amazed by the power and majesty of God, and yet still wonder why he did not order things more fairly.

Elihu suggests that Job's attitude to his sufferings is misguided, and is unlikely to end his sufferings. He should regard the misfortune as an aspect of discipline, whereby the sin is purged through an appropriately submissive attitude by the sufferer himself. Elihu seems to waver here between arguing, like the three friends, that Job is being punished for some prior sin, or that he is being tested now through his misfortune which has come about regardless of his previous behaviour. Indeed, the latter alternative has something to be said for it, since one can see how God might use suffering to help an innocent person perfect himself. Yet since Elihu insists that Job ought to repent to get out of his difficulty, and since we know from the start of the text that Job has nothing to feel guilty about, we are still left wondering what the object of the repentance could be, apart from just being human. Fortunately for the reader, God himself makes an appearance and solves the problem. He starts off by pointing to the huge contrast between the sort of knowledge which Job has of the world and divine knowledge. God describes at some length the extreme effort he has made in order to organise the inanimate world efficiently, with the implication that he is hardly likely to ignore the situation of human beings. In his response to the divine onslaught Job has very little to say. This is hardly surprising, since the whole object of his line of complaint was that God would not address him with answers to his charges, and any response is a success given Job's starting position. Job acknowledges that by comparison with God he knows very little, and must be content to accept that what God says is true is actually the case. God then proceeds to detail Job's sin, which was not anything he did before his misfortunes arose (so his friends are all wrong) but is rather his inability to accept his relatively low status as a created thing and his arrogance in challenging God in the legalistic and aggressive way in which he did. We find a lot of 'power' language here, since God is trying to impress Job with the contrast between human and divine power. The latter, after all, managed to bring the world out of chaos. Job becomes very submissive at this stage, and now accepts that the complaints which he brought against God were not just incorrect, but sinful too.

One might ask, as many have ever since the Book of Job was written, whether Job's response is the right one. Does it not rather look as though he is allowing himself to be brow-beaten by the deity's joint claim to great power and knowledge? Were I to have a servant and were I to mistreat him grievously, I am not sure that he would be satisfied if asked for a reason and told that I was stronger and cleverer than him. The point of what God says, though, is not really much to do with what he says, but lies in his saying anything at all. God has made explicit his relationship with Job, and by implication with the rest of humanity as well, and it is this quest for a response from the deity which was so important for Job. God does not tell Job what the point of innocent suffering is, but then this seems to have been just a ruse to get God to respond in the first place. At the end of the Book Job's friends are rebuked by God, but when Job prays for them his own fortunes are restored, and indeed doubled. This seems to be something of a vindication of the arguments of Job's friends. After all, they argued throughout that the innocent are eventually rewarded, and here is innocent Job receiving back not just what he started with, but even more. One wonders why God saw fit to rebuke them at all. Perhaps the idea is that by the end of the Book Job realises that human beings can have a relationship with the deity, but that relationship is not based upon a simple reward-and-punishment level. It lies far deeper than that. The fact that the innocent suffer, and it is a fact, does not invalidate that relationship, although it may lead us to waver in our belief in its existence. The happy ending of the Book is just that, a happy ending, but it could have been very different without in any way altering the central message of the text. An authentic relationship between God and humanity is based upon something much deeper than the expectation of reward and punishment.

As we shall see, the medieval commentators regarded the Book of Job as rather like a philosophical dialogue, with different interlocutors presenting contrasting theoretical perspectives on the relationship between God and the world. It certainly is not that as it stands, but it is not difficult to perceive some classical philosophical questions arising in the text. Many commentators have argued over the authenticity of parts of the text, which they have sought to reorganise in accordance with their interpretation, and there is little doubt that the text as a whole does seem to lack something in coherence. The Septuagint version tones down the aggression of Job and makes him out to be far more submissive than he is in the Hebrew version. While it must be admitted that it is enjoyable to play around with a text and move its sections around to provide a more perspicuous discussion, it is not at all clear that this is necessary for the Book of Job, because certain important philosophical issues do clearly stand out despite some evidence of confusion.

As comforters, Eliphaz, Bildad and Zophar leave a lot to be desired. The last thing one wants to hear when one is in trouble is that it is all one's own fault. Yet if we accept the simple logic of their presupposition that there is no such thing as innocent suffering, one can see the point of their rather callous accusations. Even though no one has seen evidence of Job's guilt, he must be guilty because he suffers. If he admits his guilt, he will be on the road to recovery, since God may accept his repentance, and he will have learnt something from his sorry experiences. Job's friends are prepared to accept the existence of suffering by the apparently innocent, and they ascribe other reasons for it, such as the role of suffering in bringing one nearer to God, the ubiquity of sin and the mystery implicit in God's actions. Neither Job nor his friends consider doubting the existence or power of God. The question rather is why God has on this occasion hidden his face, a question which arises many times again in Jewish history and perhaps most poignantly during the Holocaust. What is the purpose of Job's suffering? This is a question which runs throughout the Book, and it only makes sense within a system of belief in a God who can influence temporal events. One of the most interesting aspects of the Book is that this key question is never directly addressed, while being always present. Does that mean that the Book is a failure if looked upon as an extended argument?

So far it has been argued that Job is not really after an answer to the problem of innocent suffering, but rather is interested in getting an answer, any answer at all, from God. Job seems to accept throughout that innocent suffering exists, and does not use it as an argument against adherence to belief in God. No doubt his sufferings came as a great surprise to him, but he could not have been unaware before they began that people do suffer for no apparent purpose. The Book of Job seems to be an extended treatment of the idea that there is innocent suffering and no justification for it can be found. Even the discussion of the role of the afterlife is too thin to provide any suggestion that one will be compensated in the next life for undeserved sufferings in this life – not that that would have been much of a suggestion anyway. It is this rather unsatisfactory quandary in which the reader is left by the end of the Book which provides so much ammunition for Christian commentators, who tend to argue that the 'solution' to the questions raised in the text are found in Jesus Christ's mediation between heaven and earth. God shrouds himself in mystery in the Book, but when he sent his son to participate in the sufferings of the world and show how it could redeem itself he reveals himself to his creatures. This Christian strategy is appropriate, since the language of the Book seems to emphasise the ignorance which we as human beings have of the purposes of God and his intentions for us. Christianity resolves these problems by providing answers. Now, we might want to criticise these answers, but they do at least have the merit of attempting to

Must suffering have a purpose?

answer the questions which the Book raises, and which it appears to make no attempt at resolving.

Job submits himself to the divine will unquestioningly, and it is difficult not to interpret this as a mere submission to power. But were he to be entirely submissive he would not continue to insist that he was innocent of sins which led to his suffering. One might compare him here with the communists who were prosecuted in Eastern Europe by the state, and who were so convinced of the infallibility of the Party that they assumed that they must be guilty if they were charged with offences by the Party. They really were submissive, since they took the fact of their guilt to be established once the charge had been laid. Since they had total faith in the judgment of the Party, if the Party accused them they must be culpable. Job's attitude to God is not nearly so deferential as this attitude to the Communist Party. Job continues to bewail the suffering of the innocent and insists that there is innocence regardless of the fates of the individuals concerned. This implies also that Job is insisting that much the same moral considerations apply to God as to his creatures. Although God is far more powerful and wise than his creatures, the issue of innocent suffering can be laid at his door with just as much relevance as it can be applied to a temporal ruler. The fact that God is the supreme being does not show that a different set of moral rules applies to his actions as compared with ours. What is remarkable about Job is that he is prepared both to accept the greatness of God and at the same time to demand a response from God to the apparent injustices in the world. One might have expected someone who upheld the unknowability and power of God to have accepted that there is no point in querying the events in this world. We cannot understand why God has arranged the world in the way that he has, we cannot make comments about God based upon our experience of the world and so when we find something which puzzles us we should just accept it. It puzzles us because we only have a limited and restricted view of reality. One might have expected that someone who describes what goes on in this world as injustice would conclude that God does not influence what takes place here, or even that there is no controlling deity at all. Yet Job asserts both that God is the author of all that happens, and that he is clearly then the creator of much injustice.

Commentators frequently refer to Job's stance as tragic and noble, but it is not clear why this should be so. Every day of the school year some schoolchild is punished by a teacher for something which he or she did not do, and acknowledges the authority of the teacher to carry out such apparently arbitrary punishments. Within the context of the school the teacher has considerable power and can force children to undertake all manner of tasks for no apparent reason. Some pupils rebel at such exercises of authority, and get into even more trouble. Others accept that within the context of the school the sort of authority which teachers exercise is *sui generis*, incomparable with the standards of justice and fairness which apply outside that context. Most pupils, I suspect, take Job's line. That is, they appreciate that much which happens in school is unfair, but that it is mandatory because of the power and authority of the teachers. We are unlikely to call a class which has to stay in after school because some of its members were noisy noble and tragic because they accept both the authority of the school and the injustice of the punishment. One might object that this is because such an event relates to only a part of the lives of the pupils, while Job's account of human life encompasses the whole of that life. Yet it might be argued that the arbitrary nature of much school punishment is designed to prepare pupils for the arbitrary course of events in the world outside of school. If in the world as a whole the innocent suffer and the guilty prosper, as certainly is the case, then examples of such states of affairs in school help to prepare young people for the harshness and apparent amorality of adult life.

Like children in school, Job is a plaything of greater forces. His problems start when God and Satan have a wager concerning his faithfulness. Presumably Satan loses the wager, although it is worth wondering whether Job would have continued to be faithful without the theophany, without the revelation which God provides towards the end of the Book. The theme here is of the greatness and perfection of divine knowledge as compared with what we can know, and the implication is that it is presumptuous to challenge such a powerful and omniscient being as God. Job accepts this and comes to criticise his previous stand, now regarding humility before God as the appropriate strategy. It is an interesting question, though, whether God would have revealed himself to Job had the latter not challenged God to appear and answer his charges. Although God appears to criticise Job's challenge, in the end he is very critical of the response to Job's questions which follow an orthodox religious line: 'After having spoken these words to Job, the Lord said to Eliphaz, the Temanite: "My wrath is kindled against you and your two friends; for you have not spoken of Me what is right, as has my servant Job"' (42:7). This is intriguing, since the friends seem to embody those religious attitudes one might expect the deity to support. Job is rewarded for his rebelliousness by seeing God, to a degree, while the humble friends get criticised for telling Job what the religious explanation of his suffering is. Not only does Job see God, which is a very restricted honour in the Jewish Bible, but in the end he is rewarded in material terms too. For Christians this can lead to explanation along the lines of the approach to the prodigal son. This approach is not available to Jews, though, and it does look as if Job is rewarded for asking what he later on admits himself are the wrong questions, while his friends are snubbed by God for adhering throughout to the justice of God. We might think that at the very least this validates the continuation of the sorts of questions which Job poses in the Book, and we shall see that these questions did continue to be put and the validity of various solutions were considered and assessed.

Before we proceed to look at how some of these questions were taken up within Jewish philosophy, it is worth pointing out some aspects of the Book of Job which return time and again to haunt the continuing debate. Although Job is an individual, he is supposed to represent anyone at all. There is nothing special about Job or his situation. He appears to be asking for the explanation of the suffering of the innocent, but really he is asking questions about the nature of God and our relationship with him. The form in which this answer comes tells us a good deal about who we are and how we are to conduct ourselves in our world. Since the traditional explanation of God's justice as following a fair system of retribution seems to fall down in the Book of Job, we require another account of divine justice, and also a way of relating what we do to the traditions of religion. Even a cursory reading of the Book of Job reveals that the traditional explanation of how the world operates is awry, and so a new explanation will be required, one which will perhaps allow for more personal contact between the deity and his creatures. This brings out what might be called the subversive aspect of the Book, the fact that it seems to poke fun at traditional religion while all the time acknowledging its indebtedness to it, a strategy which is dramatically very effective and which has led to a vast host of commentary and argument over the meaning of the Book. The notion of the Book having meaning, just one meaning, is intriguing but difficult to defend given its multifaceted character, yet it is certainly true that the Book produces at least one meaning. This is that we have to examine critically the way in which God relates to his world. It is not enough to accept the platitudes of religion. Eliphaz and his colleagues were attacked by God for being uncritical of traditional religious explanations. Although Job was also criticised for having challenged God, the fact that he was rewarded nonetheless with a glimpse at God did not go unremarked by later Jewish thinkers. A critical view of the role of God with respect to evil and suffering in the world might also reveal important aspects of metaphysical reality. Philosophers might not expect to 'see' God, but they might hope to discover more about him through their investigations into the problem which stimulated Job. In what follows we shall see how the issue of evil and suffering was related to even broader issues in Jewish philosophy.

As one might expect, the Talmudic and Midrashic writers were just as fascinated by the character of Job as were his philosophical commentators. There exists a lot of scattered remarks, with some evidence that originally a major work devoted entirely to the Book of Job was available. The commentators were interested in a number of diverse issues, ranging over the length of Job's sufferings, the authorship of the Book and even doubts about his existence. The sufferings of Job are sometimes seen as prefiguring and representing the travails of the Jewish people. There are some important general themes, however. In the first place Job is often represented as being saintly, and as a result being rewarded with contact with God. Only very few figures in the Bible are said to enjoy such contact, and it is due to Job's excellent character that such contact is established. What is interesting about this strain of interpretation is that it thoroughly downplays the rebellious aspects of the Book of Job, seeking rather to emphasise the accounts of his righteousness and faithfulness. His accusatory appeals to God tend to be identified as reactions to sufferings, and so not something for which Job should be held liable. Job is often linked with Abraham, and one can see why. Both turned against the idolatry of their ancestors and worshipped the one God, both were opposed by Satan, both were hospitable, both had to undergo a test of faith and both became symbols of piety for future generations. The precise nature of the relationship between Job and Abraham was obviously a controversial issue in the Talmud and Midrash, since there is a variety of views about it, with some adhering to their equal status, some putting Job even higher in status than Abraham and others insisting on the superiority of the latter over the former. Indeed, for those who wanted to disparage Job there is little difficulty in finding much in the Book which can provide them with suitable ammunition. It could well be that this stress on Job's role as a rebel was undertaken to counter Christian interpretations of him as a rival to Abraham. Those interpretations identified Job with patient endurance, and so it was clearly an effective critique of such an approach to remind the reader of the many passages in the Book which represent Job in a very different light. In any case, it has to be said that representations of Job as a saint tend to restrict the reader to the prose story and the epilogue.

On the other hand, it would have been dangerous to make too much of the rebelliousness of Job, since that would be to suggest that he was adopting an appropriate attitude to God during that period of his life. It is possible to picture him as imperfectly pious, and as coming in time to understand the necessity for complete trust in the goodness of God, but this is to criticise him for at least part of his life: for the rebellious part of it. Few commentators manage to present an interpretation of the Book which successfully encapsulates it as a whole, since the Book is very diverse in its messages, and the commentators had themes which they wished to prioritise and argue for as the main meaning of the text. This is hardly surprising when one considers the metaphysical richness of the Book, with its treatment of issues such as knowledge of God and the world, providence, sainthood, rebellion, human imperfection and the nature of evil and human suffering. The richness of the text makes it very adaptable to the interests of those approaching it, and the Midrashic, Talmudic, mystical and philosophical commentators have taken advantage of this to see in the text an exemplification of the points which particularly interested them.

It is worth making a distinction between these different approaches, since they are constructed with different aims in prospect. The philosophical approaches have as their main aim the logic of the arguments in the text, and they tend to suggest that there is an underlying argument in the text which has to be sought beneath the surface of the writing. The integrity of the text as a religious work is not so important to philosophical interpreters since they restrict their analysis of the text precisely to what they take the arguments of the text to be. Talmudists and Midrashists have different aims in mind, although they use very similar structures of argument to the philosophers on many occasions. They wish to explore the way in which the text fits in with a whole range of different religious texts, and they will try to show that particular principles are common to a variety of such texts, so that unless we bear those principles in mind, we shall fail to grasp what those texts are really about. The scope of their arguments is narrower than in the case of the philosophers, since the former are limited to looking at a collection of texts belonging to a particular religion. The philosophers will often incorporate in their arguments theoretical perspectives of a much broader provenance, extending to Greek philosophy or to the philosophical techniques of the wider cultural community of which they are a part. In fact, there is no doubt that these broader theoretical perspectives also entered into the work of the Talmudists and Midrashists and informed their writings, but there is still an important distinction to be drawn between analysis which is designed to be restricted to a particular sphere of religious writing, and that which takes such writing as its object but which borrows techniques quite explicitly from a tradition of thought which is not thus limited. It is important to be very careful in not trying to pull the philosophical and the religious traditions too firmly apart from each other, despite the very real differences that exist between them. For one thing, many of the philosophers whom we shall be considering had not only philosophical concerns in mind in their writings on the topics of evil and suffering and, indeed, some of them were firmly part of the religious tradition of Jewish exegetical interpretation. Also, one has to be aware of the complexities which result when one tradition affects another. The result is often much untidier than the historians of intellectual history credit.

There is a tendency to think that it is fairly easy to distinguish between religion and philosophy because these are parts of different ways of approaching a topic, and so the methods they employ will be quite distinct. Sometimes this is true, and there is a range of both religious and philosophical topics which appear to be quite independent of each other. This is certainly not true of the topics which are being considered here. They play an important role in both philosophy and religion. It has been suggested that these two traditions of thought have different characteristics and distinct aims, but they should not be drawn apart too radically. It is clear that the traditions of religion and philosophy are so closely linked together here that it is often quite unclear where one tradition starts and the other finishes. It is far too simple to think that they embody entirely different approaches, since they use each other frequently to make the sort of points which they think are important. This is hardly surprising, since they have as their object of enquiry a fact of experience: the experience

How do we know evil? Through actual suffg? What makes something evil?

Job

of undeserved suffering. It might be thought that while suffering is an experience the fact that it is undeserved is not, and so is at a higher theoretical level than the experience itself. Such an observation would be unduly casuistical. It is clear that individuals do consider themselves as possessing the feeling of suffering when they have done nothing to deserve it, and it is this feeling which Job continually refers to God for an explanation. In the Book it is replaced with another feeling, that of contact with God, but God has not just provided Job with a more powerful feeling which allows him to ignore the original feeling. He has provided him with a feeling which allows him to regard the original feeling from a particular perspective, as being the result of an imperfect and limited point of view. So God provides Job not only with a feeling, but with an argument also, an argument which has as its result the transformation of his previous interpretation of his experience. To understand what happens to Job we have to understand both its religious aspects *and* its philosophical meaning, and we have to bring these together, since it is not possible to separate them if we are to be able to grasp what is taking place and what it means.

Although it is the aim of this discussion to concentrate upon the philosophical aspects of evil and suffering, it is very much the theme that such an aim cannot be realised without paying due attention to the religious and experiential features of such phenomena. The philosophical tradition which we are examining here was on the whole quite aware that it was dealing with only one aspect of evil and suffering, that which can be brought under the abstract and general concepts of philosophy, and that for a complete answer to be feasible a wider perspective must be added to the philosophical approach. This is not to disparage the latter, which plays a vital role in trying to understand evil and suffering, but it is to acknowledge the essential limitations of philosophy in coping with areas of human experience which have a far wider meaning than can be comprehensively understood philosophically. The Book of Job is wonderfully illustrative of this point. The constant to-ing and fro-ing between argument and experience, between dialogue and poetry, between issues and feelings reveals the richness and diversity of life in a world created by God. The philosophers whom we shall consider naturally concentrated upon those aspects of the Book which are more amenable to philosophical analysis than those which are harder to discuss formally, and yet they were also aware that they were presenting just one part of the whole view of such an explanation of evil and suffering. Most of them were content to accept that they were able to outline just one aspect of these topics, albeit a vitally significant aspect. They would argue that unless one understands the philosophical nature of evil and suffering, the experiences which are associated with those topics rest on entirely insubstantial foundations. There is certainly more to those topics than is represented by these foundations, but the latter are an essential feature of them. We shall see how those in the philosophical tradition seek to establish their view that if we are to understand evil and suffering we must use their methods of analysis. While this approach is a necessary condition of such an understanding, it is far from being sufficient, and the religious concepts of evil and suffering will always remain wider than their philosophical analysis.

CHAPTER 2

Philo

The first thinker to be considered is Philo of Alexandria, who lived from around 25 BCE to 50 CE. He was, to all accounts, an observant Jew and also a thoroughly Hellenised citizen of Alexandria. There is no evidence that he knew any Hebrew whatsoever, and he managed to argue that this hardly mattered, since the Septuagint translation into Greek was itself divinely inspired. Philo represented the assimilated Jew, assimilated in general cultural terms but not in religion, and in some ways he is thus a very modern figure, since many Jews today, like Philo, are not knowledgeable in Hebrew and rely on their secular culture to provide them with a language to approach the Bible. The language which they use is not just the language of the community in which they have been brought up, but it also involves the conceptual system of that environment. For Philo this was very much the system of Greek philosophy, which represented for him the acme of human reasoning. But once one tries to use a system like Greek philosophy to analyse religion a number of interesting problems arise. One is employing a methodology of extreme generality to discuss an entirely different system of some specificity. If the enterprise is to succeed, then it must be possible to use Greek philosophy to make sense of particular kinds of religious experience, very different kinds of religious experience from that which was described by the Greeks. As an assimilated thinker Philo was pulled in two different directions, towards the culture of Greece and at the same time to the culture for which the Bible was composed. He was obliged to argue that this is not really an enormous problem, since both cultures deal in different ways with the same issues, and those differences are more apparent than real. What is required is a key to unlock the principles which will allow those apparent differences to be seen as more apparent than real.

Philo is a highly eclectic thinker, and he produced a great deal of work, much of it rather repetitive and quite a large proportion not really his at all, but just paraphrases of current philosophical work of the time. Despite these critical comments, which might fail to account for the way in which philosophy was produced at that time, he also produced some very interesting argument, and if Harry Wolfson is correct (*Philo, passim*), he established the philosophy curriculum for the Church Fathers, the Middle Ages in both Europe and the Islamic world and much of early modern philosophy such as that produced by Spinoza.

Philo's basic project was a simple one, and involved establishing that Judaism was a rational faith. What he meant by 'rational' was in accordance with Greek, especially Platonic, philosophy. This led to a problem, since Greek philosophy seems to get on quite nicely without any Jewish revelation, while the Jewish religion seems to be based upon such revelation. Philo gets around this problem by entering into a determined project of interpreting the Bible as allegory, and relating the concepts of the Bible to the ideas of philosophy. He even suggests occasionally that the Greek philosophers acquired their understanding of wisdom from previous knowledge of the Bible, but it is doubtful whether he really believed it. He was appealing here to a popular device throughout the history of ideas whereby a thinker pretends that one system of ideas produced another system of ideas, where on the face of it the systems point in different directions. This is a cunning way to naturalise an apparently alien system of thought and to establish a basis for the argument that the systems are more or less the same anyway. The problem which Philo had was reconciling the rather personal grammar of the Bible with the impersonal and abstract god of Greek philosophy. Yet this problem is not final, since there are a host of ways of interpreting biblical language allegorically which can see it representing abstract Greek concepts, and the one God or Logos can be seen as the basis of all types of human thinking. As a Platonist Philo did not have much difficulty incorporating the Bible into his philosophy – he was very much pushing an open door. We shall come to see that the Jewish Aristotelians had a much harder task, albeit one which they were confident in tackling.

It is worth pointing out that Philo formulated most of the conceptual issues which we shall be exploring in this book. His identification of God with an abstract principle suggests that we should not relate to God as to a person in a simple sense, and that the attributes of God should be understood very differently from the attributes of human beings. The language of the Bible can then be interpreted allegorically. Now, this sets the agenda for his successors, since it allows the crucial move that God should not be regarded as responsible for evil in the world in the same way that we can be regarded as responsible for instances of such evil. Also, God cannot be regarded as responsible for evil which he could prevent in the same way as we might be regarded as thus responsible, since we should beware of understanding God's relationship to his world as on a par with our understanding of our own relationship to the world in which we find ourselves. The Bible represents the history of a particular people which has to cohere with the principles of reason as such, but the only way in which rules of particularity and universality can be brought together is to argue that they are mutually convertible. The universal rules of rationality find particular instances in the Bible, while the particular accounts of the Bible point to general issues of which they are exemplars. Philo establishes the project which later philosophers pursued, of relating reason to revelation in a manner acceptable to both, and it might be argued that the issues of evil and suffering are in many ways the key problem for such a relationship. Here we have very concrete examples of particular events, examples which dominate our attention, and to provide a universal account of such phenomena will always be a difficult task from a personal point of view.

There has for a long time been a lively controversy concerning the correct estimation of Philo as a philosopher. Some commentators regard him very highly, while others stress his eclecticism and deny him any originality or depth of thought. One of the problems with his enormous output is that it is not difficult to find him saying one thing in one book, and the opposite elsewhere. This is very evident when we come to look at his thought on evil and suffering. He works from a notion of an entirely transcendent deity, separated from evil and imperfection. We are told that:

God, alone is happy and blessed, exempt from all evil, filled with perfect forms of good, or rather, if the real truth be told, is himself the good, who showers the particular goods on heaven and earth. (*Spec. Leg.* Bk.II.§53)

He is perfect; he knows everything and can do anything. One aspect of his perfection is his inability to complete himself further. Nothing can benefit him and he needs nothing.

It would seem to follow from such statements that God transcends the evil in the world, and this is indeed Philo's claim. God may be said to have brought about the good things in the world, but not the bad things. In other places he seems to suggest that God might be held responsible for evil events, especially when these are designed to solicit repentance. His *De Providentia* deals directly with the problem of evil, and here he argues that some evil events are really surreptitious benefits. Events like earthquakes, disease and bad weather, though, are not brought about by God, but are instead natural events. He implies that when the innocent suffer we are in the realm of therapeutic and disciplinary action, and that God knows better than we do why particular individuals of apparently blameless character are picked out for punishment at divine hands. Once human beings were provided with the capacity to distinguish between good and evil, they must be allowed to have set off actions which return to make them suffer on occasions. This wicked side of humanity, though, cannot rightly be laid at God's door; Philo hints at the contribution of lesser beings in the creation of the evil possibilities of human beings. He sometimes refers to a breed of punitive angels in this respect, but generally his arguments here are based upon more solid philosophical underpinning.

Philo's Platonism made it easy for him to divide the body and soul up into two things, with physical events being labelled as gratification of the senses and so as evil, while mental events originate in the soul and are good. If we develop the virtuous side of our nature, we seek to transcend the body and cultivate our souls. We manage this if we observe the Mosaic laws and move from this world into the intelligible world where virtue, piety and wisdom prevail. Our rewards for virtue are spiritual rather than physical, as one would expect, and there is no scope for a simplistic desire for physical compensation for innocent sufferings undergone in the past. Although Philo thinks that those who obey the divine law will enjoy long life, the longevity here is not to be interpreted in terms of time, but rather in terms of quality of goodness. There is hardly any mention of an afterlife in Philo's voluminous writings, so the prospect of a heaven and hell to provide eventual restitution and punishment is ruled out. Although he does quite often mention immortality, it is far from clear what he means by it, except that it seems not to be a reward but something which happens to all. At death the soul finally manages to escape the clutches of the body, and ascends to somewhere, the precise nature of which Philo describes variably depending upon the text one examines.

If we are to be clearer on Philo's account of evil and suffering, we have to understand more of his understanding of the deity and its nature. As is well known, Philo combines the Greek conception of the deity as a pure being with the Jewish notion of a personal and responsive being. Although his descriptions of the deity are replete with the sort of abstract Greek notions of transcendence, omnipresence and spirituality, Philo's God is also said to be good and powerful, and the ultimate source of grace. This combination of seemingly incompatible properties has the interesting result that Philo stresses the need to fight anthropomorphism when we think about God. One motive behind this is the need to separate God from the evil in the world. Someone else has to be blamed for evil, and it is the participants in the creation of humanity (Philo argues that the presence of participants is implied by the phrase 'Let *us* make man...' (my emphasis) in Genesis 1:26.) This precise phrase is used because:

when man orders his course appropriately and when his thoughts and deeds are innocent, God the universal ruler may be acknowledged as their source. Others from the ranks of his subordinates are responsible for thoughts and deeds of a contrary kind, since it could not be that the father should be the cause of an evil thing to his offspring, and vice and vicious deeds are evil. (*Op.* §75–6)

Yet, one might say, what about all those instances in the Jewish Bible in which God is said to cause evil things to happen? These instances are doubtless explained by his motives in punishing and testing his creatures, yet the actions themselves are evil whatever their motivation.

Philo takes the line that if God does punish and test us, he does it through intermediaries (*Abr.* §142–6) and any text which suggests otherwise must be interpreted allegorically. We might wonder why God did not create a better world, and Philo would respond that it is due to the nature of the material with which God was obliged to work. As a result of his grace he sought to impose some aspect of himself upon matter and thus created the world, which is inevitably flawed by its inability due to its original constitution to receive more of the divine influence (*Op.* §23). Although the world is characterised by divine providence, it extends only as far as the good things in the world. The bad things which happen fall within a pattern, but the cause of those bad things is not God. Although we share in the divine soul to the extent that we have minds, we also have free will, and frequently choose to act in immoral ways. We are much hampered in this respect by the body, which seeks to dominate the rational part of us and push us in the direction of transgression. Philo dislikes the idea that the evil things in the world are there to influence us to behave properly due to their role as punishments and warnings. Indeed, he interprets the absence of threats in the ten commandments as evidence of God's intention that we decide to act virtuously out of our own desire for the good, rather than to preserve our physical wellbeing and avoid punishments (*Decal.* §176–8). In Philo's comments upon how we should seek to establish a means of determining our lives ethically there is a strong Stoic element.

How free are we in setting out to determine our lives? Philo has an interesting position on this query. God is very much involved in our virtuous decisions, but when we go astray we act entirely in terms of our own desires and intentions. It is in our interests to be virtuous, but often we fail to act in our best interests. Virtue is its own reward (*Spec. leg.* Bk. II §257–62) and we should not expect that God will reward us, or indeed punish us, like a supernatural judge. Through virtuous action we come closer to God, and our souls become closer to immortality and an ascent towards the transcendent realm. This does not come about solely through the grace which God applies to the world, because this grace is universally applicable. Since God has no needs, the only motive he has for bestowing himself upon the world is grace. We can come to improve ourselves and perfect our souls by using our natural abilities, habituating ourselves to virtuous activities and trying to stay on the right path.

Philo was working within a well-developed theory of providence and evil as presented by the Stoics. They were prepared for the objection that if divine planning enters into every aspect of the structure of the world, how can we account for the evident wickedness and suffering which is all around us? A variety of responses were thought to be appropriate here. One is to argue that if good is possible, then so also must its contrary evil be, in just the same way that we cannot talk about the truth if we cannot talk about the false, or pleasure without pain and so on. This is not much of an argument, since if it shows anything at all, it shows that there is a necessary relationship between the concepts of good and evil, not that if good exists, then evil must exist too. The Stoics were quite right in arguing that there would be no need for prudence in behaviour if we were unaware of the possible evil consequences of imprudent action, and yet this does not establish the link between prudence and the existence of evil. There may well be a relationship in thought, but not necessarily in reality.

Another tack adopted by Chrysippus, as reported by Plutarch, is to see the universe as a whole as perfect because it is regulated in accordance with a divine plan, but the universe possesses parts which only share in the perfection of the whole and are not themselves perfect. This is an interesting suggestion, and would work if it can be shown that individual moral evils can make up a perfect whole. Indeed, the argument would have to show that the perfect whole would not be a perfect whole without the individual instances of evil. A related but different strategy is that of regarding evil as a mere side-effect of benevolent principles embodied in nature. For example, it is inappropriate to think of a divine creator producing illness, since such a creator can only produce good things. But for some of these good things to work properly it is necessary for the possibility of negative consequences to exist. Eyes are carefully constructed to allow creatures to see, to be flexible and appropriate for their needs, but their very usefulness brings along with it a vulnerability to damage and disease. If the eyes were not soft and pliable they would not be much good as eyes, and if they are soft and pliable they are capable of being quite easily damaged.

Still, even if one accepted this reasoning, one might hope that the eyes of the righteous would be less at risk than the eyes of the evil, and the evidence suggests that this is not the case. The virtuous are just as capable of suffering through the vagaries of disease and accident as are the vicious. A heroic move on the part of the Stoics is to argue that nothing evil can befall the virtuous individual. This still leaves the virtuous individual with experiences which he would prefer not to possess. To argue that the divine purpose implicit in the world is concerned only with major and not petty events, such as eye disease, is to deny one of the pillars of the view that providence completely pervades the world and affects even the smallest and least significant state of affairs. A better kind of argument is that which points to the helpful side of pain and disadvantage in developing more noble and powerful personalities. In just the way that an athlete trains through subjecting his body to physical and mental hardships, so we in general should use the unpleasant events which occur to refine and perfect our abilities to act well. Many painful events are necessary for a greater good to emerge. Although the Stoic ideal of virtue is that of a passionless tranquillity, a state in which we refuse to be buffeted by

varying emotions and ideas, we are to acknowledge that our scope for
action is very limited if by 'actions' is meant self-determination. Our
role in life is pretty well determined for us from the beginning, but we
do have some scope for individual action, within the context of a
determining destiny.

Philo is clearly much influenced by these views in his account of the
role of evil. He is particularly enthusiastic about arguments which
separate God from evil. In his work *On Providence* (if it is his work) he
clearly argues that the doctrine of providence does not imply that God
is the cause of everything. In the same way as we cannot blame a just
law for the existence of crime, we cannot blame God for the existence
of criminals. Those natural events like storms and floods which cause
devastation are really aspects of natural life which on the whole
benefit people, and when they occasionally cause harm this is far less
than the good which they customarily do. Fire is very useful, but
smoke is a nuisance, and there is no smoke without fire. Philo is
obviously not very happy with this line of thought because he goes on
to account for the very differing lives of the virtuous and the wicked, as
we experience such differences in looking at the various fates of
individuals in the world. First he says that we have only a partial view
of who is virtuous and who is not, and so cannot really judge the
rightness or otherwise of what happens. He then moves to the stronger
argument that the virtuous cannot hope to be excluded from the
general organisation of events without a total reorganisation of their
constitution. Inevitably, if someone walks around in the rain, he will
get wet, and if someone lives in a community in which evil people also
live, he will be affected by their behaviour. Virtuous people do not
object to such states of affairs, since they appreciate the relative
unimportance of benefits like wealth and health, being able to
concentrate upon developing their capacity to use reason and acquire
virtue.

Since Philo argues that we can know virtually nothing about God,
we cannot understand his precise relationship with evil and suffering.
We can understand how good and evil are related by observing the
world, and we can work out that virtue is its own reward and that we
have to put up with problems because they are an inevitable part of
human life through an investigation of the relevant concepts. This
might seem to fit in well with the sort of answer which God gives Job,
an answer based upon observing nature. A difficulty which is always
going to arise, though, in such a case is that nature does not provide

much direct evidence of providence. There are certainly some examples of things fitting together well, and we do often marvel at the way in which natural organisations work. Yet it is always open to us to wonder whether small, or even large, improvements could not be made. Indeed, we ourselves are constantly changing nature to fit in better with what we see our interests as being. Now, Philo argues that the very flexibility of nature which makes it useful to us necessarily involves dangers, and there is something in this. Yet an improved kind of nature would incorporate within the same flexibility a disposition to harm us less. Could we not have rain without floods, sun without drought and children without birth defects? It might be argued that if these facts of life were to change, then we should be living in a different kind of world, and we should be different kinds of creatures. It is difficult to see this argument as particularly strong, though, since there is nothing fixed about these facts concerning the world. It may be that one day our control over the world will be such as to do away with floods, droughts and birth defects, and we shall still be human beings in such a changed environment. We might then ask why it was necessary for many generations of our forebears to suffer these unpleasant conditions when it was feasible to do away with them. Of course, we would not know how to do this until the appropriate discoveries were made, but one might assume that if some principle of providence were to govern the world then it would not drag out the discovery of solutions to our problems over such a long period.

Philo is immune from this sort of objection. He can respond by pointing out that providence need not involve what we would regard as providence. From our point of view, if we had the power to organise the world, we might well arrange it differently to accord better with what we perceive our interests to be. God is in a very different position. First, he knows far better than we do what is in our interests, and constructs the world accordingly. Secondly, we cannot work from our notion of providence to the notion of divine providence. God is not a person like us but even more so. He is entirely different from us, and his understanding of how to build justice into his creation may have little relationship to our understanding of such a state of affairs. The latter point is a very important one, which we shall see came to have a long and distinguished history. The first point is a bit more dubious. Since Philo produces what he obviously regards as evidence of providence in his description of the natural world, he can hardly object if we wonder whether the facts he describes really are evidence of providence. It is certainly true that God may be assumed to have a wider and superior view as compared with our grasp of the world, but if we are to get involved seriously in the business of assessing *evidence* of providence it must bear some resemblance to what we would call providence. After all, Philo produces arguments to show that particular aspects of nature reveal good design. He can hardly object when we criticise the design that he did not mean the design to be judged on human criteria of good design.

What scope is there on Philo's account for the individual to shape her own providence? A great deal of scope exists here, since she should appreciate that the vagaries of nature affect most immediately the less important aspects of life, the material conditions of her life. Although she may end up poor and unwell (like Job), she can always develop the spiritual and intellectual side of her nature. This point comes out nicely when one considers the so-called healers of the twentieth century who call upon their audience to have faith in God and as a result throw off their illnesses and disabilities. These healers suggest that it is within the power of God to help those in the audience who are in an appropriate spiritual condition to transform themselves physically. The lame will walk, the blind will see and the seriously ill will be cured. What many believers today say in response, in accordance with Philo's approach, is that they may be physically imperfect but spiritually they are already on the right road and the spiritual aspect of their lives is far more important than the material. They may be physically distressed, but the physical aspect of their lives is not the most significant aspect of them as people, and if they concentrate upon their religious and intellectual abilities they may become fully developed as people despite their physical problems. The healers have a notion of the person favoured by God as being in the very best physical as well as spiritual health, which one might regard as simplistic and unrealistic. We live in a natural world in which we can suffer natural disabilities, and it is up to us to minimise the importance of the vagaries of nature in our lives.

This sort of Stoicism might be regarded as an uncritical acceptance of the way in which the world is organised. Should we not expect an omnipotent and omniscient deity to organise the world in such a way that the innocent would not suffer in the sorts of ways with which we are so familiar? Not necessarily. The advantages of Philo's argument is that it works from the way in which things are in the world, and suggests that we can be expected to cope with that arrangement at no ultimate cost to our adherence to religion or reason. It is clearly more meritorious if we behave well despite the slings and arrows of fate than if we do so because we shall inevitably attract a material reward. Job does not seek a reward when he challenges God, he seeks an answer, and once he accepts the answer he is rewarded, but the reward is incidental to his acceptance of the answer. Job's real reward is his seeing God, and the material reward is a trivial consequence of the meeting between Job and God. It would be prudent to worship a deity who rewarded us by giving out material prizes, but it would not be very interesting. There is certainly something very attractive about the idea which Philo defends that what is right about virtue is implicit in the action itself and is its own reward. Any other reward is incidental to the rightness of the action. If our scope for morality is not to be cramped by the constant intervention of an all-powerful deity, we need to have room to make our own decisions, take risks and try to work out from our observation of the world what it is that we ought to do. We shall be helped in this, of course, by the teachings of the appropriate religious texts, but these require interpretation and application. Philo is certainly right in arguing that when we observe a providence ruling nature which is different from the sort of providence we would institute, were we the rulers of nature, we cannot conclude that nature is not providential. What we observe here is a different kind of providence which we only grasp piecemeal and imperfectly.

Yet we have to return to a major difficulty with this notion, the idea that while the parts which we observe are imperfect, the whole itself is perfect. There are two ideas running together here, and they are distinct. One is the argument that we cannot work from where we are to where God is. We cannot move from our idea of providence to what must be God's principle of providence. There is a lot to be said about this relationship between different kinds of language, and we shall see how it is developed by later thinkers. There are good grounds for thinking that we should be very careful before we saddle God with the same sort of ideas about how the world should be organised as we have. On the other hand, this should not be confused with the argument that we see only a part of the whole, not the whole itself, and the latter is perfect by contrast with the former. The difficulty with this argument is that it seems to be based upon evidence, but really it is not. Since we cannot observe the whole, we cannot tell whether it is perfect or not, nor even what sort of notion of perfection can apply to it. It is certainly true that we can see in nature aspects of organisation which are puzzling, and which become less puzzling once we understand more about them. Philo gives lots of examples of this type. We can appreciate that this is true on the basis of our experience. But we cannot observe the whole of nature, and while we might hope that it is perfect, or even believe that it is perfect, this cannot be as a result of evidence. We may have a deep religious belief that the way in which the world is arranged is perfect, although we can only see part of that arrangement, and we may well think that God alone can understand how the whole is perfect. This does not even have to be a religious belief – it can be a feeling we have about the world without any religious overtones at all. It is important that we appreciate that this belief is just that, a belief, and a belief for which no evidence is available. No evidence is available, and no evidence could be available to support it, since the belief itself implies the unattainability of such evidence. Now, Philo does adhere to metaphysical principles which involve such a belief, and that is perfectly acceptable from a philosophical standpoint, but it is an error to suggest that such a belief can receive any support by observing nature. The belief goes beyond nature, and any arguments for it must go beyond nature also. Philo set out some of the main ground rules in the analysis of the relationship between observing evil in the world and how it can be brought under a general theory including a benevolent deity, and these rules were much developed and extended by his successors in Jewish philosophy.

Like Philo, they had the problem of knowing how to link particular instances of providence, of divine design, to a greater whole. Sometimes it looks as though the particular instance provides evidence of providence, and sometimes the whole of which it is an instance is the appropriate object of contemplation, yet as we have seen it is hardly valid to point to either of those kinds of object as evidence. They will not serve as evidence because they exist within a context in which there is inevitably so much evidence to the contrary. As we have seen, we may accept with Philo that particular aspects of the world exhibit useful flexibility with the inevitable consequences that they may be misused or vulnerable to damage, and we may regard this as evidence of a shaping force with divine origins providing us with an environment in which we can flourish, albeit one in which we can suffer also. Since the observation of such helpful phenomena cannot count as evidence of a divine helper, given the availability of contrary evidence and the possibility of improvements to the structure of the phenomena which would make them even more helpful, one wonders at the point of observing such phenomena. It cannot be even an indication of the route to the understanding of the nature of divine providence, since Philo tells us that the latter is very different from what we understand by providence. To understand what is going on here we have to take seriously Philo as a Platonist. The particular examples which we observe are imperfect instances of immutable and complete Forms, and they serve as indications of the nature of such Forms. Our ability to identify the particulars as instances of design is itself only possible because of our ability to be aware of the Forms, and we should beware of thinking that we construct those Forms by abstracting from the particulars. To act in such a way would be to misunderstand seriously the relationship between particulars and universals on a Platonic view. The very imperfection of the particulars of our world is the best indication of the impossibility of moving from the particulars to the Forms, since those particulars by themselves provide no concept of what it would be like for perfection to be realised. The particulars presuppose the Form, and not vice versa.

The particulars are important, though. They are the things with which we are familiar, and they lead us to think about the Forms on which they are dependent. If we just concentrate upon the particulars then we will never get closer to an understanding of what it is for something to be a perfect example of its kind. To take providence as an example: if we note only examples of providence in the world we will fail to appreciate how refined this notion can become. The providence which is all around us is necessarily imperfect, as we have seen, and if we do not look for paradigmatic examples we shall be limited in our understanding of the quality. What we see around us gives us a hint of what is available at a higher level of understanding. Now, the precise nature of the more perfect form of providence is not accessible to us, at least not while we remain physically connected with the world of generation and corruption. We can form an idea of it, of course, and perhaps we had an idea of it before we entered into this world if the Platonic account of knowledge is to be followed, but while we are alive as human beings we are going to be cut off from a perspicuous view of this idea as a result of our connection with the material. Once we transcend those limitations, we can understand precisely the role which evil has in the world, and why suffering must exist in that world, but before this raising of consciousness can take place we have to be satisfied with the very limited view which is all that is possible. We can know that there is a connection between the sort of language we use when talking about evil from our present point of view and what it would be like to discuss it from a more perfect point of view, but what the precise nature of that connection is we cannot now say.

This gap between the divine and human perspectives on evil and suffering is a common theme in the treatments of the topic in Jewish philosophy. It is important to use 'treatments', since there is certainly no common approach which is followed by all the thinkers we are considering here. What is important to grasp is that the nature of the distinction between these two perspectives is a subtle one, and it is not based upon the risible strategy of suggesting that if we only understood the whole picture, then we should see what the role of evil and suffering was in the world, and the implication is that we should accept and approve of this role. It is certainly true that an individual may have a strong personal faith which is such that he refuses to regard any evil which occurs to him as really being evil at all. He treats everything which happens as coming from God and having a role in the divine plan, and he is prepared to interpret anything which happens as only apparently evil, and really good. There is nothing wrong with anyone's faith taking this form, but we should notice how distinct such a position is from an argument. An argument will provide an explanation for the existence of the apparent evil and another explanation for the existence of the explanation. A refusal to accept that something is really evil is not an argument, it is just a refusal, like refusing to accept that it is raining if one is determined to assert that it never rains. What Philo provides, by contrast, is a sophisticated explanation for the existence of evil together with a theory in which that explanation makes sense. We do not have to be Platonists to appreciate the structure of Philo's account. The radical gap which he investigates between our perspective on evil and the divine perspective is something of a theme in Jewish philosophy, and we shall see how his successors explored the nature of that gap in varying ways. Clearly this issue is going to be a crucial one here, since the nature of the gap represents a problem which fascinated and perplexed all the thinkers working within a Jewish tradition.

It is difficult to compare religions without making very crude generalisations, yet sometimes this danger must be risked in order to examine interesting features of the particular faiths. Many philosophers of religion examine the nature of the relationship between the deity and his creation, and all religions have some account of this relationship. When one looks at the three monotheistic religions which share Job as a significant figure, certain differences appear to emerge. Christian interpreters of the Book of Job often comment that the real ending is to be found in the New Testament, since there Jesus Christ comes to mediate between the human and the divine world. In Islam there have been a large number of messengers who have undertaken this intermediary role, albeit in a different way from that characterised by Christianity. There are certainly prophets in Judaism who have carried out some of these functions, and Moses is perhaps the nearest to the role of Muhammad, but the whole relationship between God and the world appears rather more distant in Judaism than in the other two religions. The fierce monotheism and the radical self-description by God at Exodus 3:14 as 'I am who [or that] I am' militates against too much familiarity between the deity and his creatures. This sets up a huge problem, though, for Jewish thinkers, since the deep chasm which appears to exist between God and his creatures has to be bridged if we are to understand what role concepts like evil and suffering are to have in a divinely created world. If God and the world are kept too far apart from each other, then the existence of evil in our world will lack any connection with God, since he will appear to be unconcerned with the events of this world or incapable of intervening in it on our behalf. It is the main task of Jewish philosophy to explain how a distant deity can nonetheless be involved in the activities of this world, yet without compromising his transcendence. As one can imagine, this task is not an easy one to carry out, and it implies the necessity to find a subtle link between God and the world. What is remarkable about the Book of Job is the continual refusal on Job's part to accept a simple answer to his problems in the language of traditional religion. He acknowledges throughout the great distance between us and the deity, and he rejects any account of that gap which reduces it by making God more like us, or us more like God. Job sets out to reconcile the apparently irreconcilable, and his philosophical successors in Jewish philosophy followed him faithfully on this path.

CHAPTER 3

Saadya

Saadya ben Joseph, generally called Saadya Gaon, was born in Egypt in 882 and died in Iraq in 942. He seems to have enjoyed a highly polemical lifestyle, championing the anti-Karaite school and the Babylonian Geonim in their long dispute with their Palestinian co-religionists. The Karaites were an important group at the time. They advocated a literal reading of the Bible without the accretions of the Talmud and the Midrash, and downgraded the significance of the Hebrew language in Judaism. While most of the Jews in the Middle East wrote in Arabic in Hebrew characters, the Karaites went so far as to prepare religious works in Arabic in Arabic script, arguing that what is important about a religious text is its sense, not the precise language in which it is expressed. The Palestinian rabbinate was involved in a struggle for dominance over the Jewish world with their Babylonian rivals, and this took the form frequently of arguments over the calendar. Saadya entered into these bitter disputes with great gusto, and only managed to get philosophical work done when out of political favour. His philosophical work is marked with the same desire to crush his opponents as is his more polemical work. He lived at a very exciting time intellectually. The works of the Greek thinkers were being translated into Arabic and commented upon by Islamic thinkers, and Islamic theology (*kalām*) came to use many of the philosophical notions imported from Greek philosophy in defence of both Islam and a particular interpretation of Islam. The Jewish community was thoroughly assimilated culturally in the local Islamic world, and had no difficulty in reading and taking part in philosophical discussions. Despite this high level of acculturation, many Jewish intellectuals wished to preserve their religious identity, and so had to use the new dialectical techniques to help make sense of the compatibility of religion, in this case Judaism, with reason.

Saadya was one of the many thinkers of his time who entered into this project. He wanted to show that the sort of things which the Bible asserts do not go against valid philosophical argument, that a rational explanation can be provided for even the most difficult passages in the Bible. This obviously has to involve treating allegorically some biblical passages which, if interpreted literally, do not make sense. Theologically, Saadya was firmly on the side of the Muʿtazilites, the Islamic school of theology which advocated an objective standard of justice and an areligious concept of rationality. For the Muʿtazilites God does what is just because it is just, while for their opponents, the Ashʿarites, God does what is just because whatever God does is just. That is, 'just' means 'what God does'. Saadya spends a lot of time in his philosophical works showing how rational the Bible is despite some apparent difficulties in making sense of particular passages. We shall see that it is not correct to see Saadya as a thoroughgoing Muʿtazilite, since he was impressed by aspects of Ashʿarism, and incorporated them in his approach to theology. Saadya is a more eclectic thinker than is often thought. He took the standard line in the Middle Ages within both the Jewish and Islamic philosophical communities on the relationship between reason and revelation. They cannot disagree, but they may appear to disagree. The very general rules of reason are often unhelpful to our efforts to work out what we ought to do on particular occasions, and they are inaccessible to many people. The Bible uses anthropomorphic language, which we know through the use of reason cannot be literally accurate, but it may help many people to work out how they ought to behave and what they are to believe. Prophecy is necessary because it reveals religion to everyone, while philosophy will always be limited to a minority of people with intellectual interests. The fact that they express themselves differently, because they are addressing different audiences, is not in any way an indication of contradiction. Reason and prophecy express the same truth, albeit in different ways, and Saadya sees it as his task to show how compatible these two different ways of arguing are.

Saadya's approach to the Book of Job is a complex one, and heavily influenced by contemporary theological controversies in the Islamic world. It is buttressed by his developed philosophical and theological views expressed in other works, but he says that he was compelled to address the 'story of Job' (as Maimonides goes on to call it, in accordance with Islamic usage) because many people were confused by its message. He is clearly in no doubt that the message is to do with theodicy, since he calls Job the Book of Theodicy (*Kitāb al-taʿdīl*) or, literally, the 'Book which confirms justice'. This is very much his theme in discussing Job; the emphasis is firmly on justice and how to reconcile the notion of divine justice with the course of events with which we are familiar in the text. Saadya seems to have objected to the confused and confusing nature of much Midrashic commentary on the Book of Job. The various Midrashim tend to interpret Job as in some ways guilty, unbeknown to himself, of committing sins which are met with divine punishment, and Saadya felt, quite rightly, that this is to distract the reader from the real point of the Book. If that was all the Book was about, one might say, then it is hardly worthy of the interest which it receives from the reader. But it is not just the line of interpretation which Saadya dislikes, it is also the whole process of Midrash, with its mixture of argument, lexical analysis, comparison with other biblical texts, speculation, stories and a hermeneutic approach which seems to be able to arrive at quite arbitrary conclusions. What is required is a more 'scientific' approach to the text.

Saadya was writing at a very exciting time in the history of ideas. He was a strong opponent of Karaism, the movement in Jewish theology which stressed literal interpretations of the religion without any Talmudic accretions. The Karaites were a powerful and persuasive movement, and for a time it looked as though they might be able to overturn the entire Talmudic interpretation of Judaism. Whatever one might say about the Karaites, and this is not the place to analyse their thought, it made intellectual Jews examine the whole basis of their approach to religious texts. In Islam at that time there existed the protracted dispute between the Muʿtazilites and the Ashʿarites on how to work theologically, a dispute which largely concentrated upon the notion of divine justice. The Muʿtazilites argued that there are objective constraints on the notion of divine justice, so that if God is just he must balance the rewards and punishments which he gives his creatures in accordance with their deserts. It would be unfair to do otherwise. The reward for virtuous believers need not come in this world, but it must come at some time or another. Saadya uses this as an argument for the necessity of an afterlife, since it is patently true that some virtuous people have miserable times in this world which then have to be compensated by rewards in a future life.

The Ashʿarites were repelled by the idea of any constraints upon the actions of God. They pursued a metaphysics of morality which interprets moral expressions in terms of God's will. Justice then becomes whatever God does, and he is not in any way obliged to act in a manner which accords with our notion of justice. A later and celebrated Ashʿarite thinker, Ghazālī, suggested that insisting on a balance between rewards and punishments is to interpret God as like a capricious sovereign, who first of all slaps his servant and then makes it up to him by some financial compensation. The Ashʿarites pursued their belief in the overwhelming power of God to the extent that they denied the objectivity of events in the material world, interpreting natural phenomena as having no reality in themselves but only through their relationship with their creator. In reality, then, the world consists of atoms which exist only momentarily and through divine influence, and which can at any time be reassembled in ways which make a nonsense of our understanding of the course of nature.

Another important intellectual movement at the time of Saadya was the development of Peripatetic philosophy in Arabic. A programme of translation and discussion of Greek scientific texts was being prosecuted in Baghdad, and among these texts were many of the works of Plato, Aristotle, Alexander of Aphrodisias, Porphyry and Galen. The translations were surprisingly good, especially when one considers that they had to follow a rather tortuous route from Greek into Syriac and then into Arabic, and they led to the development in the Islamic world of a powerful school of philosophers, the *falāsifa*, who based their thinking upon the processes to be found in Greek thought. Perhaps the greatest *faylasūf*, Fārābī, was a contemporary of Saadya, and there is no doubt that the latter was heavily influenced by the techniques of the *falāsifa*. In Saadya's theoretical work these very varied influences are obviously present, but they rarely get in the way of his characteristic clarity of expression and depth of argument.

In his commentary on Job Saadya employs a mixture of techniques from theology (*kalām*) and philosophy (*falsafa*). While both sorts of argument are equally rational in themselves, the *falāsifa* promoted the superiority of their methods. The main distinction, they claimed, was that their arguments were demonstrative in form, starting from certain propositions and resulting, via a valid decision procedure, in certain and necessary conclusions. The arguments of the theologians (*mutakallimūn*) are by contrast dialectical, starting from premises which are accepted because they occur in some system of thought and belief, but which have no stronger rational background than that. The process of dialectic is to take premises and explore their

implications. Even if those implications do not reflect badly on the
initial premisses, then we still do not have any justification of those
premisses as they stand. In his commentary on Job it is clear that
Saadya employs both theological and philosophical techniques, as
one would expect. The structure of the commentary to a degree
reflects the structure of the text itself, which is often dialectical,
consisting as it does in many places in conversations between the
leading protagonists. While Saadya wants to impose a clear theological line on the text, he also wants to employ rigorous philosophical
techniques to clarify the leading ideas and relate them to wider and
more complex theoretical issues. Given the morass of potentially
confusing Midrashic interpretation into which the Book had fallen (in
his view), this is all too necessary.

In his introduction to the commentary Saadya sets out clearly what
his intentions are. The whole emphasis is upon theodicy. We are told:

> Plainly, his bringing creation into being from nothing is the ultimate act of
> grace. For he created the entire world and settled it with human beings for
> their benefit . . . Likewise, his giving us life, and the other acts of providence
> by which he governs us and orders the passage of our lives are all expressions
> of grace and bounty, as the prophet said 'Life and favour hast Thou wrought
> with me' (10:12) (*BT*, p. 124).

One interesting minor point to make about this passage is the
description of Job as a prophet, a very Islamic idea which nonetheless
helps to interpret him as a producer of messages. The idea that human
beings are the point of the creation of the world is an early indication
of Saadya's Muʿtazilite sympathies. Once we are told that creation is
for the benefit of human beings, we know that somewhere an
argument will be required to show that despite appearances they do
benefit from it in accordance with their merit. We do not have to wait
long for such arguments, because we are told that 'God's creating
suffering, sickness and injury in the world is also an act of beneficence
and in the interest of humanity' (*BT*, pp. 124–5). It is worth pointing
out at this stage that were it not for the assertions, and they are just
assertions, of the purpose of the world being for us, we might assume
that since God created the world out of nothing as a perfect act of
grace he was not constrained by considerations for our welfare in his
creation. This idea of the point of creation being humanity is one of
the main objections which the Ashʿarites have against the Muʿtazilite
school. They see it as demeaning to suggest that the deity had us in
mind when he created the world, and one of the points of insisting

upon its creation out of nothing is to guarantee that he was not limited to creating it in a particular way out of a particular matter.

For Saadya there are three purposes resulting from the phenomenon of human suffering – education, punishment and testing. Suffering can help discipline us and point us in the right direction, that is, the direction in which we shall ultimately benefit. Saadya has both a retributive and a deterrence view of punishment, in that our suffering helps to clear our guilt while at the same time making us motivated to avoid the actions which led to the pain. The third purpose is obviously what the Book of Job is about, namely:

The third case is that of trial and testing. An upright servant, whose Lord knows that he will bear sufferings loosed upon him and hold steadfast in his uprightness, is subjected to certain sufferings, so that when he steadfastly bears them, his Lord may reward him and bless him. This too is a kind of bounty and beneficence, for it brings the servant to everlasting blessedness. (*BT*, pp. 125–6)

As it stands, this is a rather perplexing statement. If the master knows that the servant will bear the sufferings, why subject him to them? Saadya goes on to strengthen his claim even further by asserting that it is not unjust for a creator to kill his creature in the midst of his normal life span, provided that he is promised recompense. Indeed, he further claims that such sufferings are a sign of divine benevolence, since the future reward is greater than the span of life foregone.

He obviously feels unhappy with the way in which he has made his point here, since he gives a variety of examples to try to show how reasonable his view is. He points out that we may grow accustomed to a particular form of existence, and may dislike being obliged to move onto a different form even if it is to our advantage. This certainly has some merit as an argument when applied to changes within our lives, but when we die we might wonder how we are going to benefit in the future. Instead of saying that if we deserve to benefit, we shall benefit in our next life, Saadya takes the course of claiming that God's wisdom is superior to that of his creatures, and he knows best. As it stands, this is not much of an argument, but is rather an excuse to close the discussion. We may not understand how we are to be compensated in the next life for our undeserved sufferings in this, and we might expect to be made aware of what arrangements we can look forward to when we face death. Appealing to the mysterious wisdom of the deity is perhaps not really enough. It might be said further that

were we to know to what we are going when we die, we might be in a
position to bear our mortal lives more equably.

Saadya points to three kinds of benefit which God institutes. First,
he created us, then he promises to remunerate us for our actions and
lastly he will recompense us for our tribulations which he has caused
and which we have borne stoutly. These latter are there not due to our
sins, but for a future benefit – they point to the future and not to the
past. If we really understood the future, we would understand how
much better off we are as a result of the divinely imposed suffering
compared with how we would be without it. Saadya backs this up
with some rather Ashᶜarite principles. God is completely just and can
do no wrong – 'Indeed, the very notion of being able or unable to do
wrong is inapplicable to him' (*BT*, p. 127). This is very much in line
with Ashᶜarite interpretations of the sense of moral language, in terms
of what God does and does not do. If God does something, then it is
right that it be done, and its having been done by God provides the
rightness of the action. 'Right' means what God does.

What the Ashᶜarites wished to avoid was the relativisation of
values, the reduction of the meaning of moral language to what would
suit us. Even worse in their eyes was the insistence that God himself is
constrained in his actions by the moral requirements of his creatures.
Saadya suggests that God cannot be unjust, because one would only
be so motivated if one were ignorant of some fact about a case or
wished to twist one's understanding of the facts to one's own advantage. Clearly, neither of these two things can be said of God, since he is
assumed to be omniscient and omnipotent. This is not quite correct,
though, since one might wonder whether divine injustice arises
through indifference to the lives of his creatures, and an all-knowing
and all-powerful creator could just not care what happens to his
creation. Saadya probably thought that he had covered this, for the
time being anyway, when he pointed to the ultimate act of grace as
being that of creation. Yet it might be argued that for some creatures
it would have been better had they never been created. For example,
they might suffer so much while alive that it would have been
preferable for them never to have been born, unless one believes in a
compensatory level of pleasure in the next life. Even if one does so
believe, it still raises questions about the *point* of the initial suffering.

Saadya deals with this issue when he refers to Job as having been
tested, passing the test and attaining bliss in the hereafter and more
than he could have hoped for in this life. There are four possible

reasons for Job's sufferings. One is that they are unjustly caused by God, a possibility which everyone in the Book rejects and which does not make sense if justice is equivalent to God's actions. He considers the possibility that God causes the righteous to suffer just because he wants to. He can also reward the unrighteous for exactly the same reason; as the Book has it, 'The tents of the plunderers are safe, and the strongholds of those who outrage God' (12:6). Yet all Job's companions inform him repetitively that God would not cause suffering to anyone who did not deserve it. This is why they continually try to turn Job's mind to his past actions and thoughts in order to discover where and when he sinned. As Saadya says, 'What drove them to this conclusion was their rational recognition that the Creator, being just, will do no wrong' (*BT*, p. 129). The correct view is presented by Elihu. The greatest reward is provided by God for those of his servants who endure the trials and tribulations which are inflicted upon him. Indeed, the purpose God had in creating human beings is to test them.

Elihu's position is taken to be quite simple. He argues that when we suffer there can be only two explanations. Either we are being affected by prior sins, or we are being tested. If we know that we have not been guilty of sins in the past, then we can be sure that we are being tested. Neither explanation for our suffering shows that God is unjust. Many readers find the Book of Job enigmatic because they confuse these explanations of his sufferings, and tend to concentrate upon his possible sins in the past. This is to go against the whole purpose of the text, which is to show how God may test perfectly virtuous individuals, and explain how such testing is compatible with divine justice. Saadya gives some rather unfortunate examples to help illustrate his point. In his *Book of Beliefs and Opinions (Kitāb al-Amānāt wal I'tiqād,* p. 214) he refers to the way in which children may suffer pain which will eventually be compensated, and compares this to the discipline which a father might try to impose in order to keep his children from harm. This analogy might work partially for older children, but is difficult to accept in the case of those very young children who spend most of their short lives in apparent pain and with no apparent enjoyment of life. Does it not seem gratuitously cruel to put them through this torture in order to benefit them eventually in the next life?

Saadya has an answer to this sort of objection. Could not the Almighty have provided them with their future reward immediately, without their having to submit to unpleasantness first? Might not this

seem to be an example of superior grace to that with which we are
familiar at the moment? He replies that the benefits of rewards by way
of compensation are greater than those which are immediately
conferred as a result of an act of divine grace (*BBO*, pp. 214–15). We
can see why this might be so for mature adults. If in order to win a race
I have to get hot and tired, I benefit by the feeling of triumph at the
end of the race, and to have such feelings without doing anything to
deserve them is in a sense absurd. Robert Nozick produces an
interesting example in this respect, called 'the experience machine'.
Suppose that we could plug ourselves into a machine which would
perfectly copy those feelings of success without the tiresome necessity
to undergo any exertion to succeed in reality. Would such sensations
be equivalent to the experience of winning, or whatever feeling is at
issue? The answer is taken to be that more is involved in having a
particular experience than just having that experience – a whole
context has to accompany it and give it its specific meaning. It is not
just the feeling which we are after when we undertake certain
activities (*Anarchy, State and Utopia*, pp. 42–5). So there is some scope
for Saadya's argument that it is better to suffer discomfort in order to
reap an eventual pleasure than to be presented with the pleasure right
at the beginning. We might want to limit such an example quite
strictly, though, since it does not seem to be very persuasive when we
are dealing with very young children, or with great degrees of pain
and discomfort.

   There are a variety of reasons for allowing the evil people in the
world to continue with their impious behaviour. They may eventually repent, they may produce virtuous children, they may have
produced some virtuous deeds, they may be employed to punish those
even worse than themselves and they may be there to benefit the
virtuous. Finally, they may be allowed to linger in order to make their
punishment even harsher. The important point to grasp here is that
there is a purpose and a reason behind the actions of both the virtuous
and the wicked; they both have a part to play in the structure of a
world which has been designed in order to enable human beings to
achieve the greatest possible benefit, and if we are unable to understand why this is so we have to reconcile ourselves to the fact of our
limited understanding of God's purposes and justice. The world was
created for us, but we have to work hard in it to get everything out of it
which we can, since it represents an arena of testing and trial. It is
better for us that it be so rather than just a place where benefits are

handed out, since we are thus able to take on moral development and improvement against the very evident obstacles which surround us. If we deserve to succeed then we will enjoy the appropriate benefits, albeit maybe in a future life. If we do not deserve to succeed, we shall experience the appropriate punishments, although not necessarily in this life.

For Saadya the attitude which the virtuous and the wicked have towards their actions is very important. If the latter come to repent of their sins they may well be eventually pardoned by God; if the former come to regret their good deeds they may be punished. Indeed, Saadya has an ingenious explanation for the prosperity of some evildoers. A virtuous person comes to regret his good deeds, and then starts to prosper. This seems to all who observe it a most unjust state of affairs. One would hope that the wicked would fail to prosper and the good be rewarded for their virtue. According to Saadya, what is happening here is that the wicked person is receiving reward in this life for his past virtuous deeds, while the appropriate recompense for his evil awaits his arrival in the next world. The reverse also happens, so that a virtuous person who turns evil and is rewarded in this life when he goes awry is matched by an evil person suffering misfortune when he repents of his past deeds and decides to turn over a new leaf. Punishment has both a retributive and a consequentialist point. God seeks to be just in the way in which he parcels out benefits and evils, but he also tries to test people, to see whether a problem in their lives might cause them to stray from virtue. It used to be a practice among Victorian householders to leave coins hidden in their furniture to check up on their servants' ability to clean and be honest. These little trials would ensure that the employer kept himself informed of the honesty of his employees. God only tests those who could benefit from the testing process, he does not bother to test those whom he knows would fail the test because of their moral weakness.

Saadya has an interesting discussion of why God does make clear to those he tests that he is testing them. Job is a patient man who endures the test and is eventually rewarded for his faith and virtue. Yet had he known from the start that this was only a test, albeit a rather drastic test, he would undergo a far less traumatic trial. Other people would assert that the patience of the virtuous was not so remarkable since they know that they will eventually be compensated for their sufferings. Even the entirely innocent may be made to suffer for their ultimate benefit, and Saadya has in mind here the sufferings of children. He compares this to the way in which fathers may force their children to drink unpleasant medicines for their ultimate advantage. There is even the implication that the more that God loves someone, the more that individual will be tested. We might recoil from such an argument, wondering whether it would not be better in the case of entirely innocent children for them not to have to undergo suffering, especially great suffering, for some eventual reward. Saadya seems to regard children here very much as the possessions of their parents, and the sufferings of the former are part of the testing of the latter. The point which he seeks to make is that the evil in the world is fairly distributed even when we cannot understand precisely how this takes place. The fact that we cannot tell is part of the divine purpose in testing us, and sometimes we have to be tested through others and their negative experiences.

This account might appear to be rather banal and involve a concept of God as a glorified bookkeeper, totting up balances and adjusting deficits and credits on a moral scale. It also seems to reduce the world to a realm in which balance must be present at all times when the broader view is taken, which might be thought to be a rather prosaic view where evil is concerned. Surely there is more to evil than just the ability to punish and test people. Saadya would agree with this point, and would argue that evil nonetheless plays an important part in the arrangement of a rational and just universe. Our sufferings are supposed to raise the spiritual character of our behaviour to a higher level than they would otherwise achieve. The motivation for our actions should not be based upon prudential considerations, or at least not always so based, and the educative function of evil makes us aware of the power and influence of God in the world. He sees all our actions and assesses them, punishing some and rewarding others. We are free to choose how to behave, and we must expect that our behaviour be taken seriously at a higher level of existence than that on which the behaviour itself takes place. Yet it must be admitted that we are led to conceive of a deity dispensing justice much in the way of human justice, albeit on a much grander and longer-lasting scale. Since Saadya argues that the world is both just and rationally analysable, he assumes that we can lay down the sort of ground rules for justice which must apply. There is mystery in the world to the extent that we cannot see exactly how what goes on fits into a scheme of rational justice, but no mystery at all about the existence, and indeed omnipresence, of such a scheme of rational justice.

This of course is in marked contrast to the way in which the Ashʿarites interpreted divine justice. For them there is no rational objectivity which the deity must follow if he is to be just. We can make no demands upon him because he can do whatever he wishes, and whatever he wishes is just. The sort of organisation which we as human beings count as justice provides no clues at all to the notion of divine justice, since there is an enormous gap between us and the deity, and any attempt at assimilating human and divine justice is erroneous. The kind of account which Saadya presents of the existence of evil might be thought to confirm the Ashʿarites in their position. Surely there is more to evil than just recompensing the wicked and educating the potentially virtuous. The neat scheme which Saadya constructs is consistent, but leaves out a great deal of the spiritual sense of evil. It constrains God to behaving like us, but do we want God to be thus limited in his actions? It also involves interpreting some aspects of suffering in very artificial ways. Job as a prophet teaches the wider scope of evil than that which might be immediately available to us on confronting our experience, but the very human interpretation he gives to it follows from his view of our relationship with God. This is a close relationship, since God is rather like us, but perhaps too close to describe adequately the depth of that relationship.

Saadya tries to justify aspects of evil in the world which the Book of Job itself avoids. It is very difficult to justify punishing someone through the sufferings of someone else, especially children. One's immediate reaction is to say that it is wrong to test someone through someone else. If I deserve to be punished, or need to be tested, then it is only I who should be addressed by the punishment or the task. No one else should be involved directly unless they also are part of the target of the project. In the discussion of the Book of Job by the Jewish commentators this point was developed when it came to wondering what it meant when at the end we are told that Job's children are returned to him. Does this mean that he gets back the same children? If everything is doubled, does he get back twice as many children? Since this might not seem very desirable, some suggested that he got back twice as many sons, but the same number of daughters. What is of interest in this discussion is the idea that children cannot be lumped together with everything else as possessions. There is something very morally dubious about the idea that Job's children die as part of the test, and then are returned to him, either the same or different children, at the successful completion of the test. The questionable nature of this is not mitigated by the fact that he passed the test, and even if he were guilty of sins and/or failed the test, one might well think it completely wrong to make or allow others to suffer in order to go through some sort of process with Job. These are different people, they are not possessions of Job and they should be respected as individuals. The suggestion which Saadya countenances that we can be tried through others is difficult to accept morally.

On the other hand, there is a point to this sort of notion. It grasps the fact that when we go awry, we take others with us. When we abandon the right path ourselves others are inevitably implicated. Our behaviour has a wider context than just involving ourselves. When we are told that everything starts to go wrong for Job, this had to involve his family. If Job was to represent the individual for whom everything started to go sour, it would not have been possible to exclude his wife and children. His wife had to start to complain, and his children had to suffer also. Had Job fallen ill and his material possessions disappeared, and yet his family stayed together as a unit, his sufferings would not have been so extreme as they ended up becoming. He would only have symbolised the individual who was partially abandoned by God. Satan's test is only meaningful if everything was taken away from Job, not just some of what he held dear. From a symbolic perspective, there is a good deal to be said for such a picture of total loss. When things do fall apart, other people as well as things are part of the disaster. If there was to be a test, then Job's children had to play a part in it. If we see the things which happen to Job as being a symbol of how things can go wrong for an individual, for any individual, then his family must be involved. It does happen that for certain individuals terrible things happen to them and to their families. We are entirely familiar with this. People of outstanding moral character bear children with severe physical disabilities and low life expectancies, whose lives are not only brief but unpleasant also. Healthy, bright and attractive children are killed due to entirely haphazard circumstances. All this is personified in the Book of Job.

It is inevitable also that others will suffer when we suffer for our sins. If I am a thief and I go to prison, then my family will suffer even though they are entirely innocent of any crime. If I am a thief and I am never caught, they will still suffer through their association with me, since it may be assumed that on the whole living with a thief will have deleterious moral results on the family unit. It is a shame that the innocent suffer in this way, but it is a fact in the sort of world which we inhabit. The Book of Job represents the terrible things which happen to people as brute facts, things which just happen and which we can often do nothing to prevent. Saadya cannot accept this at face value. His commitment to Mu'tazilism means that he thinks of the events of the world falling under an objective standard of justice which must regulate the balance between innocent pains and pleasures. If the innocent do suffer, then they must eventually be compensated for their suffering. If they are not thus compensated, then the situation is unjust. Of course, he has great difficulty fitting such a theory of justice onto the Book of Job, since it is precisely the message of the Book that that theory of justice is vacuous. There is no evidence of such justice in this world, and little reason to hope for it in another life. It is the refusal of Job to accept such a simplistic notion of justice which makes the Book so interesting. It fortunately will not fit the ethical strait-jacket which Saadya has prepared for it. If we are going to find a notion of justice in the world it will have to be far more complex than that suggested by Saadya. It will have to be at least as complex as that which we find discussed in the Book of Job.

We need to accept, though, that the 'thoroughgoing' Mu'tazilism of Saadya picks out something very important in the Book of Job, and that is the idea that there must be a rational explanation for the sort of things which take place. That is, in a divinely ordered world, it is open to us to wonder what the divine plan is, and to expect such a plan to exist even if we are unable to examine its workings. Perhaps Saadya expects rather too simple a solution to be provided, and this accusation could be thrown at the whole Mu'tazilite movement. It would be wrong to think of their opponents, the Ash'arites, as opposed to rationality, since the latter were just as concerned to provide a rational explanation for the role of God in the world. The difference lies in the way in which they do it. What the Ash'arites argue is that there is no way of positing an objective standard of justice by looking at the events in the world and connecting these with the notion of a benevolent and omnipotent deity. The standard of justice must itself be determined by God, and then it could be at least partially available to our understanding. In some ways this encompasses more accurately much of the Book of Job, especially the latter sections in which God asks Job how much the latter understands of the construction of the world and how human power and comprehension relate to what is applicable to God. God seems to be following an Ashᶜarite position here, hinting at the way in which he has established a specifically divine notion of justice which mere mortals such as Job can only partially grasp. Job's apparent acquiescence in this form of explanation makes him come over as rather more of an Ashᶜarite than as a Muᶜtazilite, and this leads many aspects of Saadya's analysis to seem forced.

What remains valuable in Saadya's approach on this point is his feeling that an objective standard of justice is a desideratum. It is not enough to say that just because God acts in a certain way then that way is just. It is always open to us to wonder how we are to relate that sort of justice to the notions of justice which apply within our own world. We have to distinguish here between two claims. One is that the form of divine justice which applies is not entirely comprehensible by us given our limited point of view, and this is compatible with Muᶜtazilism. The other, stronger, claim is that there is no point in looking for evidence of divine justice, since whatever God does is an example of divine justice. This latter position is just as rational as the former, but it seems to make much of the enterprise upon which Job starts nugatory. Both Muᶜtazilites and Ashᶜarites want simpler explanations for the existence of evil and suffering than the Book suggests, and these explanations leave out a great deal of what is interesting in the issue. If the Muᶜtazilites are right, then Job is searching for an understanding of how an objective standard of justice applies to the world and for a long time is unable to find out. Once he succeeds, the problem is solved and the Book comes to a logical conclusion. He establishes that there is such an objective standard, and once he knows what it is he is satisfied. On the Ashᶜarite approach, the enterprise itself is mistaken, and the problem is dissipated once Job realises that there is really no problem at all, just a basic misunderstanding in questioning divine action. Neither form of analysis seems to do justice to the text, though, which is as impressive as it is precisely because it does not end up with a neat solution. It ends up with very much the same questions hanging in the air awaiting an answer as we observe at the beginning, and the interesting feature of the Book is that Job is praised for raising those questions, not blamed for misunderstanding what he thought the problem was. Since Saadya's commentary works on very much of an Ashᶜarite/Muᶜtazilite axis, it tends to lack the dimension of the original Book and so fails to represent accurately its richness and complexity.

Saadya does hit on an important theme when he explores the notion of an objective standard of justice. There is an understandable view that such a standard of justice must exist, and that it is right for us to seek it in our interrogation of a divinely characterised creation. The search for a solution is valid, even if the solution itself is unavailable to the searcher. It is certainly true that one might conclude that since the solution is unavailable to us, then there is no point in searching for it, and this would provide ammunition for an Ash'arite form of analysis. But if we follow this line we will be obliged to accept that there is a vast gulf between us and the deity, so vast that the only basis upon which we can understand him and his effect upon creation is faith. Clearly this is not a line which Saadya could accept, and it is certainly more radical than the Book of Job would justify. It is the people who have simple faith who are criticised in the Book, not Job. He is praised for asking his questions and challenging divine justice to declare itself. Saadya's concern to establish the objectivity of justice does succeed in bringing out one of the themes of the Book, and of the tradition of the debate in Jewish philosophy, which is that there does exist just such an objective standard, although it may be unavailable to our understanding. The search for an understanding of that standard is acceptable and even obligatory if we are to grasp how we ought to live, and we can use appropriate religious texts to help us here. Discovering such a standard is going to be a long and difficult task, however, and although Saadya clears the ground usefully by arguing for its existence, his analysis is not sophisticated enough to work out what it might actually be.

Part. II chapt. X - XII; XXII-XXIII
Council for True Perplex Chapt. IX

What do
How does he
support the not - that god does not
Create evil? Why is this important

How is man
nec cause,
to sin no fining?

CHAPTER 4

Maimonides

Philosophy in the Jewish world continued to be influenced by the sorts of issues which had earlier arisen within Islamic philosophy, and many Jewish thinkers went on to explore the notions of evil and suffering. It is hardly surprising that they employed the technical apparatus of Islamic philosophy to try to get clearer on the problems which they were considering in Jewish philosophy, since Islamic philosophy during the Middle Ages represented some of the most exciting and daring thinking then available. This approach was continued with enormous philosophical élan by the giant figure of Jewish philosophy, Moses Maimonides. He was born in Córdoba in 1135 and died in Egypt in 1204. He spent most of his life in North Africa and Egypt, his family being obliged to flee the Almohads in Spain, but he remained a symbol of all that was remarkable in medieval Spanish culture. During its domination by Muslims Spain witnessed a flowering of intellectual thought by all the three religions, but especially by Islam and Judaism. It is customary to see this time as a Golden Age of some sort, a period of inter-religious harmony and co-existence, but this is far from the truth. There did exist during the Islamic era in Spain periods of relative toleration and co-operation between the diverse ethnic groups, but this was by no means the norm. When non-Muslim communities were tolerated this was often due to their usefulness to the Muslim rulers, and once that usefulness had diminished the toleration diminished also. Spain was also the territory over which competing Berber tribes from North Africa fought, and the frequent disruption and occasional outbursts of religious fanaticism was very unsettling for non-Muslim groups, and even for those Muslims who did not come from the right part of the community. Despite these political problems, Islamic Spain experienced an extraordinary development of a whole range of intellectual pursuits, ranging from astronomy to medical science. At the heart of these developments lay philosophy, which was pursued by some of the best

minds of the time and came to have a huge influence upon Christian
Europe through the translations of the works of Averroes, Avempace
and Maimonides himself. The Jewish community in Spain was
culturally at one with the Islamic community, with the exception of
their religious differences, and the works by the Islamic philosophers
such as ibn Ṭufayl, ibn Bājja (Avempace) and ibn Rushd (Averroes)
were much read and studied by Jewish intellectuals. Jews in Spain
shared the arrogant attitude of their Muslim peers towards philosophical and other kinds of intellectual thought which emanated from
the eastern part of the Islamic world, much as German Jews nearer to
our own time disparaged thought from beyond the German-speaking
world.

Maimonides played a full part in the political life of the Jewish
community in the Islamic world, producing religious works intended
to guide them in their difficulties with rulers who did not always
respect religious diversity. As a doctor and a businessman he was very
involved with the practical side of life, but his main claim to fame lies
in the huge output of legal and philosophical works which continue to
be studied and argued over today. His two most important works are
the *Mishneh Torah* of 1180 and the *Guide of the Perplexed* of 1190. The
former is a compilation and systematisation of Jewish law which
attempted to bring order and rationality into the organisation of
religious law. The *Guide* is a philosophy book, but far from an ordinary
one. Maimonides starts off by examining some key terms in Hebrew as
they appear in the Bible, and ends up by presenting a whole
metaphysics which seeks to show to someone skilled in science how
religion fits in with the Aristotelian view of the world. It is one of the
most-discussed and interpreted books in Jewish philosophy, and some
have argued that its real message is cleverly hidden beneath its
apparent argument. Some passages are so difficult to understand that
an enormous variety of interpretation has been suggested. To a degree
the controversy surrounding the book has a lot to do with its central
feature, the fact that Maimonides seems to be doing something like
traditional Jewish philosophy and yet he is really offering some very
radical answers to the traditional questions of that philosophy. We
shall see when we come to discuss his approach to evil and suffering
that he insists that Jewish philosophy cannot continue to go on in its
previous direction.

Maimonides represents Spanish Jewish thought at its most self-
confident. He claims not to think much of those Jewish predecessors,

but there can be no doubt that the metaphysics he constructs is built up partially on the many significant Jewish thinkers in Spain whose works were much read by intellectual Jews in the twelfth century. As an exile from Spain he may have had an over-affectionate attitude to Spanish culture, but he embodies some of the principal features of that culture. What are these features? First, they are based upon a tendency in Andalus to try to look at texts in a new and original way, without being too respectful about the accretions of previous commentators. Then there was an emphasis upon thought having a scientific basis, in this case largely being identified with Aristotelianism. Lastly, and perhaps of greatest significance, there was much confidence in natural science and the ability of reason and experiment to discover the truth. That is not to say that revelation was ignored, quite the contrary, but given the great upsurge in astronomical, medical, mathematical and philosophical effort in Andalus it became evident that a number of effective techniques had arisen to answer quite basic questions about the world and the people in it which were not specifically religious techniques. If religion was going to continue to be worth studying by intelligent people, it must be shown to fit in with all these discoveries. At the time of Maimonides there was not only scientific optimism but also philosophical optimism, and we shall see that Maimonides sets about defending a scientific view of evil and suffering as philosophically respectable, but at great cost to traditional religious attitudes.

Before we look at what Maimonides had to say about evil and suffering, it is important to say something about the approach which is being taken to Maimonides here. Maimonides is a highly controversial figure in Jewish thought. His works are often regarded as laying down the principles of orthodoxy when they deal with law, but when he discusses philosophy there is a lot of argument as to his meaning. Many commentators argue that Maimonides was intent on reconciling religion with philosophy, and his philosophical works have to be read in the right way if we are to appreciate how he sought to carry out his intention. Maimonides himself refers to the ways in which a writer can conceal his real opinions in his writings, and this has often been taken to be a broad hint that the intelligent reader should look for clues which indicate how Maimonides was hiding his real as opposed to his declared opinions. This has led, as one might expect, to a good deal of detective work by commentators who each think that they know where the real opinion lies, and each of whom can produce a good argument for a particular interpretation. Why did Maimonides write in what has been taken to be such a cryptic way, producing such difficulties for his readers? Was it just because he enjoyed wrapping his words in mystery?

Like most writers of Islamic and Jewish philosophy, Maimonides had in mind a particular audience for his writings. Indeed, his major philosophical work, the *Guide of the Perplexed*, is addressed to a specific reader, to an individual who was knowledgeable in both the secular and the religious sciences, and wonders how to reconcile them. An Aristotelian possesses an account of the world which is entirely naturalistic, so that no principle is required which comes from beyond that world for an explanation to be satisfactory. Yet Judaism seems to suggest quite specifically that such an external principle of the world is necessary if we are to understand the world, and that principle is embodied in the deity. Maimonides was here addressing a problem which only a very limited number of people in the Jewish community would have, since very few people would be troubled with a knowledge of Aristotelianism in the first place. Most Jews would follow the principles of their religion, to some degree or other, without bothering about its metaphysical underpinnings. Maimonides felt that it was very important not to interfere with the beliefs of ordinary believers while trying to settle the doubts of the more sophisticated members of the community. It would be very harmful to the faith of the unsophisticated if they were to be confronted with some of the philosophical problems which arise when considering basic religious notions, not because these notions cannot be philosophically analysed in ways which are entirely compatible with faith, but because the ordinary believer would be unable to understand how this reconciliation was effected. As a result his faith in Judaism might be weakened. So it is incumbent upon an author to express himself on at least two levels, on the level of the ordinary believer and on the level of the more sophisticated believer, when discussing important religious ideas, since the author has at least two audiences, both of whom deserve an argument. The problem is that they cannot be presented with the same argument.

There is a good deal of controversy over the relationship which the two arguments have to each other. Maimonides might have been presenting the ordinary believer with an argument which is incompatible with the more sophisticated believer's argument, since it is not possible to bring religious and philosophical arguments any closer. That is, Maimonides' main aim could have been to placate the ordinary believer, so he writes in such a way that he is confirmed in his faith, while the more sophisticated believer understands what is wrong with the ordinary believer's argument and turns to its reformulation in a way which fits in with his interests. There is a good argument for this possibility in the apparent incompatibility of religion and Aristotelianism. That incompatibility would imply that Maimonides had to treat the ordinary believer's version of the truth as very much a distant version. Only the philosopher would really be able to understand the truth, and only the account which would satisfy him is worth having from an epistemological point of view.

On the other hand, Maimonides might have been suggesting that both the ordinary and the more sophisticated believer have access to the truth, but their routes are different. They get to the same place in the end, albeit along different paths. This is a feasible view if one thinks that it is possible to reconcile religion with philosophy. One might think that if this is really Maimonides' view, then he would have no qualms about frankly acknowledging it. But what worried Maimonides is that the faith of the ordinary believer would be threatened by his attempt at grasping the philosophical explanation. This might seem rather condescending. Does it not imply that the less intelligent have to be satisfied with more basic and figurative descriptions of the truth? It does, yet it need not be regarded as condescending. The ordinary believer may just not have the time to consider more complex issues, nor the inclination to do so. The formulation of his faith in the Scriptures and in the practices of his religion may be entirely satisfactory to his personal relationship with God. If he tries to understand the philosophical explanation and fails to do so entirely he may feel that his simple faith has been threatened and come to abandon his religion. Also, he may come to suspect the value of philosophy, since if he continues to adhere to his religion there must be something wrong with the arguments of the philosophers who appear to wish to threaten that religion. It would be far better, Maimonides suggests, for such a believer to stick with the formulation of religion which is in accordance with his attitudes and abilities. It is only the individual who is genuinely bothered by philosophical issues and who has the capacity to do philosophical work who needs to be addressed philosophically.

There is good reason to think that Maimonides was careful in his formulation of his arguments because he did not wish to interfere with the beliefs of the ordinary member of the community, not because he thought that those beliefs were incompatible with philosophy. This view has the advantage that it is actually in accordance with what he says, and there is a good deal of evidence in his arguments that he thought, like most of his medieval colleagues, that philosophy and religion are different routes to the same end. Had he thought that they were really two entirely different approaches which yielded completely different answers then it would have been difficult for him to have continued with his role in the Jewish community as a leader and spiritual authority. It must be admitted, though, that many commentators take the opposite view, and regard Maimonides' language as hinting at the total incompatibility between religion and philosophy, an incompatibility which he wishes to keep quiet for prudential reasons. It would be remarkable if he had such a view, given the tradition in both Islamic and Jewish philosophy of writing in much the same way as he wrote and maintaining the compatibility between these two approaches. What is certainly true is that he derives some very unusual conclusions from his arguments, unusual in the sense that they imply that changes are necessary in our understanding of basic religious concepts. That is, if his arguments are correct, it will be necessary to look anew at the way in which religion is interpreted. Some of his conclusions are difficult to reconcile with traditional religion, and this has led some commentators to argue that they are irreconcilable. Yet there is no reason to accept such a strong conclusion. Like so many of his predecessors, Maimonides is establishing an interpretation of important religious concepts which obliges us to think carefully about what we mean by them when we use them, because the ordinary religious use is based on an interpretation which can be limiting and misleading. What is needed is a new and improved understanding of those concepts, one which gives a better indication of their real meaning, and only if we have such an understanding can we be said to use them in their fullest sense. Only then can we really understand what it means to have the corresponding religious experiences, since these have a wider reference than ordinary believers may normally acknowledge. Maimonides was not setting out in his work to criticise religion, but rather to raise it to a new level of intellectual awareness which would do justice to its complexity.

Maimonides provides a complex and intriguing account of evil
which was very much part of the continuing debate in both the
Islamic and Jewish philosophical world. He seems to be of the view
that one source of evil in the world is due to the composition of things
out of matter. Matter is irretrievably limited in its capacity to be
perfected. Although the species itself may be perfect, the individuals
which constitute the material exemplars of the species display varying success in achieving perfection, and some are inevitably rather
far from perfect and so able to endure the vagaries of natural forces
which lead to suffering. Of course, the fact that certain individuals
are able to experience evil does not necessarily lead to the conclusion
that they will experience evil, but Maimonides operates with a
metaphysical principle which closes this gap. He employs the principle of plenitude so popular among the *falāsifa* (Leaman: *Introduction*,
pp. 32–6; *Averroes*, pp. 31 and 75; *Moses Maimonides*, pp. 57–8, 178)
according to which every possibility, if it is a genuine possibility,
must at some time be instantiated. So if matter is a source of
deficiency, and if some instances of a species are material, then those
material things will occasionally be deficient. This is hardly a new
idea, and Maimonides quotes Galen as being amazed by the view
that we could be creatures which emerge 'out of menstrual blood and
sperm' (*GP* Bk. III, Ch. 12; Pines, p. 444) and yet avoid pain and
suffering.

This might work as a rhetorical device, but on closer examination it
seems a rather poor argument. Why should not an omnipotent deity
create perfect creatures which are generated in what might be
regarded as rather sordid ways yet which nonetheless are insuscept-
ible to pain and suffering afterwards? Here we would have to say that
God could have created perfect creatures had he wished to, or indeed
no creatures at all. The point of creating creatures which inevitably
experience pain for at least some of their lives is to give them the
possibility of transforming their situation by the use of their own
intellect and will and thereby increasing as a result of their own efforts
in their individual perfection. We have seen how there has been much
discussion in the past of the educative function of suffering, and
Maimonides might well appeal to that point here in defending the
apparent willingness of the deity to contemplate working with
deficient material. Maimonides makes rather similar points when he
considers what is involved in the gradual eradication of idolatrous
practices from the Jewish people through the imposition of contrary

yet in some ways similar practices. God could, when he led the Jews out of Egypt, have transformed them immediately into the sort of people he wanted them to become. Then they could have spent less time in the desert preparing for the entry into Israel, an entry which could only be accomplished once the appropriate cultural and religious transformation had taken place. Yet in the difficult and challenging task of transformation lies the ability of individuals to take responsibility for their own characters and relationships, and this leads (so it might be argued) to a more interesting and valuable form of existence than that which would be available through immediate and perfect divine intervention.

So one sort of evil which affects us is due to our material constitution. Two other kinds are much more under our control. There are evils which result from political events such as war and ill-government, and these ultimately are to be blamed upon the selfish and inaccurate judgments of people. Then there is the related form of evil which we quite readily impose upon ourselves, through our greedy and inappropriate attitude to the world and its resources. The world is structured in such a way that we can easily satisfy our natural requirements in it if we are moderate in our demands and limit ourselves to those requirements. As Maimonides wittily suggests, 'the more a thing is necessary for a living being, the more often it may be found and the cheaper it is. On the other hand, the less necessary it is, the less often it is found and it is very expensive' (*GP*, Bk. III, ch. 12; Pines, p. 446). As a result of our greed for both material possessions and high reputation we constantly come into conflict with others and pervert the natural ability of the world to treat us all equally. Although Maimonides distinguishes this form of evil from that arising through political association, there is clearly a connection here, since the institution of different prices on goods which become scarce and highly valued is only possible within a particular institutional and hence political framework. He makes an important and useful contrast here between the wants and needs which human beings acknowledge. As a result of our imagination we think we need a whole variety of things which often we want only because other people want them. Were we to use our intellect, our rational capacity, more fully, we would appreciate that many of our wants bear little relationship to our needs, and would as a consequence forego the struggle with others for those illusory and inessential goods. When Maimonides becomes more explicit on the role of providence in the world we shall see that a constant theme is the evil resulting from the subjection of the intellect by the imagination.

Clearly the exact relationship between God and the world is going to be important if we are to form an accurate view of the nature of evil in a world created by a god. Maimonides distinguishes between five different views here. The first he credits to Epicurus (entirely wrongly) and has everything in the world occurring as a result of chance. The contrary view is taken to belong to Aristotle and identifies divine providence with natural law. The scope of providence is limited, though, to the level of the spheres and the species. The individuals which are part of the species escape from the general force of providence. The third view is that of the Ashʿarites, which interprets the universe and everything in it, however small in size and importance, as existing and changing solely due to the influence of divine providence. Furthermore, the deity is not in any way limited in his actions *vis-à-vis* the world by external standards of right and wrong. He sets the standards himself through what he does and what he wishes to do. The fourth view is attributed to the Muʿtazilites and has the world directed by God with wisdom and justice, with undeserved suffering in this world compensated by God in the next. A notion of justice exists which is independent of the notion of God, although God is careful to employ it in his government of the world.

The fifth view seems at first to be the view acceptable to Judaism on Maimonides' account. It is the view that human beings have freedom to act as they wish, and the consequences of their actions reflect their moral worth (*GP*, Bk. III, ch. 17; Pines, p. 469). Yet Maimonides seems to identify himself most closely with what he takes the Aristotelian view to be, arguing that divine providence is limited in its scope to the heavenly spheres and species, with the individuals falling under these influential bodies and universal groups being governed by chance. The only exception here is the case of human beings, and then only some human beings, who are able to key in to high levels of abstract thought. When human beings are able to perfect their thinking and link up with the divine overflow they come close to being identical to the species of human being itself, and since providence is concerned with the species rather than the individual, such human beings are able to live in a way which is governed by providence. Maimonides extends this theory a little when he asserts that providence applies to us in proportion to our ability to think abstractly, and even if we are as perfect as human beings can be in the development of

our abstract powers, providence only guides us while we are employing those powers. When we do something else, providence deserts us
(*GP* Bk. III, ch. 51; Pines, pp. 624–5).

This might seem a bit unfair on the intellectually unsophisticated
member of the community who nonetheless carries out his or her
religious duties scrupulously and obeys the law. It looks as though
providence is uninterested in these people, and yet they are precisely
the sort of people whom one might have expected providence to
support. To a certain extent this criticism is misguided, since it is
based upon the idea of God as an omnipotent and omniscient ruler
who is interested in the individual fates of his creatures. This is not
Maimonides' view of God at all. The more we think of God as
someone just like us, but more powerful and knowledgeable, the more
we go astray. God is radically dissimilar from us, and when we come to
wonder what role providence plays in our individual lives we must
free ourselves from the model of servants and master. Virtuous people
cannot expect to be rewarded in the way that valuable servants might
tend to expect to be rewarded. Hence the rather brisk attitude which
Maimonides adopts, as we shall see, to Job and his complaints.

Yet the simple believer might still wonder why providence is to be
reserved for the intellectually gifted. After all, it is not the fault of the
simple believer that he or she is a simple believer. In some ways this
state of affairs might be laid directly at the door of God. He has made
people differently, and their differences should not, one might think,
lay them open to different levels of reward and punishment if they
have no control over them. One of the features of an acceptable faith
might be said to be the ability to include within it a whole gamut of
levels of intellect and interests, excluding no one who is prepared to
accept the main principles of the faith (*Moses Maimonides*, pp. 146–7).
There should be routes for everyone to God, and all routes should be
equally assessable in so far as rewards and punishments are concerned. It might be argued that even the simple believer is able to tune
into the active intellect through the perfection of his religious practice,
which brings him as close as he can get to a rational grasp of the
principles underlying his belief. He has the same understanding of
religion as his more intellectually adept peers, although the former's
understanding takes on a different appearance from that of the latter.
For example, through belief in an afterlife he grasps the wider
significance of his actions, but finds this easier to understand if
formulated in terms of his continuing in some sort of existence after

death. The more sophisticated believer knows what difficulties attend such a view of the afterlife, and she can view that future state in an intellectually more respectable manner than can the simple believer. But to a degree they both understand the same point and both can participate in the same divine overflow with its corresponding providence.

The inequality between the simple and the sophisticated believer becomes more evident on death. Since the latter have perfected themselves as far as they could there is no need to regard their death as an end to their lives as thinkers. They have passed away into the realm of abstract intellectual thought, and death is nothing more than the sudden absence of the material body around which the thinking takes place. In some ways death is to be welcomed, since it increases the ability for intellectual thought to continue without the potential for confusion by the body and its tendency to choose imagination rather than intellect. What happens at death in the case of perfect human beings is that contact takes place between the material and the active intellect, so that the thinking things becomes part of the object of thought (*Moses Maimonides*, pp. 114–15, 123–4). It is important to point out that what remains is an entirely impersonal kind of immortality, since all that survives death are the thoughts, not the thinker. And not just any thoughts, but only thoughts which are abstract and capable of functioning without participation by our physical constitution. My memory of what I had for breakfast has no future after my death, but my memory of Pythagoras' Theorem will survive me, but not as *my* memory. Individuals whose lives have been dominated by thoughts of breakfast and who were uninterested in mathematics and similar intellectual activities will completely disappear with their bodies, but those who did manage to think abstractly will have the 'consolation' that those thoughts will survive them, albeit not as their thoughts. In so far as providence watches over those abstract thinkers, it watches over the thoughts rather than the bearers of the thoughts, and the only 'reward' which the latter can look forward to is the pleasure in having the thoughts themselves.

This is where Job goes wrong. He thinks that because he has been virtuous, he deserves good things to happen to him. Yet Maimonides points out that Job is only described as righteous and not as wise (*GP*, Bk. III, ch. 22; Pines, p. 487). He is a simple believer and

While he had known God only through the traditional stories and not by way of speculation, Job had imagined that the things thought to be happiness, such as health, wealth and children, are the ultimate goal. For this reason he fell into such perplexity and said such things as he did. (*GP*, Bk. III, ch. 23; Pines, p. 493)

Job was unable to appreciate, due to his simplicity, that the events in the world affecting individuals are purely natural events which take place without any divine intervention or moral balance. People just do lose their wealth and children, they just do fall ill and even perish, they just do suffer extreme reverses of fortune. Job naïvely expects God to act like a wise and kind parent, rewarding and punishing his creatures in accordance with their deserts. Maimonides insists throughout that we must not regard God in this way. He also holds to the view that only the intellect is really significant, since only the intellect presents a route for human perfection, and Job mistakenly thought that material and familial possessions are important and are to be regretted when they are lost.

This turn in the argument might well seem highly unconvincing. There is something to be said for the idea that one might lose great wealth and be consoled since one was still able to think rationally about abstract topics, and such thinking represents the most important part of us as human beings. In some ways wealth might even be seen as an obstacle to intellectual work, since it might distract one from pursuing such work. Yet the full complement of troubles which beset Job would seem to make even limited abstract thought unlikely. Maimonides himself goes on in the *Guide* to argue that one requires a reasonable level of health, wealth and general material contentment for intellectual work to be possible in the first place. There has to be some sort of balance between satisfying our material and social needs, and being able to engage in intellectual work. In the case of Job, poor, ill, grief-stricken and putting up with the dubious advice of his friends, this balance seems unavailable. Were Job able to ignore his present discontents through concentration upon abstract thought he might impress Maimonides but probably not many other people. We expect people to be seriously affected in their abilities to perform intellectual work by personal disaster, and it would appear to be extraordinarily cold-blooded were Job to be able to shrug off his troubles and get on with some serious thinking.

Since Maimonides does emphasise the importance of our material aspect, it is perhaps incorrect to take him at his word here in disparaging all non-intellectual life. He might just be pointing out that there is more to human life than just material and social possessions, and that many people tend to place too great reliance upon those features of human life which are most transitory. By contrast, abstract ideas are eternal and continue after our death, and we should, if we are able, spend time on perfecting our intellectual abilities. Even Job can come as near to this as possible by performing his religious duties and seeking to understand the nature of the world in so far as he can by adhering to religious doctrine and law. This represents the only possible route to a better grasp of the nature of reality available to those who, like Job, are not able to engage in serious intellectual work. The difficulty which Job and those like him have, though, is that they are liable to understand religious language to mean that they can know what God is like, and that they can have certain expectations of him. Yet there is no link at all between the language we can use to describe God and the language which we use for our everyday purposes, except for the actual phrases themselves, and this has to be acknowledged:

so that you should not fall into error and seek to affirm in your imagination that His knowledge is like our knowledge or that His purpose and His providence and His governance are like our purpose and our providence and our governance. If man knows this, every misfortune will be borne lightly by him. (*GP*, Bk. iii, ch. 24; Pines, p. 497)

Why does Maimonides think that the conclusion follows from the radical distinction between divine and human providence? On the surface it might seem to increase our misfortunes to know that there was no wise and just ruler looking after us. Many people find the idea of a powerful and caring God an important part of their religious faith, and a highly consoling notion. When they are told by Maimonides that they must abandon this image, their misfortunes might seem heavier rather than lighter.

We can work out Maimonides' reasons for the conclusion, though. First, if we believe in a God who is a powerful and caring super-being we are going to experience frequent disappointment. We are going to suffer when we find out that the wicked sometimes prosper and the virtuous sometimes suffer, and we are going to be confused in just the way that Job is confused. Secondly, and perhaps more significantly, it is important to have as accurate a grasp of our relationship with God as we can acquire. If we base our lives upon an incorrect notion then we are condemned to leading inauthentic and confused existences. We should not wait for God to do things for us, to help us and listen to us when we address him in prayer. We have to take responsibility for our own lives and we should try to perfect ourselves by improving our ability to reason and to develop intellectually. There is no reason to believe that Maimonides would rule out divine intervention entirely, but the general point is that our reward and punishment lies very firmly within this life, and we should take up an accurate attitude to the role of the deity in this life, foregoing the view of him as a fair referee who is going to regulate the game of life in accordance with just rules. When God responds to Job by emphasising the scope of divine knowledge in its general organisation of the world he is providing an account of his concern for the structure of the world, not for everything individual in it. Maimonides would concur with this model, and if we are to look for divine providence we should look at structures and not at aspects of those structures. If we examine the structure of the universe as a whole we find it is replete with order and grace, according to Maimonides, as befits the creation of a rational deity. He is not on the whole going to concern himself with all the minor aspects of that structure, and the sooner we realise it the better.

Perhaps one of Maimonides' motives in attacking the importance of human desires in our lives is his wish to replace the arguments of Saadya with something more solid. The latter had argued at some tedious length that a just deity could not but compensate both us and even animals for undeserved suffering, and the model he clearly has in mind here is recompense for physical suffering. How could a world which is inspired by divine grace leave wickedness unpunished, righteousness unrewarded? The existence of an afterlife in which a final reckoning is made for sins and virtues is the only possible solution to the calculations of who deserves what treatment, given the very evident lack of moral balance in this life. As we have seen, Maimonides will have nothing to do with such a theory. It represents God in far too human a manner, and holds over the notion of divine justice a standard which comes from somewhere else, from our conception of what arrangements are fair. Maimonides quite clearly sees that this is not just an argument about the nature of providence, but concerns a whole range of important theological points, such as the point of the law and the nature of creation (*GP*, Bk. III, chs. 17, 26, 31). Saadya does not really believe that physical pleasures and pains are the sole criterion of human good, nor does Maimonides think that physical pleasures and pains are unimportant aspects of a valuable human life. It is a matter of emphasis, but where one places the emphasis is very important. Both Saadya and Maimonides agree that God rules the world with providence, but the former expects this to mean that he is concerned to balance pleasures and pains with deserts, which implies that these are highly significant aspects of what passes for a valuable human life. It also implies that God is just like a human judge, but more so, and one does not have to accept the very radical theory put forward by Maimonides on the difficulties of describing the deity to be concerned at Saadya's suggestion.

It is not just that Saadya represents God as rather like a judge, a very human judge, but also that as a judge he seems to be particularly unpleasant. He makes it all right in the end, but seems to torment people for no other reason than to test them, or for no reason at all, with the ultimate promise that compensation will be available. Al-Ghazālī, as we have already mentioned (p. 51), poked fun at this Muʿtazilite notion by comparing it to the actions of a king in slapping a servant and then later paying him a sum of money in recompense (*Introduction*, p. 133). Is this how we should view the deity? Furthermore, Saadya's argument that the world has been created for the benefit of human beings is taken to be misguided by Maimonides. If this was God's aim, then he seems not to have been very successful, in the sense that one could think of different and more helpful ways in which the world could be organised. God has rather established a natural world which manifests in its structure his grace and perfection, and if we are to appreciate his providence we have to look at the world as something we are in, not something which was made for us. This is the meaning of God's response to Job, which is in terms of his power and intellect. We cannot hope to match either, but we can come as close as possible to perfecting ourselves by developing those characteristics of ours which are rational and abstract, and most similar to the principles underlying the universe.

But how can Maimonides say that the universe is a perfect creation given the amount of undeserved suffering which goes on in it? First, there is the necessity for the deity to create with the participation of matter, and matter is a continual source of limitation. Maimonides is consistently rude about matter, whose temporary nature offended his admiration for the abstract and eternal. Yet as we have seen we would not be the creatures we are without the contribution of matter, and if there are to be mortal beings at all matter is inextricably involved. Of course, one might query the reason for the existence of any material things from a moral point of view, but Maimonides would probably say that God had freely chosen to create a world of corruption and generation, and this world gives us scope to participate in, to a degree, the divine intellectual perfection. Yet

> Everything which can be generated from any matter at all is generated in the most perfect way in which it can be generated out of that particular matter. The deficiency appertaining to the individuals of the species corresponds to the deficiency of the specific matter of the individual. The ultimate sense and the most perfect thing which can be generated out of blood and sperm is the human species with its familiar nature consisting in man's being a living, rational and mortal being. So this type of evil must necessarily exist. (*GP*, Bk. III, ch. 12; Pines, p. 444)

God knows everything in the world through his maker's knowledge, through his understanding of the formal principles whereby he constitutes the world. God not only knows how things will turn out, but he also knows how they might turn out were they to take other directions, and we are free to escape the deficiencies of the world by perfecting our intellectual powers. The nearer we come to perfecting ourselves, the farther we go from matter, which ultimately is an irrelevance and a hindrance. There is evil in the world, as there is matter, but there is always available to us the option of transcending our material form of existence and coming close to the divine reality through our intellectual thought. This is where God's providence lies.

Yet this is not always how he puts it. He quite often seems to accept a simple-minded view of providence not dissimilar from Saadya's approach:

> It is thus one of the fundamental principles of the Law of Moses our master that it is not at all possible that He, may He be exalted, should be unjust ... all the calamities which befall men and the good things that come to men, be it a single individual or a group, are all of them determined according to the deserts of the men concerned through equal judgment in which there is no injustice at all. (*GP*, Bk. III, ch. 17; Pines p. 469)

This seems quite clearly to be the sort of exoteric doctrine which ordinary believers are obliged to accept, since they cannot really be expected to do the intellectual work which is involved in working towards a more philosophically respectable position. It is not so much the difficulties which ordinary believers would have with understanding a sophisticated view of providence, but even more the entire metaphysics which goes with it. It is much better, Maimonides frequently urges, not to stir up a hornet's nest by mentioning these difficult theories to those unable to deal with them. It only results in weakening their religious attachment and in a misunderstanding of

the theory in any case. What is involved here is not just an understanding of providence, but of the complex cosmology upon which it
rests.

What we have to appreciate here is the big gap which exists
between God and his creation. Maimonides' view of God's creation is
heavily influenced by the doctrine of emanation, according to which
there is a hierarchy of intelligences ranging from the first intelligence
created by God leading to the lowest intelligence controlling this
world, and all maintained in existence by the preceding intelligence,
and ultimately by God. God's relationship to the world is entirely
indirect and mediated through a long range of spheres and intelligences. So any notion of providence which is going to survive such a
distant relationship to God must be based upon the principles of
thought and influence present in the intelligences. Yet there can be no
notion of providence present in the intelligences and spheres themselves; they do not present an appropriate realm for moral assessment,
since they are just perfect in themselves and follow an eternal and
rational path – very distant, one might think, from the paths followed
by human beings, with the apparently arbitrary distribution of
rewards and punishments on our constantly changing and imperfect
earth.

As we have seen, Maimonides argues that if we are to enjoy the
benefits of providence, we must key in to the active intellect by
perfecting our intellectual abilities. We are free to do so, and our route
to intellectual perfection involves moral activity too, only if we first
have adopted a successful political and moral role in our society. A
problem arises here, though. Job in the exoteric version was a virtuous
and pious man who fell foul of fortune and suffers terribly, returning
to happiness only when he admits God's power and foresight and is
accordingly rewarded for his steadfastness. In the esoteric version,
which is clearly accepted by Maimonides, Job is an ignorant person
who takes literally the sort of language he finds in religion. So he
expects the pious to be rewarded and the evil to suffer. Since Job has
no intellectual grasp of how the world works or how it is possible for
human beings to attain greater felicity through increased understanding of the world, his fate is very much dependent upon chance. When
Job comes to understand the real nature of reality, he comes to the end
of his sufferings, since at this stage he acknowledges the relative
insignificance of material pleasures and ambitions. When he realises
that his wealth, children and body are unimportant, he is in the

process of uniting with the active intellect. The Book of Job represents this by describing the return of his previous possessions doubled as compared with before, and 'solves' the puzzle in the text. The puzzle is what it was that persuaded God to end Job's sufferings. On the exoteric version it is to mark his fidelity, yet he does not appear to have been noticeably faithful throughout his ordeal. He continually questions and complains about the justice of his sufferings. On the esoteric version the sufferings end because Job transcends them. He no longer regards them as important, and the happy ending of the story may be regarded as ironic.

As we have seen, there are features of this view of providence which raise important questions about Maimonides' concept of God. God seems to have very little grasp, if any, of what is going on in the world, so that the traditional idea of God's providence has to be abandoned. God appears to be lacking in knowledge. Also, since it is up to us to direct ourselves in the appropriate way to tune into his providence, he lacks the power to raise us once and for all to that level of intellectual perfection which would ensure our permanent perfection, in so far as mortal creatures can be perfect. If God is powerful enough to have created the world, then presumably he created the evil in it as well as the good. If the evil in the world is independent of God, then he is lacking in power. If he were not lacking in power, why does he not provide us instantly with the ability to perfect ourselves, rather than having to use the system of rewards and punishments to goad us into line? A perfect deity should be concerned about all of creation, not just human beings, and especially not just intelligent human beings. If providence consigns most people and everything else which lives to an inferior and imperfect life, how can we say that the creator of the world is good and cares for his creation?

Maimonides' response to these objections, is to defend his notion of God. God is not like us and we should beware of thinking that he ought to be and act like us. His power is represented in his ability to do whatever is logically possible, and in creating the world he acts perfectly and well because he both enables other creatures to become as perfect as possible and produces as great a variety of beings as possible. The assumption here is that it is always better to exist than not to exist (*GP*, Bk. III, ch. 25; Pines, pp. 504–6), something which Job challenges initially. We tend to think that the world was created for our benefit, or for the benefit of the world itself, but this is totally wrong. This is to conflate God's creativity with human creativity. If

suffering did not exist in the universe then there would be a lack of
variety, and God would not have created as much variety as it is
possible to have. Human beings could have been created so that from
the start they would be perfect, but this would mean that there were
no creatures such as ourselves in existence, thus leaving a gap in
existence. The fact that we are constituted of matter is not evidence of
God's weakness and inability to create us out of pure form, but rather
evidence of his intention to people his world with as great a variety as
is conceivable, and the fact that he can do this is a sign of his power
and perfection rather than a reduction in these qualities in the deity.
The creatures inferior to human beings cannot share in providence
since they do not have the right mental constitution. Were they to do
so, they would not fulfil the roles in the variety of nature which God
has established. It does not follow that they necessarily suffer as a
result of this. What does follow is that their lives are arbitrarily
directed by chance, and they cannot share in the sort of perfection
which is available to human beings.

Maimonides was very impressed by a saying of Rabbi Akiva to the
effect that 'Everything is foreseen, yet freedom of choice is given' (a far
pithier remark in Hebrew, consisting of only four words – see the
Talmud, *Avot* 3.19). What the phrase seems to mean is that God
knows exactly what is going to happen, but in spite of this we are not
compelled to act in particular ways. A problem arises here, though,
and it is one which has been discussed thoroughly in the literature of
religious philosophy. How can we really be free to act if God knows
what we are going to do? We may have the illusion of freedom, since
we do not experience God's foreknowledge during our own activity,
but this is just an illusion, since he does know exactly what we are
going to do. There seems not only to be no scope for free activity on
our part, but also very limited scope for ethical behaviour. If we
cannot help but act in the ways in which we do then surely we can be
neither blamed nor praised for our behaviour. Yet Maimonides seeks
to escape this dilemma by making a radical distinction between
human beings and other created things in the world. There is no
doubt, according to Maimonides, that in so far as we are natural
creatures we must be subject to the influences and laws of the natural
world. It would be extraordinary were this not to be the case. Those
quite common Midrashic passages which emphasise the deterministic
structure within which we act are capable of being misleading here.
They imply that we have no more freedom to choose than do the other

animals in the world, or even as in the case of inorganic things. Yet we do have choice, and this choice depends upon our decisions about the appropriate objects of our thinking.

There are two kinds of providence, general and special. The former relates to the way in which the world is organised, and governs the actions of all the beings under it. We can attract special providence if we concentrate upon God himself, if we regard God in the right way. The use of light imagery here is interesting (*Introduction*, pp. 88–9). Maimonides says:

Just as we perceive God by means of the light which He sends down upon us, about which the Psalmist says, 'In Your light shall we see light' (*Ps.* 36:10); so God looks down upon us through this same light, and is always with us beholding and watching us ... Note this particularly. (*GP*, Bk. III, ch. 52; Pines, p. 629)

If we are to take the imagery seriously, it is worth noting that when light is thrown on something, it becomes accessible to viewers, but it is very much up to the viewers to look, to make the effort. God is watching us, but he is said not to be doing much else. If we are to attract this special providence, the effort must come from us. It is up to us to align ourselves in such a way that this light falls upon us, and we can do this by turning to God, by concentrating upon knowledge of God in so far as we can have such knowledge. The normal idea of providence is of some arrangement which God imposes upon the world. It is a way in which God helps us, or at least those of us whom he wishes to help. On Maimonides' account there is such providence, and it does apply to everything in the world, but only through the laws of nature. As we know, the laws of nature need not be especially beneficial. Someone dying of cancer would not perhaps regard God's connection with the laws of nature as entirely provident. The special providence which really can help us escape from the demands of the laws of nature is something which God provides which we can avoid, unlike universal providence. Not only can we avoid it, but we have to work very hard to achieve it.

How can we achieve this special providence? Most believers can get near to it by following the rules of the Law, but their motive is important here. If, like the majority of the community, they have a rather simplistic notion of God as someone who rewards the virtuous and punishes the guilty, they may be motivated in their worship by prudential considerations. In a sense they adhere to religion because of what they hope to get out of it, and this is obviously a lesser motive than those who worship God solely from love of God. This contrast is made clear throughout the *Guide*, and the significance of Maimonides' negative theology is in its attempt at purifying the notion of God so that it becomes an appropriate object of love for its own sake, in itself and not for any other reason. This comes out nicely in his analysis of the *Shema*ᶜ, a highly important prayer in the Jewish religion, a prayer which is said just before death when possible. The first part of the prayer deals largely with the love which Jews are to have for God. The second part describes the benefits and penalties, which are on offer to believers consequent upon such love (*GP*, Bk. III, chs. 27–28, Pines, pp. 510–14). It is quite clear which form of worship Maimonides thinks is superior to the other. In his account of Job he shows how there can be a development of the individual from one form of worship to the other. At the start of his travails Job complains that he does not deserve what is happening to him, and God should help him to escape from his problems. Once God responds to Job's complaint, the latter realises that his whole attitude is mistaken.

What does God tell Job? According to Maimonides, he does nothing more than show Job a series of natural objects and events. This might seem to be not much of a reply. What Maimonides takes it to mean is that divine providence is very different from the sorts of providence of which we have experience. We cannot understand the way in which God rules by looking at ways in which human beings rule:

The term 'rule' has not the same definition in both cases; it signifies different notions, which have nothing in common but the name. In the same manner, while there is a difference between works of nature and productions of human handicraft, so there is a difference between God's rule, providence and intention in reference to all natural forces, and our rule, providence and intention in reference to things which are the objects of our rule, providence and intention. (*GP*, Bk. III, ch. 23; Pines, pp. 496–7)

This is just one aspect of the familiar but challenging Maimonidean thesis about meaning, namely, that there is no semantic connection at all between divine and human attributes (*Moses Maimonides*, pp. 101–2). We may foolishly expect God to intervene in the laws of nature to help us as a result of our prayers and virtuous behaviour. We might well expect this if we worship God in order to benefit ourselves materially. The highest form of worship, by contrast, involves seeking to know God out of a motive of nothing more than love. God will not as a result of such an attitude towards him suspend the laws of nature in favour of the worshipper, but the worshipper will be in a position to appreciate more surely the way in which the world is organised, and will consequently be able to acquire an appropriate attitude to that organisation and her place in it. She is free in the sense that she can change her character to be able to love and know God in a selfless manner.

There are a variety of ways of taking Maimonides' remarks here. One is to concentrate upon the way in which he argues that free will is compatible with determinism, and to suggest that the scope for free will which human beings appear to have is as a result of the divine will. In just the same way that God created the world at a certain time, and in which he selects individuals to prophesy, so he also excludes human beings from the confines of causality (*Moses Maimonides*, pp. 40, 46). If we were entirely predictable in our actions there could be no merit in our lives, and so the whole basis for reward and punishment would be nugatory. Yet it is clear from Maimonides' account of the Adam and Eve story that he thought that we do have the ability to choose freely what to do, and are responsible for our choices. An exponent of such a view (and Yeshaiahu Leibowitz is a good example in his *The Faith of Maimonides*) would point to the passages in the *Eight Chapters* and in the *Mishneh Torah* which do stress the significance of free choice and the ways in which the deity leaves scope for such choice. Clearly, such a view is far easier to accept from a religious point of view than the more intellectualistic position that Maimonides also seems to hold. On this position God does not intervene in the world. His providence extends to us all through the laws of nature, and some special people can, by their own efforts and abilities, come to grasp the organisation of the world which they inhabit and so are able to make even wiser decisions about what they should do than are the majority of the population. The sorts of people he has in mind here for this special providence are the prophets like Abraham, Isaac, Jacob and Moses, who were able not only to achieve a high level of intellectual awareness of God through contemplation but also to participate widely in political and social life to the extent of forming and strengthening the religious community. This is clearly the ideal form of human perfection which Maimonides had in mind. What is interesting about this form of perfection is that it leads to a form of providence which consists of achievements which are its own reward. God does not give these paragons rewards for their behaviour; this would be to trivialise the relationship which they have with God.

How does this special kind of providence work? We have to bear in mind here the existence of two levels of morality, a social level at which we should endeavour to control and moderate our dispositions and a more intellectual level which is only attainable through submerging the animal part of ourselves as far as can possibly be managed. Some laws relate to the proper development of people as members of a community, and it is only if we can fit into such a society that we will be in a position to undertake more rigorous intellectual work, work which 'contains neither action nor morality' and which is 'irrefutably superior' (*GP*, Bk. iii, ch. 27; Pines, p. 511). The sort of knowledge we have at the higher stage is very far from being practical knowledge. Religious law at this stage 'imparts true opinions concerning God ... and the angels ... making people wise and intelligent ... encouraging them to understand the universe' (*GP*, Bk. ii, ch. 40; Pines, p. 384). The apparent conflict in Maimonides concerning the role of law in human development has often been commented upon, especially when it comes to considering the role of the commandments. Sometimes he argues that the role of the commandments is to develop appropriate moral qualities in us, using very Aristotelian language to interpret such qualities as being characterised by some sort of mean. This is very much the language of the *Shemonah Peraqim* (*Eight Chapters*) and the *Mishneh Torah*. In the *Guide of the Perplexed*, though, he sees the commandments as primarily concerned with stamping on physical desire, which is far from Aristotelian. We have already seen how Maimonides in the *Guide* treats matter as an irretrievably negative feature of reality. This goes a long way from acknowledging the composite nature of humanity as the basis to philosophical reflection, very much the sort of Aristotelian starting-point with which he is often connected.

Maimonides has such an unusual understanding of the purpose of the law because of his interpretation of what it is to imitate and follow God. To imitate God it is not enough to do the sort of things which the deity does, as be merciful, benevolent, gracious and so on. God is not a merciful, benevolent and gracious agent in the way in which we can be merciful, benevolent and gracious agents. He has no psychological characteristics at all, and to talk of him as possessing such characteristics is to misunderstand how he should be regarded. He has an essence which is indescribable and unknowable, and we can only talk about him if we are clear that our language does not actually set out to ascribe attributes to him. The kind of attributes which Maimonides allows are attributes of action, since these do not actually describe God but only the world. We ascribe the sort of qualities which we might ascribe to ourselves to the world, because we know that God is the ultimate author of the world, and we say that a particular natural event is merciful by using metaphorical language. Yet we must beware of moving from such acceptable language to thinking that we have discovered anything about the deity. He is not like us, and we cannot use any evidence of his actions to derive conclusions about his mental state prior to the action. God is far above the sort of considerations which we have, or which we might like him to have, for the everyday events in the world of generation and corruption. His connection with such contingent phenomena is bound to be very distant, since he is a necessary being, and as such completely independent of such phenomena.

This brings us to an important point here. Although it is commonplace to record Maimonides' rather disparaging remarks about ibn Sīnā (Avicenna) by contrast with Al-Fārābī and ibn Rushd, there should be no doubt but that his main distinction between God as a necessary existent and the rest of existence as contingent is entirely within the scope of ibn Sīnā's methodology. One of the reasons why we cannot refer to God acting is that a necessary being does not act in the way in which we act. Acts emanate from the essence of a necessary being, they follow from the nature of that being, and they are not arbitrary actions which might or might not occur, but they necessarily follow from the nature of their originator. The idea is that the deity is an overflow overflowing, which avoids the necessity to use language reminiscent of matter. One of the problems with ordinary descriptions of action is that they seem to imply a lack in the agent, since otherwise why would he act in the first place? Yet God cannot lack anything. If God's action occurs as a result of an emanation then this is akin to a necessary and automatic process. What happens does not happen because God has done something, but it happens because it follows necessarily from the nature of the deity, and if we are to attain the highest level of knowledge available to human beings we must seek to understand the nature of God and the world which follows from him.

It is clear that for Maimonides there exists a hierarchy of kinds of providence, with both a practical and a theoretical providence being available as a result of the divine overflow on to either the imagination or the intellect, via the active intellect. The former consists chiefly in the ability of human beings to conduct their lives prudently, which as we have seen Maimonides thought important but far from the whole scope for providence. When someone has been perfected intellectually he 'has become rational in actuality, I mean he has an intellect which is actualized. This consists in his knowing everything about all the beings that it is within the capacity of human beings to know in accordance with their ultimate perfection' (*GP*, Bk. III, ch. 27; Pines, p. 511). Neither form of providence will save people from all misfortunes. The prudent person will take care not to take rash decisions and will have a good grasp of the way in which she should set about her practical tasks, but this only makes misfortune more unlikely to occur, it does not rule it out completely. To take an example, the person who has perfected herself morally and physically can still find that things go wrong. Although she acts well and fits in nicely with her community, people may still come to dislike or to resent her. Although she may take care of herself physically, she may succumb to illness at an early age and in an undeserved way. By contrast, as the Book of Job never tires of telling us, we may behave like fools and obnoxious characters and nonetheless thrive and live to a ripe and prosperous old age. That is as it should be, since we operate in the contingent world which is characterised by unpredictable and apparently arbitrary events, where our wellbeing is for at least some of the time at the mercy of forces which we can neither control nor comprehend. All that we can do is to seek to increase our opportunities of getting along in such a world by forming appropriate moral and practical dispositions.

There is, then, a form of providence which can be attained through 'the perfection of the body' (*GP*, Bk. III, ch. 27; Pines, 510). Since this providence is related to the body it is, as one would expect, rather limited and transitory in nature, in keeping with the body which it preserves. A higher level of providence is possible for those on a more perfect level through having perfected the soul, and 'It is clear that to this ultimate perfection there do not belong either actions or moral qualities, and that it consists only of opinions toward which speculation has led and that investigation has rendered compulsory.' This sort of perfection is more noble than that of the body and 'is the only cause of permanent preservation' (*GP*, Bk. III, ch. 27; Pines, p. 511). While the body is mutable, the soul is taken to be potentially permanent, at least by virtue of its concentration upon abstract and scientific knowledge. This superior type of providence is not available to the ordinary believer, who has only piety and good deeds to recommend him. Maimonides states quite bluntly that 'the thing which necessarily brings about providence and deliverance from the sea of chance consists in that intellectual overflow' (*GP*, Bk. III, ch. 51; Pines, p. 625). The things which we have as a result of our ordinary lives, our wealth, health and so on, are not really essential parts of our lives. They are things which we have at one time, and which can be withdrawn at another time. Of course, we may value such possessions, because we imagine quite wrongly that we ought to have them, that life is inconceivable without them. Yet we are mistaken here. Job's enlightenment consists in his becoming aware of the inessential nature of such aspects of his life, and then his suffering comes to an end. Knowledge of God is the proper object of our lives, and if we can come to have it, in so far as it is available to us, we must regard the physical and moral requirements of us as human beings as relatively unimportant.

There are two interesting aspects of this argument. One is that the route to perfection, and accordingly to providence, is one which is open to us and attainable entirely in terms of our own effort. This is true for both kinds of providence, the lower and the higher. The idea of a personal God either helping or preventing the realisation of either kind of perfection is not part of the story. It is part of the story which we get in scripture, but this must be understood metaphorically. It is clear, for example, that the Satan who brings about Job's troubles is 'the evil inclination, and the angel of death are one and the same' (*GP* Bk. III, ch. 22; Pines, p. 489). This evil inclination Maimonides identifies with imagination (*GP*, Bk. II, ch. 12; Pines, p. 280, see also *Moses Maimonides*, pp. 42–3). By contrast, 'good inclination is only found in man when his intellect is perfected' (*GP*, Bk. III, ch. 22; Pines, p. 490), and so the active intellect is available to all those who undertake this higher level of thought and life. The traditional idea that our relationship with providence comes about through the effects of a supernatural being upon our lives is only partially true, in the sense 'that that intellect which overflowed from Him ... toward us is the bond between us and Him' (*GP* Bk. III, ch. 51; Pines, p. 621). Once we understand this we appreciate that the availability of happiness lies in our own hands if in anyone's, and our own efforts may make it more or less attainable. It is no good complaining to God, as Job does initially, when things go wrong. God cannot do anything about it, but we can.

Sometimes Maimonides sounds almost mystical in his description of the highest form of providence:

If a person's thought is free from distraction, if he apprehends Him, may He be exalted, in the right way and rejoices in what he apprehends, that individual can never be afflicted with evil of any kind. For he is with God and God is with him. (*GP*, Bk. III, ch. 51; Pines, p. 625)

This does not mean that nothing unpleasant can affect the perfect individual, but rather that such an individual will not be aware of anything affecting him at all. He will be contemplating far more important things than the pain in his tooth or the gap in his bank balance. Maimonides does seem to be advocating an asceticism here which goes against much of the rest of his thought, especially in the *Mishneh Torah* and *Shemonah Peraqim* (*Eight Chapters*). As we have seen, though, this latter work can be seen as a description of a lower form of providence, or a stage of the growth of the higher form of providence. Although it is tempting to contrast the earlier and more theological discussion of providence with that present in the *Guide* along the lines, perhaps, of an Aristotelian notion of the person by contrast with a Neoplatonic notion, this can be misleading. The idea that the proper end of human beings is intellectual contemplation is very much present in Aristotle, and Maimonides works with this idea to claim that when we are intellectually at a peak in our development we have reached a high point as human beings. This sort of work is that most suited to us as human beings, it differentiates us most surely from the rest of contingent creation and establishes what for us is our proper role. Certainly there are other things which we can do, and they have a point since they are enjoyable or important to us as social and material beings. If we think they are important we are misled by the forces of imagination, the evil inclination which seeks to draw our attention away from what really concerns us as human beings. Once we realise that these changeable aspects of our lives are meaningless to our real role as human beings we can no longer be troubled by the arbitrary events of the world of generation and corruption.

Yet, one wants to say, this is far from the case. My toothache continues to trouble me even while I am doing mathematics. My concentration upon syllogistic reasoning may distract me for a time from my hunger, but not for long. How can Maimonides assert with any hope of support that the perfected intellect exists under complete providence? We hardly seem to be being looked after if we are in pain or want. Is he calling for adherence to an ascetic attitude to the body, whereby its demands are regarded as meaningless? This is not his view, although he is certainly attracted to a type of asceticism.

Maimonides is arguing for what might be called a muscular form of providence. It is up to us and our capabilities whether or not we attract providence. If we attract the very highest form of providence through our intellectual endeavours then we direct our minds and ourselves in precisely the direction in which it is most appropriate for them to be directed. This does not mean that by some magical process all our physical and social problems vanish. How could they? What is required, on Maimonides' account, is that these problems are put in their proper place, as inessential aspects of the most important part of us, our intellect. They may well prevent the intellect from doing its work to its utmost, which is why he recommends taking care of the physical and social aspects of our lives before we undertake serious intellectual work. Yet the carrying out of such work does not imply that everything else about our lives is immediately rescued from contingency. Our minds are capable of relating to the eternal and permanent ideas of reason because they can know such objects, to a degree. Our bodies are not capable of being anything more than bodies. So Maimonides argues that there can be no permanent providence affecting our bodies, since our bodies are incapable of anything permanent at all. They are irretrievably part and parcel of the world of generation and corruption.

The most interesting version of this kind of view in our time is undoubtedly that presented by Lenn Goodman. He argues along the sort of Aristotelian lines which Maimonides employed that the appropriate role of natural justice is to be found in nature itself. The consequences of virtuous and wicked actions are aspects of the actions themselves, not something which God attaches afterwards as a reward or penalty. As we have seen, Maimonides strenuously argues that it is impossible to know more about God than that he acts in particular ways, a conclusion we can reach by observing the laws of nature. This is an aspect of what is involved in Moses only being allowed a view of God's back (*GP*, Bk. I, ch. 54). Yet there are plenty of passages and prayers which call for a more positive understanding of God and his motivation. God appears to threaten us in some places with the consequences of rejecting him, and in other places he hints at rewards for faithful service. Now, we should not accept these passages literally, since that would be to treat God anthropomorphically. God is not like a powerful ruler or an autocratic father, although he is sometimes described in these ways. The reason for this sort of description is to wean the community gradually off their idolatrous thought processes, which involve making a person of the deity. Weaning has to be done gradually, since only in that way can it work with rather than against human nature. God could, of course, have changed our characters instantly to skip the stage of thinking of God as rather like us to get us immediately to the stage of understanding that he is very different from us and only to be grasped by our intellectual powers. This would make it impossible for us to engage upon the exciting process of seeking to change our way of thinking for a more accurate alternative. This might strike one as rather a strange way of describing the process of improving one's view of God, but it has a lot to be said in its favour. To take an ethical example, I may be rather mean with my money, and God could suddenly change me into a generous person. I could wake up tomorrow with an entirely different disposition in so far as charity is concerned. In such a case I should not have done anything; on the contrary, it would have been done to me. In different circumstances I may never become perfectly generous, but the process of acquiring more generous dispositions is an interesting and meritorious one and can play an important part in our own transformation of our lives.

How does God work through nature? He accomplishes this by setting up a particular form of nature in the first place. He maintains it in existence and participates constantly in it, not just on special occasions. When we look at the world we perceive a situation in which God's justice is at work. The rewards and punishments for actions performed in the world are intrinsic to those actions. How so? Is it not possible for someone to live the life of a scoundrel and have a rather merry time of it? If like Maimonides we do not think he will be punished in the afterlife, then he can have an even better time, knowing that if no one punishes him in this life there is no one to punish him in the next life. According to the strong Aristotelian views of Goodman, this is to misunderstand the meaning of crime. Goodman's book *On Justice*, with the subtitle *An Essay on Jewish Philosophy*, continues the tradition of Maimonides into the present century, combining it with much of the thought of Alasdair MacIntyre, and argues forcefully throughout that the Maimonidean approach encapsulates a persuasive and specifically Jewish approach to the issue of justice. To assess the value of his approach it is worth looking at some of the examples he gives to show that crime does not pay. These examples have something in common in that they all urge that the notion that the consequences of crime are separable conceptually from the act itself is mistaken. Crime does not pay not because criminals get caught, or do not in the long run benefit by their actions. Crime does not pay because it is crime, and it is of the essence of crime to go against the rules of living well, as we ought to live.

Take the example of rape. Goodman argues very sensibly that what is wrong about rape is not that it is a violation of someone else's property. He argues that

rape is not a good. Still less is it a freedom. Behind such assessments lies the notion that rape is somehow a pleasure enjoyed rather than a fixation acted out. The assumption does not square with the phenomena. Whatever is experienced by a rapist seems hardly to contribute to his happiness or well-being. And it is scarcely material penally whether a rapist enjoys the experience, undergoes an orgasm or (as is often the case) does not. The 'gain' is a phantom. While acts of violation involve a certain license, in that boundaries are transgressed, mores flouted, dignities degraded, they do not add stature to character, value to experience, or any enhancement to the latitude of liberty. (*On Justice*, p. 56)

This approach to understanding human action is based upon the idea that we can identify what our well-being is, the well-being of us as human beings. Suppose we are confronted by an amoral individual who claims to enjoy committing rape. He claims he enjoys the experience. Actually, if Goodman's description of rape is at all accurate it is not relevant whether the rapist achieves orgasm during his crime, since he can enjoy everything else about the experience, the humiliation, the violation, the violence and so on. These might be far more important for him than an orgasm. Goodman claims that if we examine the facts we can appreciate that rape is not really pleasurable. It is just something that certain people find a compulsion to do. He goes on in the book to call the criminal irrational, since his activities destroy him as a human being.

This sort of Aristotelianism clearly fits in well with religion. It suggests that there exists a set of moral descriptions which are applicable to things in the world as a result of the nature of those things. Everything has a purpose or a design, and we can judge whether it has achieved its end by observing it. If it has not, then we know that it is bad or wrong, while if it has then it is good or right. We can take rape as an example here. We have to ask what the point of sexual intercourse is to decide on the status of rape. Many Aristotelians would argue that sex is a means for people to find out about each other, to enjoy being together and to enter into activities which are mutually pleasurable. Some would further see the point of the activity in the generation of offspring, and so would deny the acceptability of taking active steps to prevent this taking place, a position which is familiar to us as that of the Roman Catholic Church. This is not relevant for our purposes here, since it adds a further complicating factor. What is relevant is the notion that it is basic to sexual relationships that they are based upon consent, and if this consent is breached, the relationship immediately goes awry. It is not the way it ought to be. This is true even if the people involved in the violation enjoy, or appear to enjoy, the experience. Now, we have to be careful what we say about this sort of example. It is certainly true, as most people would agree, that the activities of the rapist are not conducive to the development of human beings as we should like them to develop. The rapist is the person who is determined to have his way regardless of the wishes of others, and if in fact the others do not object to the violation this is entirely irrelevant to the judgment of his crime. He is prepared to act as though the feelings of others have no significance, as though only his desires deserve satisfaction. He may deceive himself about the feelings of others, but this is a further sign of his descent into moral depravity.

It is quite easy to see what is wrong with rape, and it would not be difficult to show someone who shared our sort of moral outlook that rape was a crime and should be severely punished. Yet this sort of argument would not work with the individual who sees the world in an entirely different way, and who does not seek to enter into our approach to social life. Such an individual may be the extreme egoist who crops up occasionally in the textbooks of moral philosophy, the person who is determined to get what he wants come what may, and who requires a reason not to behave in that way before he will desist. The Aristotelian will try to persuade him against rape by pointing to the nature of consensual sexual relationships and hoping that he will see that the point of such relationships is negated by violation and force. This suggests yet again how appropriate Aristotelianism is as part of a general religious point of view. The Aristotelian has a problem in that her arguments are often based upon a description of something in the world which, she argues, has a certain character such that to behave towards it in a different way is to misunderstand its character. When we move on to the moral plane, though, it is difficult to find such clear-cut cases, and we might wonder whether the Aristotelian really has access to the way in which things are through her description of them. Are human beings really only able to flourish or live well by following the sort of rules specified by the Aristotelian philosopher? This is far too large a topic to consider here, but it is worth pointing out how helpful it is to the Aristotelian if her system can be embedded within a religion. For then the way in which the world provides evidence of how we ought to live and how nature should work has a higher justification than is available by mere observation. She can talk about the purpose which God has in creating the world, or a particular kind of world, and the role which God wants his creatures to perform. In that case we do not only have to rely upon our observations of the world, but we can appeal to an additional and higher level of authority. There has in the history of philosophy been a great deal of discussion about how Aristotelianism was seen as an enemy of religion when philosophy entered the culture of Judaism, Christianity and Islam, but it is worth mentioning that there are aspects of Aristotelianism which it is entirely appropriate to embody within a religious framework, and vice versa. As so many of the medieval philosophers realised, religion and Aristotelianism could do a lot for each other.

The difficulty with Aristotelianism, though, is that it is not always easy to show that the Aristotelian solution to a problem is the only rational solution. For example, for the egoist the Aristotelian view of sexual relationships is seriously flawed. The egoist has a different view of such relationships which abandons entirely their consensual element. The Aristotelian would have to argue that the question of consent is not an incidental aspect of such relationships but an essential aspect of what makes them what they are. The egoist wants some evidence which he has to accept before he goes along with this view. He wants to be able to say that while the Aristotelians see sexual relationships in one way, he sees them in another way, and there is no objective standard which will adjudicate as to which way is better than the other. We are getting into rather deep water, but it can be seen what sort of difficulties the Aristotelian gets into when trying to persuade an opponent of the appropriate description of a form of human relationship. She has to do it in such a way that there is no feasible re-description which can produce alternative moral answers, and the contortions which Goodman gets into when describing rape are a good example of how difficult this is. Perhaps this is a useful indication that the Aristotelian who wishes to operate by moving easily from the realm of facts to the realm of morality is mistaken in the very possibility of such a jump.

This is even more noticeable when we get into the area of

identifying God's justice operating in the world. As Goodman says, Maimonides also talks about the providence which stems from God operating all the time in the course of nature. It is this general providence which is at all times available to us. How do we know? We can observe it in the workings of nature. We can see how the world is organised and we then come to grasp God's role in it, at least to a degree. Goodman puts it thus:

We do not hold that God exists and acts, governs and judges despite all the evidence – clinging to the claim out of sheer doggedness or brute faith, without experience to give definition or confirmation to give direction to our trust; and we do not hold that God is just in the trivial sense that for God all is right by definition. Our faith is founded in evidence – in our experience and appraisal of the world. What we see when we see God's justice at work ... is a factual state of affairs, to which evidence is relevant. (*On Justice*, p. 154)

There is a necessity to the way in which the world is organised, but it is not a logical necessity. It cannot be logical, since things might have different natures and actions different consequences, and so Goodman refers to 'the higher, metaphysical necessity of things' [*sic*] being what they are' (p. 155). It is God who lies at the source of this necessity. He has created a particular kind of world, and if we observe the workings of that world we can discover, to a degree, how it incorporates a system of fairness and justice to all in it.

Goodman is following in a very distinguished tradition here, and it is clear that Maimonides would approve of this sort of approach. After all, Job comes to understand the role of God in the world once God talks about the significance of natural events and his role in their production. As we know from Maimonides, there are problems in being more precise about God's role in the world since we are severely restricted in what we can know about God, and we must eschew anthropomorphic language as much as possible. Even in the Messianic age, according to Maimonides, the course of nature will not be different. It will be we who are different and as a consequence life will be much improved. The implication is that the Messianic age will come about through our own efforts and not through an external event such as God sending an individual to bring this state into being. He might well send the Messiah, but only at such a time as we are in a fit condition to receive him, and this will be due to our own efforts and ability to perfect ourselves.

But is it really true that there is evidence of God's justice in the world? There is certainly evidence of organisation and creatures having particular characteristics which often slot together in appropriate-seeming ways. A large variety of different life forms have an opportunity to flourish and play their part in the arrangement of the whole, and this might well be called fair. As far as we are concerned, human beings have a great deal of scope to arrange their lives in efficient and satisfying ways, and we are able to improve our moral character by gradually working on our dispositions to act and also to extend our intellectual range by concentrating upon theoretical issues. Of course, things often go wrong, and people are afflicted by natural and social disasters of one type or another, but this is supposed to form an appropriate context within which we have the opportunity as a community to better ourselves ethically and in intellectual ways. If it were the case that the virtuous were automatically rewarded by God for their virtue and the guilty punished, then our motives for behaving in particular ways could easily become entirely prudential, thus excluding a whole realm of moral thought and activity from our lives. When we look at the world we inhabit we see plenty of reasons to think that it has been organised fairly, albeit not always to our advantage, in that it gives humanity scope to do many of the things which it ought to do and freedom to develop in a variety of alternative directions. Maimonides clearly thinks that if we look at nature we find evidence there of God's general providence, and it is up to us to make the best of it that we can. We can in addition try to attract special providence through our own intellectual effort, but this also is really just a kind of natural providence, since it does not occur haphazardly but only to certain individuals who have worked with nature, with their natural abilities to understand nature, and who as a result can think at a higher level about theoretical matters than most of their peers.

When one thinks about this line of argument one is struck by one feature of it, namely, that it is a rather strange way to talk about seeing and assessing evidence. It might be better to talk about it being possible to see the world in a particular way, as a teleological rather than a determined system, with purposes and ends and patterns. We should be clear that this is just one possible way in which the world can be interpreted. There are alternatives far less suitable for the Aristotelian or theistic enterprise. We can only interpret what we find in the world as 'evidence' of justice if we are going to interpret that world in a certain sort of way. This highlights the rather intimate connection between religion and Aristotelianism. If we see the world as having been created by God then we shall regard it as containing things which point in a particular direction. If we see the world as being a teleological whole, then we shall interpret its contents as having ends and essences which are to be realised. There is a tendency for philosophers to use Aristotelianism and theism to reinforce each other, but such an approach is mildly circular. Both doctrines can be made to appear similar on how the world is, but it is important to bear in mind that there are other ways of interpreting the world. How do we assess the different approaches here? This is, of course, an enormous question, but one way to deal with it is to look at how plausible as a description of the world's events each alternative theory is. Since the sort of theory which Maimonides and Goodman present is supposed to be based upon evidence, it should be possible to assess the strength of that evidence within the terms of its own theoretical framework. If it fails to look convincing even then, we might well have qualms about accepting the whole theory itself.

How attractive is this way of looking at the world? There are obviously many advantages to the Aristotelian approach, especially its dependence upon the way things are in the world. We look at the world, observe how things are organised and work from that basis, and so the notion of finding evidence in the world for God's justice is not difficult to accept. Is there really evidence for this, though, or is it just a determination on our part to see the world in a particular way? If it was what normally goes under the name of evidence it would be possible to consider alternative explanations for the phenomena for which we are supposed to have evidence, and those alternatives should be less satisfactory as explanations than the Aristotelian explanation. This is not the place to consider the enormous issue of the merits and problems of Aristotelianism, but it is worth pointing out how difficult it is to identify the events in an Aristotelian world with a personal God unless we already have the notion of such a God. Aristotle's God is quite impersonal, and the importation of a personal God by the medieval philosophers filled a significant gap in the system of Aristotelianism. Yet there remains a structural problem with such an import, in that the system it is designed to supplement gets on very well without it. Then there is the problem of showing how a world which works well by itself needs a God who has to have an impact upon the world, and that impact has to provide evidence of his intentions in the construction of the world. We can talk about evidence here, but it is a very strange type of evidence, and one concerning which we ought to be wary.

A good indication of how etiolated the Aristotelian system of description is can be seen in the account of rape. The notion that the rapist gets satisfaction from his activity and that rape forms part of his happiness cannot be allowed, since it goes against the sense of sexual relationships on the Aristotelian account. Now, however much we may deplore rape as an activity, there is no denying that some men find it an enjoyable and important part of their lives. If they are in important positions, or just lucky, they may never be caught and punished and so rape may form a regular feature of their lives. It is certainly true that we can find good arguments against the moral acceptability of such a lifestyle, yet such arguments will need to be based on firmer foundations than a particular understanding of the practice of sexual relationships. It is worth pointing out yet again how helpful theism is to Aristotelianism here, in that the former can provide additional support for the meanings presented by the latter. The appropriate definition of sexual relationships can be given a religious definition which apparently backs up the 'natural' definition provided by the Aristotelian. This takes us even further away from the notion of evidence, though, and places far more emphasis upon the religious aspect of the definitions of the phenomena involved than on the 'natural' aspect. This might not be a problem if one is working from a religious framework already, but it is important to understand that the conclusions of any such argument owe far more to the theological premises than they do to any independent judgment concerning the nature of things in the world.

This is not really a problem for a Jewish philosophy provided that it is both Jewish and philosophical. Yet if we look at the sort of account produced by Maimonides we might begin to worry that God has been provided with very little room for manoeuvre, since it is up to us to attract his providence. Once we have attracted it, we receive it, and until we do we get nothing, or at least only the general providence which everyone gets. This makes it difficult to perceive God's role in the world, and one might wonder whether the world would get on just as well without divine intervention. Even if one wanted to give God a role in the world it might be enough for him to have brought the world about and then left it to get on by itself. This has certainly seemed to be a good explanation of the existence of evil in the world, since it might be assumed that the evil arose after God left his creation to its own devices. Maimonides places the emphasis very firmly on us to sort out the evil in the world. There is no point in expecting external intervention to rescue us from our plight. We may appeal to God to save us from our sufferings, but if we really think that he could do so we are guilty of an inappropriate conception of the deity. We can see evidence of God's justice by looking at nature, and there is nothing else available to us in this respect except what we learn through the Jewish religion. If we are not happy with what we observe in nature, we are mistakenly expecting God to create a world in which he constantly intervenes for our benefit. This would vitiate our capacity to make independent decisions and set about transforming and improving our moral and intellectual characters. The interesting question with which Maimonides leaves us is whether the evil and suffering in the world has become on his account so distant from God that the best means for us to alleviate and cope with such phenomena is to follow a strategy which is not religious at all. We shall see how his successors grappled with this kind of issue.

How far is it true to say that Maimonides' treatment of the link between God and the world is too distant and weak for a traditional account of our relationship with God to be feasible? As we have seen, this is certainly not the conclusion which he would want ordinary believers to acquire when they were wondering about these issues, because they would then find their religious commitment seriously weakened, if not entirely destroyed. The ordinary religious formulation of how God watches over us and helps us is to be preserved for unsophisticated believers, since for them this is their route to knowing God. More sophisticated believers will understand that this sort of religious language is in fact symbolic of a deeper and more rational understanding of our relationship with God. We might express the contrast between these two approaches in a more common-sense way as replicating to a degree different sorts of relationship which we may have with each other. For example, there are people who find it difficult to believe that their friends and lovers are really their friends and lovers unless they are frequently demonstrative in their affection. Such people will require as evidence of friendship and love certain actions like the giving of presents, or declarations of affection, or just being in close proximity to each other. This would be an analogy of the simple believer, who may expect to receive some reward for his belief, or some acknowledgment from God of his attention to his creation. Now, the more sophisticated believer, like the equivalent friend and lover, might require none of this. This individual believes that the other person is in a relationship of affection without requiring any evidence. They may sit together without exchanging words, or even sit apart and merely think of each other. There may be no practice of exchanging gifts or even communicating on many occasions. Yet the relationship between such individuals may be just as affectionate, or even more so, than the more demonstrative relationship. It might even be argued that the less demonstrative relationship was likely to display more maturity in its participants, in that they have come to appreciate that there is more to feelings of affection and friendship than can be expressed, and so it can be appropriate to embody those feelings in non-expressive ways. It might be argued that those who required constant avowals of affection are unsure of their relationship, and so call for reassurance to be frequently supplied. Perhaps they are also unaware of the diversity of ways in which affection may be expressed, and reciprocated, and as a consequence they insist upon a limited and relatively crude form of response.

Maimonides might use such a formulation of ways of relating to God to show how acceptable from a religious point of view his account is. There would be nothing wrong about the idea that we have to attract divine providence through our own efforts, since this could be taken to reflect a mature and intelligent attitude to our relationship with God. From a moral point of view it puts the onus on us to develop our characters in appropriate sorts of ways, and prevents us from expecting God to pull our chestnuts out of the fire on our behalf. From an intellectual point of view it obliges us to work out what our relationship with God can be, given the restrictions which exist on what we can acceptably say about him. These restrictions mean that we cannot relax into holding on to a cosy and anthropomorphic conception of the deity, and so we have to work out for ourselves from our observation of the world (including ourselves) and our understanding of religious texts what notion of God is feasible. The important point that the elucidation of the fact of evil in the world has on us is to force us to re-examine and redefine our relationship with God. For those capable of this sort of intellectual work it is not enough to sink into the platitudes of religion as Job's friends do, and even ordinary believers are supposed to use those platitudes only as stepping-stones to more sophisticated and rational conceptions of their relationship with God. Job is continually trying to work out and develop what sort of idea of that relationship is appropriate, and Maimonides provides a good deal of support for the idea that Job is asking exactly the right kind of question.

CHAPTER 5

Gersonides

Philosophy of the style practised by Maimonides and Averroes went on to have great popularity in the Jewish world, but in the Islamic world not much work in the subject continued outside of Persia. The prosperous Jewish communities in Provence and the Languedoc took to philosophy with relish, resulting in two huge controversies in the early thirteenth century over the writings of Maimonides and in the early fourteenth century over the allegorical interpretation of the Bible. There is a well-known saying of Yedaya ha-Penini that if Joshua arose to forbid the Provençal Jews from studying the works of Maimonides, he would be ignored. They would sacrifice their lives and fortunes in defence of the philosophy of Maimonides. I think we can accept that there is some exaggeration here, but the general point is valid that there came to be a large translation project turning Jewish and Islamic philosophy into Hebrew and using it to make sense of Scripture. Whereas interest in philosophy in Spain had been very much the preserve of the élite in Jewish society, in Provence it seems to have been much more broadly distributed, and there was a lot of interest in even the more technical aspects of philosophy, such as logic. By far the most outstanding figure in this period is Gersonides, Levi ben Gerson, who lived from 1288 to 1344. Gersonides was a very considerable astronomer and mathematician, who also concerned himself with using philosophy to understand the Bible, and his large set of philosophical books, *Wars of the Lord* (altered by his opponents to Wars Against the Lord), deals with a number of the main issues in the philosophy of religion of the time. Gersonides was an original thinker, but he found it difficult to escape from the domination of Maimonidean thought, selecting as his escape route the philosophy of Averroes.

Gersonides and Maimonides employ very distinct philosophical styles. Gersonides attempts to follow the approach to philosophy of Aristotle and Averroes, stating clearly what the point is and seeking to analyse it. Maimonides, by contrast, writes in a far denser manner, with lots of allusions and hints to deeper matters. In some ways this is a reflection on the very different cultural backgrounds within which they worked. In Provence philosophy was a popular and respectable activity, despite the occasional bans by the religious authorities. It was too widely dispersed among the community for any rabbinic ruling to destroy it. In Maimonides' time philosophy was under great suspicion, and the philosophers themselves were very concerned at the possibility of weakening the faith of their co-religionists by being too frank in expressing their opinions. Interestingly, all the philosophers whom Maimonides himself recommends others to study embody the Aristotelian principle of clear expression and exoteric exposition, yet he himself followed a different approach. Given the rather embattled context within which he operated, this is hardly surprising. In Provence Gersonides had the cultural space in which to develop fully the implications of Spanish philosophy, both Jewish and Islamic, and he took his opportunity well. Gersonides bases his approach to philosophy on Averroes, and so comes to less radical answers than does Maimonides. Averroes constructed a theory of meaning according to which the relationship between ordinary language and the language describing the attributes of God is equivocal, but not in a strong sense. When we say that human beings are wise and then that God is wise we are using the same notion of wisdom in both cases, but it is being used in such a way that not all its features apply to both sorts of subject. God is paradigmatically wise, and our wisdom is a pale reflection of his. Yet the same notion is being employed in both cases here. Maimonides produces a far more radical theory, according to which there is no relationship whatsoever between our wisdom and divine wisdom except that we use the same word in both cases. This makes our route to God rather difficult, and we shall see what implications this has for our understanding of the role of evil and suffering. For Averroes and Gersonides there is a more accessible route to God, and Gersonides writes of that route sometimes with the same sort of confidence which he has in natural science.

Gersonides discusses the problem of evil in a number of places, both throughout his more general works and in two specific books, a volume of his *Wars of the Lord* (*Milḥamot ha-Shem*) and a commentary on the Book of Job. The latter is a very searching examination of the Book, and Gersonides is very much influenced by Maimonides in his approach. In spite of this undoubted influence, he was also determined to take a different path from his predecessor, and this he certainly does in the text. One noticeable feature of the commentary is its length, which Gersonides says is due to the extreme importance of the contents. As he puts it:

The subject to be discussed in this commentary is whether God extends His providence to the individuals of the human species, as it follows from the fundamental principles of the Torah, and consequently calls them to account for their acts, or not. If we posit that He does extend His providence to human individuals, it would follow that we may attribute injustice to God, on account of the imperfect order of events in matters of good and evil accruing to men, since it often occurs that the righteous suffer and the wicked prosper. It is this doubt which swayed the philosophers to assume that God has no knowledge of any of these particular incidents. (*J*, p. 3)

Gersonides credits this philosophical view to Aristotle, and is scathing about the ability of his predecessors to unravel the meaning of the text. Even Maimonides is said to make only brief comments on the opinions of different characters in the Book of Job. For Gersonides, the Book presents a number of different philosophical positions, characterised as the opinions of the different participants in the story, and it is the task of the commentator to analyse these logically distinct arguments and come to some conclusion as to where the greatest degree of validity lies. This methodology runs throughout his approach to the text, which is on the whole highly systematic and clear.

He starts off by presenting the reader with a summary of his general theoretical perspective on the issue. Most evils which apply to human beings come from either a material or an accidental cause. By talking about material causes he means those explanations of our behaviour which originate in us, either through the constitution of our nature or as a result of our attitudes. Some of these causes affect us because of the way in which we have been naturally constituted. Some affect us through our inability to act prudently, through our inability to apply reason to our lives because we have been overwhelmed by natural influences. Then there are those natural events like earthquakes and floods which affect us adversely, and which originate in some natural event. Although the purpose of such phenomena is on the whole benign, on occasions they accidentally bring with them negative results, such as people being killed or injured.

These natural events have as their proximate cause the motions of the heavenly spheres, and as their ultimate cause God. Such events are thoroughly rational, and we can use our ability to reason to understand them and cope with them. The important message of the Book of Job is that we must appreciate how to apply reason to our misfortunes, and in this manner explain them. Although we are told that Job was a virtuous and observant individual, we are not told that he was wise, which Gersonides takes to indicate that he lacked wisdom. Through his sufferings Job is eventually brought to the state of wondering whether it would have been better not to have been born at all, and he comes to doubt that God knows what goes on in the world of generation and corruption. After all, a blameless person like Job comes to suffer while the evil people in the world may well flourish. Eliphaz rejects this approach. He argues that the unpleasant things which affect the good and the evil people in the world have different characteristics. For the evil they are punishments, and far severer in scope than the trials and reprimands affecting the virtuous. Then there is the argument that we can have some understanding of what is going to happen to us through our dreams, a common idea in medieval philosophy. This notion originates in Aristotle and is based upon the theory that our imagination can operate swift logical reasonings which enable us, while asleep, to grasp the ways in which the organisation of the world can result in particular consequences for us (*Introduction*, pp. 111–12). Finally, Eliphaz runs through the argument about general providence and its results for the sublunar world. The general organisation of the world is evidence of divine benevolence, and it is just unfortunate that in some cases suffering results. If God did not keep his eye on things, the cunning planning of the evildoers would bring about even worse results than those with which we are familiar. The conclusion which Eliphaz reaches is that the misfortunes affecting Job must be due to previous sins on his part, or those of his family, and the advice was to return to God and hope for mercy.

Bildad produces the view that the evils which befall the virtuous eventually result in their advantage. Conversely, good things may happen which in the end turn out to be highly disadvantageous. Job points out that this suggestion goes against experience, at least if we are limited to things happening in this world. Gersonides has an interesting interpretation of Job's angry comments upon his fate. He describes these comments as an attempt at separating God from the evil events which occur in the world, thus preserving God's beneficence, albeit at the expense of his power. If God does not know, and cannot alter, the contingent events in the world, then he cannot be blamed for what takes place there. There are two arguments for this conclusion, one of which has a sound Aristotelian pedigree. This asks how an immaterial being like God could know what goes on in the world given his lack of sensory equipment (*Introduction*, pp. 108–10; *Averroes*, pp. 71–81). Job asks God 'Have you eyes of flesh or do you see as man sees?' (10:4). The next verse 'Are your days like the days of men, or your years like man's years?' (10:5) implies that God's distance from the spatio-temporal world makes it impossible for him to grasp what goes on within such a context. He may certainly be allowed to enjoy knowledge of necessary and eternal things, but the idea that God is aware of everything which goes on in the world is to identify him with the 'darkness' of that life (10:22).

Zophar has an interesting development of Bildad's argument. He suggests that we have difficulties in knowing whom to classify as good or evil. This is because the ascription of such terms depends not only on what we see people do, but also on their dispositions for good and evil. Someone who is capable of doing great good may not achieve the perfection which is compatible with his character, and may seem to us to be highly virtuous. Yet the few good things which he does not do and which would complete his route to perfection count very heavily against him *sub specie aeternitatis*. Conversely, someone who finds virtue very difficult to pursue might perform a few good deeds, for which he is heavily rewarded, and ordinary observers may find this difficult to perceive. The few virtuous actions which he performs represent his route to perfection, the only route which is available to him, and for which he is rewarded accordingly.

Job's response to such arguments is to appeal to our experience. We know from our experience that the wicked prosper and the innocent suffer, and his friends imply that God is unjust through their efforts at excusing him. Surely, Job continues, it is inappropriate for God to extend his providence to the least important parts of creation. The most appropriate object of contemplation for the deity is himself, and there is no reason to think that he would concern himself with the trivial and seamy events of our world. As the most perfect thinker, God must have as the object of his thought the most perfect material, and that cannot consist of us and our problems. This leads Eliphaz to challenge Job's claim not to have sinned. After all, the idea that God is unconcerned with our world is in itself a sin, in that it leads people to question the purpose of prayer and the point of virtuous action. At this stage the debate becomes rather repetitive, with Job pursuing his point that experience suggests a great similarity in the sufferings of the wicked and the virtuous, while his friends try to differentiate between them. Experience suggests that Job was righteous and always sought to follow God. Although he grants that the wicked on occasion also suffer, he wonders why such people are often allowed to prosper before the suffering, and the purpose God would have in tolerating them. Not only do the wicked prosper, but they often cause suffering to others, and die peaceful deaths with no evidence of punishment during their lives. All this is evidence from experience that God does not punish people in this life for their actions.

Elihu refers to the influence of the heavenly bodies on the fates of human beings. God has ensured that good will come to the inhabitants of the earth, albeit not necessarily to the individuals who deserve it. The argument to a certain extent is based upon the idea that the organisation of the events in the world are determined from without, and there is nothing that can be done once that organisation is set up. But there is an additional argument, namely, that human rationality is capable of warding off evil if correctly applied. In this way Elihu can dodge the objection that a benevolent God would not have caused so much evil to come to virtuous people. The latter can avoid evil by paying attention to the warnings which come to them through their use of reason. Gersonides gives a broader explanation of how this is to work when looking at the fate of the Jewish people as a whole. When the nation turns away from the right path, it receives two sorts of warning. A prophet may warn them of what is in store, or suffering occurs in order to avoid even greater suffering should the people not change their behaviour. Providence can intervene in the causality of the heavens and prevent what would otherwise inevitably occur from taking place.

Elihu has to respond to two complaints made by Job. The first is that from Job's experience a good man may unfairly suffer through the influence of the heavens, and so there is no justice in the world. The second complaint is that it is unfair for God to provide people like Job with life, since they are going to suffer unfairly in their lives. They would be better off had they died soon after birth, or had they not lived at all. Elihu takes Job to task for his points here. Job is held to be a sinner, despite his self-justification, through his assertion that there is no point in following the path of religion. Interestingly, this sin is labelled as particularly serious because it is a sin in opinion rather than in action, which offends reason and not only our physical capacities. If people come to agree with Job on this point, they will eschew moral behaviour and social control. But the more significant problem is that

real human happiness consists in conceiving God in the best way possible. This view is concurred in both by philosophers and by the followers of the Divine Torah, for to a philosopher who knows the value of reason and the greatness of the being to be apprehended by it, it is very clear. And since the possible right conception of God can be attained by us only through the proper conception of his deeds and the manner of his activity, especially as regards the things in this sublunar world, it follows that when his conduct of the world is hidden from us and we form an erroneous view about it, like the one held by Job, we are prevented from the possible right conception of God. (*J*, p. 210)

Job's complaints lead him into sin, and so serve to explain his suffering.

Elihu is taken in addition to adhere to a theory that God could not intend injustice, since the world is the very best mixture of types of things that can possibly exist. Had God wished to produce evil, then the world would be a lot worse than it is. If we still wonder why the world exhibits apparent injustice, we must conclude that there is something wrong in our grasp of the situation, not that God is unjust. God need not punish the wicked immediately, since their actions do not affect him, and in so far as they affect the more righteous people in the world, such people can through the use of their rational faculties avoid the evil if they adopt the right strategy. Elihu presents a highly intellectual interpretation of providence. God is taken to be perfectly knowledgeable in actuality, while we are only potentially thus knowledgeable. Providence is the possibility of our potentiality achieving actuality, and helps the wise and virtuous escape from the occasionally negative effects of the heavenly bodies upon us. God enables such people to perfect themselves and benefit as a result, while the wicked do not enjoy this option. The amount of providence we get is entirely dependent upon the amount of effort we put in. What Job should have done is considered how the suffering he experienced might have been directed at helping him avoid some act of rebellion against God towards which he was evidently inclining.

God discusses the organisation of the world in order to show Job that it is neither appropriate for him to judge the divine actions, nor is it acceptable to doubt divine providence. A judge must have complete knowledge of the object of his judgment, something which human beings clearly cannot possess, and the punishment of the wicked through the evil in the world is to the ultimate benefit of the righteous. God could have given men the strength of the leviathan, which would have guarded them from all harm, but then they would not be human beings. Similarly, if it would have been possible that the favourable position of the stars should at all times influence the welfare of the righteous, then it would do so. What God has done is supply such individuals with the means, by using their reason to unite with the active intellect, to avoid the force of negative natural forces. He has thus enabled them both to make free decisions and offered them an escape route from the evil in the world. The conclusion is that Job is wrong to accuse God of importing injustice into the world, and when he comes to realise this and repents, his fortunes suddenly improve and his previous prosperity and happiness return. Although there are clearly some Maimonidean themes running through Gersonides' approach to this topic, the latter is keen to disentangle himself from his distinguished predecessor. Maimonides finds a useful escape route from the problem of reconciling divine providence with omniscience in his doctrine of the complete equivocality of divine predicates. That is, he argues that the way in which we can say that God knows is so different from the way in which we can say that we know that there is nothing in common between these two types of knowledge except the name itself. It is a constant theme in Maimonides' work that we must beware of moving from what we know about ourselves and our world to making assumptions about the deity, since there is no such route available to us. This is a useful move for Maimonides to make, since it entirely avoids the problem of accounting for divine knowledge of evil which could be prevented in the world of generation and corruption. Once it is accepted that God's knowledge is totally unlike our knowledge, one can say that one has no idea how God knows, so that the issue of why he does not rectify obvious evils in the world just does not arise. This sort of argument Maimonides adopted in large part from Avicenna (ibn Sīnā), a philosopher who had a great impact upon him despite his occasionally rather disparaging references to him (*Introduction*, pp. 110–17). Avicenna argued that God could really only be thought of as knowing about eternal and unique events, since any other form of knowledge would imply change in him, and an improper interest in events too insignificant for God to concern himself with would demean him.

This debate became very heated in Islamic philosophy, and al-

Ghazālī famously classified Avicenna's argument as one of the key signs of heresy, since any orthodox Muslim must accept that God knows exactly what is happening in the world of corruption and generation. After all, it seems to follow from Avicenna's thesis that God cannot know that Muhammad prophesied, or whether individuals behave immorally or otherwise. How, in that case, would he know whom to reward and whom to punish, who was a Muslim, and so on? Gersonides rather suggests that Maimonides feels that the idea that God does not understand contingent facts is challenging to religion, in this case Judaism, and so he develops his doctrine of the complete equivocation of divine predicates such as knowledge. But Gersonides argues that we do not have to take so drastic a step to avoid Ghazālī's charge of irreligiosity. Ghazālī's most famous opponent in the Islamic world, Averroes (ibn Rushd), produced a theory which is designed to sidestep the very points which Ghazālī makes here, and it is this theory which Gersonides adopts to berate Maimonides.

Averroes criticises Ghazālī's insistence that God's knowledge should be like our knowledge. Since God is so different from us, any demand that he be like us in his capacity to know demeans him and fails to grasp the real nature of the difference between him and his creatures. Averroes charges Ghazālī with representing God as a kind of super-being, just like us but more powerful (*Averroes*, p. 14). This clearly is the sort of unsophisticated view which many ordinary believers have, and Averroes is quite right to point to its inadequacy as a theoretical notion of the deity. How, then, can the sort of God which Averroes thinks we can discuss be said to do and know things? Like Avicenna, Averroes asserts that God's knowledge is very different from human knowledge. Yet there is a link between human and divine knowledge, albeit a far weaker link than that which Ghazālī seeks to establish. The sort of knowledge which we can have is a pale reflection of the sort of knowledge which God possesses, but it is nonetheless a reflection of the same thing. God knows himself and through that knowledge he knows the whole system of the contingent world. This does not imply that he knows every detail of the contingent world – this would be beneath his dignity – but rather that he is aware of the rational principles which underlie that world. It follows that God is aware of the principles behind human action, but not aware of precisely what will happen in the future. This latter knowledge might seem in any case to make the future determined, in which case it might be problematic to blame human beings for their (inevitable) actions.

Gersonides employs Averroes' strategy here to try to work his way from under Maimonides' insistence upon the irresolubility of the issue of divine knowledge. Yet it must be acknowledged that some of the most important aspects of Maimonides' thought do also crop up in Gersonides. In particular the limiting nature of matter seems to be retained. As one might suggest, if Gersonides is right and God can know particulars, then he would organise them in the very best manner, since he is perfect. Yet from our experience of the world it is quite evident that things could be better organised, in the sense that there is a great deal of apparent disorder and unfairness in the world of our experience. It might seem to follow that God cannot then be said to know particulars, since if he knew them he would not allow such disorder to prevail. But Gersonides rejects this approach. He argues that we must differentiate between a perfect order and the best possible order. God could bring about the former were he to be working with immaterial things, yet since he is obliged, by the nature of things, to work with matter, what he creates will be influenced by that matter. And the influence will be predominantly negative, since matter is not in any way mediated by rationality. What God does is operate on the very best principles available to him, but the material he uses sometimes produces results which are undesirable. This is in no way to criticise the way in which God organises the world or to criticise his capacity to carry out such organisation. It is simply of the nature of matter for arbitrary and unpleasant events to emerge on occasion. For Gersonides as for Averroes, God can know particulars, because ultimately they arise from his knowledge of himself and consequently his world, but he knows them in ways which are not inappropriate to his sole concern with abstract and necessary principles. He knows those aspects of particulars which reflect the divine consciousness, the rational aspects, but not those aspects of them which are outside that consciousness. Any other conception of divine knowledge misrepresents the dignity of divine understanding.

What notion of providence goes with this theory? Providence is generally available to all creatures through the influence of God on the world in general, by importing order and pattern into the world. Gersonides has a complex account of how events in the world of corruption and generation are determined by events in the heavenly spheres, so that the movements of the higher spheres lead to corresponding movements and changes in the lower world. Maimonides argued that human beings in general escape this determining influence of the heavenly spheres, and that divine providence is available to us precisely in so far as we are exempted from the workings of the higher spheres. Gersonides accepts that there is a difference in the providence affecting human beings as compared with the providence affecting the rest of creation, and yet that it is possible for individual human beings to escape the general pressures of the determining superior spheres by individual effort and intellectual attainment. As far as the rest of the animal kingdom is concerned, providence benefits them by looking after the whole genus, but not individual members of the genus. The case is different for human beings. We are able to acquire rational concepts and so align ourselves with the contents of the active intellect, the system of principles governing the universe. In so far as we perfect ourselves and match the workings of the active intellect, we receive a proportionate share of providence. This is not an entirely intellectual process, since it is also important to be virtuous, but once someone has reached a high level of rational growth he or she is rewarded by providence passing on information about the shape of forthcoming events. The perfected individual is then able to avoid evil and pursue good as a result of his own efforts. Although there is scope in Gersonides' account for the existence of miracles in exceptional cases, it is important to grasp that this application of providence is an entirely natural event. The individual who has perfected himself rationally should be no more surprised at benefiting as a result than the individual who has trained hard for an athletic event should be surprised at success.

Although Gersonides' account is in important respects close to that provided by Maimonides, it is also quite distinct. The main similarity lies in identifying providence with what is under our control, or at least largely under our control, through the development of our rational powers. Gersonides' insistence that the workings of the heavenly bodies affect us as well as the rest of creation, and his more composite description of what it is to perfect oneself, are more useful than Maimonides' concentration upon our rational abilities. In so far as we are natural creatures we are affected by everything which controls nature. Gersonides recognises this when he insists that all natural things are subject to the laws of nature. This does not exhaust the topic, though, since we are able, he argues, to transcend our physical limitations through the use of reason. Yet we have to work towards this form of perfection via our natural constitution, and it is important to organise that constitution in appropriate kinds of ways. Although they both agree that evil is basically equivalent to matter,

Gersonides argues that God can have knowledge of individual material things, albeit very different knowledge as compared with the sort of knowledge we have. Basing himself as he does on Averroes, he is in a position to argue that the organisation of the natural world is itself evidence of divine wisdom and justice, whereas Maimonides is rather in the position of someone throwing up his hands in horror at the events of the natural world and saying 'What do you expect?' Maimonides implies that one could not hope for a better organisation of the natural world precisely because it is a natural world, and as such subject to the vagaries of matter. Gersonides argues that the natural world is informed by principles of divine rationality, and so it is appropriate to ask of that world whether it accords with our notion of justice. God can know what goes on in the world, although in a special way, and he cannot be excused responsibility for the events of that world.

The problem with such a view, though, is that it leaves a good deal mysterious. When we observe a cruel and unmerited natural disaster, for example, we might wonder how it fits into the divine plan, and we should be obliged to conclude that we could not understand its role in such a plan. Maimonides can avoid this by his theory that there is no relationship between our attributes and the divine attributes, so that we can form no idea at all of how God might seek to intervene in the world from our observations of that world. Indeed, Maimonides' radical theory of meaning is designed precisely to avoid such a question being raised in the first place, suggesting as it does that the ways in which God will seek to structure the world bear some resemblance to the ways in which we will attempt to organise what is under our authority. Gersonides' arguments against the Maimonidean position are well chosen. In particular, as he rightly says, it does not follow from the difference which exists between us and the deity that there is no relationship at all between our understanding of concepts relating to us and those appropriate to him. Maimonides presents many fierce arguments to try to establish this point, but it may well be that Gersonides has a shrewder view of this issue than his predecessor.

Let us take the existence of evil as an example here. For Maimonides nature is irretrievably evil and gets in the way of all attempts at perfectability, although there is a possibility of transcending such physical shackles through intellectual progress. Yet the deity is said to have created this matter, and we might wonder why he chose to bring about matter with such awkward characteristics for its inhabitants. If Maimonides believed that matter was already there waiting to be informed by the creator then this would not be such a problem, although the problem would shift to that of accounting for the relative lack of power in a deity limited to working with pre-existing matter. Gersonides also has a low view of matter, but a positive attitude towards nature and its organisation, and he is quite happy to think of looking at the way in which the world is structured for clues as to the intentions and capacity of God. Maimonides is very much opposed to such an exercise. As a result he is unable to capture much of the traditional sense of religion in his theory. Gersonides' God is interested in the actions of individuals, and he is then in a position to reward and punish them in accordance with their actions. He can be thus interested because he can have knowledge of even contingent individuals, although in a very different way from that available to the contingent individuals themselves. Such a deity is much more like the traditional God of religion, the Jewish religion in particular, and seems to adopt the appropriate attitude towards his creation. When observing that creation, one observes at the same time the hand of God in the everyday events of the world.

Yet as a result of his connection with the world Gersonides' God has to answer some embarrassing questions about that world. Let us agree that there are all manner of ways in which rational creatures can mitigate the evil in the world, and we are still left with examples of unavoidable evil which affect undeserving individuals. The Averroistic line which Gersonides adopts involves arguing that were we to be able to view the world *sub specie aeternitatis* we should understand how these sorry events fit into the best possible rational arrangement of the world. Since we are limited to our particular point of view as a result of our finitude we cannot really understand the role of such evil. This is not a terribly attractive strategy. It means that a great deal of trust must be placed in the idea of a deity who knows why everything has to take the shape it does take, without the possibility of examining any evidence to support such a conclusion. One might think that there is no need for such evidence, since we should trust the deity to organise things properly even though we cannot see how he has done it. There is certainly something in this, but it perhaps raises more questions than it can answer. God is taken to represent benevolence in its most perfect form, and our concept of benevolence is only a pale reflection of his. We can see why our limited point of view might fail to show us how God has fashioned the world in the best possible way, but we should expect some mechanism by which we could move from our understanding of a benevolent world to God's understanding of such a world. Unless we can make such moves there does not seem much point in adopting the account of meaning which Averroes offers. It seems that we cannot make those moves, since as soon as they seem to be blocked by the apparent difference between our point of view and the divine point of view regarding evil we can go no further. We have to conclude that God's rule is the most perfect rule, and we cannot really understand why. But if we cannot move from where we are to where God is, to a degree, there does not seem much point in the whole enterprise. One might as well agree with Maimonides that there is a semantic gap between our language and divine language such that no bridges are possible to bring them together. To say that they can be brought together, but in a way which it is impossible to specify, seems to be vacuous.

Gersonides is critical of the way in which Job displays a lack of trust in God's benevolent organisation of the world. Job cannot see how the existence of evil in the world is mitigated by divine justice, and so he concludes that no such mitigation exists. But Job seems to be justified in his doubts. There seems little force to the idea of divine justice where there is no evidence for its existence. But Gersonides has a stronger argument in his favour. If he is right in thinking that he has shown that God has knowledge of individual contingent events then God is at least morally connected with such events. Human beings have a choice. We can either allow ourselves to be dominated by external forces (the heavens) or we can develop our intellectual powers so as to make contact with the active intellect and escape such domination. If we choose to do nothing for ourselves intellectually and so come under the sway of determining forces we can hardly blame those forces for misfortunes which occur. We could have avoided them. If we take seriously the idea of a contrast between the human and the divine points of view then we can accept the idea that there can be much more to the divine point of view than is available to us. The analogy which Gersonides makes between God and a judge is a useful one. If I go to court to seek legal redress for a wrong which I think I have suffered I am convinced that the judge must rule in my favour. I see the issue from only my own point of view. The judge, however, is concerned not just with my point of view but with justice as a whole, and she will seek to reconcile my point of view with that of the other people involved, and with justice as a whole. I may well be totally unable to understand how she came to her decision, and I might blame her for ruling against me, but that does not show that she is wrong and I am right. One must assume, and hope, that she is able to take a broader view, abstracted as she is from the emotions and partiality of the participants in the case.

We do not always require evidence that someone else has a better and more comprehensive grasp of the situation than we do. We frequently take it on trust, when we have reason to assign trust to someone else. If it were the case that we were continually being asked to trust someone who never produced any evidence of being trustworthy, then we might come to doubt the wisdom of our behaviour. But this is not the case with God. As Gersonides points out, there are often occasions when things look as though they have been organised contrary to our interests, but longer and deeper reflection reveals us to be wrong. This certainly does happen occasionally: the idea of undeserved suffering as part of an educative process is a useful one. It shows us that we are at the mercy of events which are unpredictable and yet which can have major implications for our lives. Unpleasant experiences can quite easily be seen as educative, as Gersonides sees Job being persuaded, and they lead us to a happier state of affairs than is available were we to think it possible to pass through life unscathed by the vagaries of the contingent world.

These comments apply when we are thinking about what might be called minor disasters, but they do not get much grip when major disasters occur. The educative nature of the experience of being shepherded along with one's family into a death camp might well elude us. Saying of such an experience that it came into the category of 'benevolent' when seen from God's point of view would be to place a great deal of trust in the deity. Still, if we accept along with Gersonides the possibility both of free will and determination by external forces we have to accept that evil people can allow themselves to be driven to evil actions, and if God were to seek always to limit the scope of such evil the room for free action in the world would be severely constrained. Our ability to escape evil by developing our intellect might help us avoid some of the threatening actions which confront us, but it will not act as a global guarantee of safety. The whole point of providence here is to save us individually from the claims of matter on our thinking, not on our bodies. We may come to put the unpleasant things which happen to us physically in their proper context when we have extended our intellectual abilities, but there are limits beyond which we cannot go, and however perfected our intellect may be it cannot forever hide from us the sufferings which we are undergoing as natural and social creatures. The fact that the world is characterised by a modified determinism (I owe this expression to Gad Freudenthal) means that there is always the possibility of occurrences which we can neither predict (because they are due to the free will of human agents) nor prevent (since external forces have a huge impact upon what goes on in this world). We might agree with Gersonides that there is a good deal to be said for such a world from a religious point of view, yet wonder whether there really need be quite so much evil in it.

Gersonides tends to argue that the structure of the world is precisely as it is because that is precisely how it is best for it to be, a form of argument which he found and admired in the works of Averroes. As we have seen, when it comes to the issue of evil, this approach involves placing great trust in God, since there is a good deal of evidence missing which would validate a belief in a benevolent God. It is always available to us to assert nonetheless that the deity knows why everything is as it should be, but such a claim is made despite the evidence rather than on the basis of the evidence. Of course, believers would have a different concept of evidence from non-believers, and the texts of religious authorities have a privileged status which no amount of observation of the world can be said to replicate. Maimonides avoids this difficulty of comparing human with divine organisation by bluntly refusing to accept the possibility of any such comparison in the first place. This results in a refusal to enter into the traditional religious debates regarding theodicy, since the initial premiss which one needs to accept before the debate can get under way, that there is some link between human and divine predicates, is missing. Gersonides does get involved in the traditional debate, but he cannot make much progress. He is stuck at the point of saying that were we only to share the point of view of God we should see why the world has to be organised in the way in which it is organised. It can only be a matter of faith to believe that God does embody such a point of view, which indeed is no bad thing in a religion, but the important attempt at providing a rational move from our observation of the world to God's observation does not really get started. As far as the analysis of evil is concerned, Gersonides' aim is to provide a rational account of its existence in a world controlled by a deity, and only limited progress is made in this direction.

But there is one interesting aspect of Gersonides' approach, which is consequent upon his use of Averroes' theory of meaning. This suggests that there is a connection of meaning between attributes we apply to ourselves and those we apply to God. It follows that we should be able to get some idea of what God is doing with respect to evil by looking at what we do, and we can try to fill in the gaps by working out what a perfect creator would do about evil as compared with imperfect creatures such as ourselves. For example, I am in my sitting-room now, but I can hear someone banging away on a typewriter in the room next to mine, and I can work out from the noise I am making that a similar process must be going on next door. Since I am a finite creature I can only imagine what is going on there – the walls restrict my field of vision – but this will not be a problem for God. He is infinite and is aware of everything which takes place, so that we should have little difficulty in conceiving of what it is like for him to be doing something rather like the things we do, albeit in a different and more perfect way. But this is not at all the sort of relationship which either Averroes or Gersonides had in mind. It is not a relationship between two similar things, or between one thing which is a smaller example of something else, like a slice of cheese cut from a substantial round. The meaning of the attributes applied to God is taken to be the paradigmatic use of the names, while its application to the world of generation and corruption represents a very weak imitation of those names. There is then, a connection between the names, but it is a very weak connection. Yet the connection is much stronger than is the case with Maimonides, for whom there is no connection whatsoever between divine and ordinary predicates. So Gersonides does suggest that there is a route along which we might find some indication of how God organises the world in the best possible way, and the only place we can start to find out is where we are now, working from our point of view.

Yet it seems that we cannot move very far from our point of view when we set off along the route to finding out what God's approach to evil is. We know how we might organise the world were we to have the power to do so, and we do know how we cope with evil in so far as it is under our control, and we might then wonder how an infinite being might set about the same sort of task. Unfortunately, although there is a connection between our organisation of the world and God's organisation of the world, the connection is too limited for us to be able to work out from how we do it to forming a conception of how God does it, with the sole exception that we can think of him doing it perfectly, while we are limited to being imperfect organisers. If he organises it perfectly, and it seems imperfect to us, then the problem is not with his organisation, but with our limited perception of what he does. This comes out quite nicely in the Book of Job when Job is confronted by a God who responds to his complaints by showing the mortal how limited his perception of creation is as compared with that of the deity, and how restricted in power he is compared with God. The implication is that were Job to be able to understand more about the context within which God was working, Job would then understand why he did the things he did and why the world was the way it is. Job is impressed with this implication, for all that God has to do to bring his complaints to an end is to demonstrate the differences in the abilities of human beings and those of higher intelligence to understand the nature of the world around them. Job is impressed by the contrast between divine and human power and knowledge, and accepts that God knows why the world must take the shape it does.

Job might be impressed by this argument, and Gersonides seems also to be impressed by a version of it, yet should we be? It does have something going for it. Clearly the viewpoint of an infinite being is going to be distinct from that of a finite creature, especially a finite creature who has been created by the infinite being, and we must acknowledge that a whole range of knowledge is available to God which is inaccessible to us. Some of this divine knowledge would, were we only able to grasp it, explain what seems to us to be very difficult to understand, why there is so much evil in a world created by an omnipotent, omniscient and benevolent being. Would it be unthinkable for God to give us an insight into aspects of the solution to the problem? If he did, we would then know that he has organised the world in the best possible way, and we could adhere to our religious practices with an awareness of the rational basis to the belief in the essential rightness of how things in the world are arranged. There are a variety of responses to such a suggestion, but from the viewpoint of Gersonides there are perhaps two main points which should be made. First, if it was made entirely clear to us, or fairly obvious, why the world was the way it has been created, then there would be no role for faith. Religious commitment would be an entirely rational process of saluting the creator who had made such an obviously wonderful job of his creation. Secondly, even if we were to be shown how the world is arranged in the best possible way, would we understand it? Can a finite consciousness understand how an infinite arrangement makes sense? As a mathematician Gersonides might have thought that this could be possible for arrangements of numbers, but it is very different when we are talking about the arrangement of the world. We are not just thinking here about what might be an infinite variety of things, but also an infinite variety of ways in which they might be organised. Even if we could be shown part of that organisation over and above what we are shown through our study of natural science, we would fail to understand how it played a part in the best possible arrangement of matter. We lack the perspective for this knowledge to be available to us in any more than a piecemeal scientific manner.

Although we cannot understand what God understands, we can make moves to understand part of what he knows. These moves are essentially slow and painstaking, and will result in only a glimpse of something which God sees all at once and perfectly, but it is the mode of knowledge which is available to us, and indeed the only mode of knowledge which is available to us apart from insights into the nature of reality available through religion. Through our scientific work we can build up something of a picture of how God operates, but it will be always only an aspect of the whole which is essentially restricted to him. In that case the theory of meaning which Gersonides uses is quite suggestive, since it is based upon the idea of there being a connection between our point of view and the divine point of view, albeit a rather loose and weak connection. This gives us scope to develop our understanding of God as we increase our knowledge, and it might also be said that it establishes the possibility of increasing our understanding of ourselves. As Job developed and changed through his experiences, so we are able to regard the distance which exists between us and God as a challenge to be overcome in so far as we can, as an opportunity to change ourselves in order to come closer to God. Since Gersonides relates our language about ourselves with our language about God, there is a semantic bridge between the finite and the infinite, and so there is some prospect of getting from where we are to where he is. We cannot expect to complete the journey, but while we are on it we can expect to discover a great deal about ourselves and how we should relate to others, not to mention how the world is. We can, in other words, work out what the nature of our relationship with God is, and so what role the evil in the world has as part of the divine plan. Gersonides defends the possibility that we can make progress along these lines, although we should not think that we would ever be in a position to achieve a final solution to these problems.

CHAPTER 6

Spinoza

It is a big jump from Gersonides to Spinoza (1632–1677), but perhaps not as large a jump as it might seem. Spinoza was a descendant of Spanish Jews and although he lived in the Netherlands he received a thorough grounding in the works of Spanish and later medieval thinkers. He has often, and accurately, been described as being one of the first of the modern philosophers and one of the last of the medieval philosophers, and it is certainly true that he embodies both approaches. He took Maimonides and Gersonides to what he took to be their logical conclusion, and the notion of a personal God largely disappears as a result. Even early on he was prepared to stick his neck out in his defence of what he took to be the truth, and when he produced good arguments to challenge the accepted views of the authorship of the Pentateuch he got into serious trouble with the Jewish community, who eventually excommunicated him. Spinoza certainly was not the only member of the Jewish community to get into trouble with its religious authorities. The spirit of the Renaissance and the influence of the medieval thinkers which so ably supported and helped to create that spirit led quite a few Jewish intellectuals into what were regarded as heresies. The reaction of the Jewish authorities might seem justifiable when one considers the desire which they had to keep a low profile in what was a fairly tolerant host community that had allowed them as refugees to set up home in the Netherlands, and the idea that people from the Jewish community were producing material which challenged not only Judaism but religion as a whole was not something which they wished to be widely disseminated. Whatever can be said about the circumstances of Spinoza's expulsion from the community, it won him the admiration of the Romantic movement in later centuries, since the idea of an individual setting himself up outside of society and grinding lenses for a living while writing philosophy along a geometrical system was immensely attractive to the Romantics. Add to this the amount of discussion which Spinoza produces on God, albeit a very natural God, and his argument that we can transform our emotions and desires, and you get the image of the heroic and noble outsider so beloved of the Romantics.

It is not clear that by the time of Spinoza there was a new way of doing philosophy or looking at the world, or whether we just see the culmination of the work of the medieval philosophers. Certainly Descartes is a very new intellectual figure, yet a good deal of the apparently novel reorientation of thought away from God and towards human beings was a making explicit of what was there already in the thought of Maimonides and Gersonides. One of the important differences between Spinoza and his predecessors is that he was not writing for the Jewish community, but for anyone interested in the issues he was discussing. It is true that the works of Maimonides and Gersonides also had a much wider audience than the Jewish community, but this was not something which they intended nor expected. Maimonides seems even to have been rather surprised to be asked for permission for his *Guide* to be translated into Hebrew, so that Jews outside the Islamic world could read it. Spinoza was definitely writing for the philosophically inclined public at large, and his references to Judaism are rather disparaging by contrast with his references to Christianity. He continues on the project of making religion and rationality concur, but this is only accomplished by a very radical reinterpretation of what theological terms mean, which has an illuminating influence on the analysis of evil and suffering. Spinoza seems to go back to the Stoicism of Philo, but bases that attitude upon a far more complex and persuasive metaphysics.

Spinoza has a most unusual answer to the problem of evil, and that is to recommend a total reversal of our customary reactions to negative events. In a universe which is entirely given over to the causal mechanism determining the course of events, there seems to be nothing left but to adopt a Stoic resignation in the face of catastrophes and personal difficulties. There seems very little, if any, room for the decisions of the individual to have an impact. Although Spinoza's approach is very different from that of his medieval predecessors (with whose work he was very familiar), he does in the end come to much the same conclusion with his stress on the significance of reason as a route to relative salvation. The use of reason enables us slowly and gradually to determine what is to happen to us. While we must rationally acknowledge our determined status in the world, we can use this realisation and all that goes with it to become active and influence what happens to us. What we have to do is to internalise those pressures which push us into certain directions by acknowledging and making them a part of ourselves in a self-conscious manner. This is to follow the route from being passive to becoming active, taking control of our fate through an understanding of how out of our control it is, at least initially.

To grasp Spinoza's argument here, we have to see how close his account of the mind is to the view put forward by the medieval philosophers sympathetic to Aristotle, especially Maimonides and Gersonides. They all identified the human mind with the processes which go on in it. If the mind is equivalent to its thoughts, then to think is to act, and to act is to take up a mental attitude which is determined by a previous thought. The distinction between true and false ideas can be explained by the nature of their occurrence in the mind, since false ideas do not have a history which justifies their inclusion in the process of human thoughts. Such ideas (and Spinoza would not want to give them the status of real ideas) do not reflect the system and organisation of the world, they offer a different and fallacious way of combining thoughts.

Let us take an example. Job is struck down by physical and psychological troubles. What is happening here is that he is overwhelmed by a combination of external forces which is stronger than his own *conatus* or essence. This *conatus* is not a separate thing which Job possesses, it is just the ways in which he behaves when in contact with the world and internal thoughts. It represents the system of ideas and images which the individual acquires through his contact with his causal history, both internal and external. When it looks as though he is about to be destroyed by his problems, Job's ability to maintain his essence when confronted by external forces appears to be weaker than his ability to preserve himself. One of the interesting features of the Book of Job is that the attack upon his well-being is not only from without, from external causes, but also from within, from the destructive influence of his depressive and potentially impious thoughts. This brings out nicely a Spinozistic view that when negative facts influence us, they then become part of us, part of our history, and so in that sense not external to us at all. This is not only the case for the psychological force of the attack upon his *conatus*, but it is also very much the case for the physical deterioration which he suffers. Job changes, and the physical changes become a part of what it is to be Job after certain physical influences have had their way with him.

Once Job is in the position of trying to cope with a constant supply of misfortunes, his troubles seem to take him over and dominate his thoughts, which given the nature of his problems is hardly surprising. His *conatus* will try to defend himself from such negative thoughts, since according to Spinoza 'The mind tries to think of those things which increase or assist the body's power of activity' (*E*, III, P12). Different people will undertake this reaction in different ways. Job seems to be determined not to allow himself to be changed by his sufferings, and indeed by the end of the Book he seems to be in much the same position as he was at the start. Spinoza would argue, though, that he should realise that the sufferings he has to experience are not just external forces from without, but they also change him. They become part of his history, part of his way of experiencing the world and come to define him, along with many other parts of his causal history. He can be overcome by his sufferings, and suffer them passively. He may accept them as part of himself, but continue to despair at their effects upon him. Or he may actively be able to take up a reflective attitude towards his situation. This latter need not make it any less painful. Is this, though, just a description of the desirability of adopting a calm and collected attitude to misfortunes which strike us down in life? If so, it might seem a rather truistic and shabby view.

Spinoza's argument is far deeper than this. Pain is the result of a damaged *conatus*, and as such tends to dominate our other ideas and ambitions. No way of thinking about the pain will make it any less unpleasant in terms of the sensations which we are obliged to experience, or to forego. Yet if we grasp the relation between the pain and other connected issues we are at least in the position of forming a more adequate idea of what is happening to us. The grasp of the role of pain in our constitutions will not make it less painful, but in perceiving the necessity of that feeling and its place in our history we can become as active in our relationship to it as possible. The more adequate our ideas about our misfortunes become, the more able we become to integrate those misfortunes into our histories, understanding all the time how they become part and parcel of us. Then we are not only in the position of passively experiencing unpleasant feelings, but can take up an active stand in also conceiving how those feelings are very much an aspect of who we are and how we came to be who we are.

The individual who uses reason to make sense of what is happening to him achieves a *conatus* which is on the way to becoming more adequate and self-determined. What has to be realised is the difference between two types of explanation of what has happened. Job picks out God as the cause of his misfortunes, and when we are considering the explanation for apparently contingent events in our lives we might well point to some putative cause which we would label as the cause of our present situation, such that had that prior event not occurred, then neither would the subsequent events. For Spinoza this is an error. We fail to understand that an infinity of prior events has led to what affects us now, and that there is nothing contingent about it at all. Although the deity is obviously taken by Job to be an eternal and necessary being, his bringing about his misfortunes is very much like one contingent event leading to another. God decided to test Job, and as a result certain consequences followed, but God might have decided not to test Job, in which case he would not have suffered those consequences. It looks as though the situation in which Job finds himself is explained by the single decision of God to set off a course of events, rather in the way in which my decision to let my child borrow my car sets off the course of events which ends in its damage.

Most people spend their lives in a state of mental confusion, allowing their imaginations to connect quite arbitrarily certain images of events which may bear little if any relationship to what has actually taken place. Our imaginations are further confused by the inclusion of varying emotions and obsessions which connect to the objects of our thought. If we manage through the use of our rational powers to connect our present situation with eternal and demonstrable truths, we are on the way to achieving more complete and intellectually adequate ideas which permit us to direct ourselves in ways no longer at the mercy of our confused passions. Just as it is natural for us to experience such confusion, so it is also natural for us to seek to rise above it. Physically we are creatures which seek to preserve our own lives as members of an environment, while the psychological principles which correspond to this are the need to preserve the integrity and distinctiveness of our thought as against the continual stream of impressions represented by our perceptions and feelings. As thinking creatures our *conatus* tends to act naturally to allow active thinking dominance over a passive sequence of images. The more this sort of thinking comes from us, the more individual and free we are, and the less at the mercy of the vagaries of those things in the world which affect us.

Although we are told that rational people are freer than less rational people, this does not mean that they have much of a choice about what to do. Given the sorts of creatures which we are, the ends which we should seek are already determined by our natures. The only choice we have is how we approach those ends. We can try to achieve pleasure and avoid suffering by following our impressions of the causes of pleasure and pain, and thereby we eventually fall into confusion and frustration. Or we can think rationally and clearly about where our wellbeing lies, directing our own actions and enjoying the feeling of being in control of what we do. What choice does Job have in confronting his misfortunes? He considers blaming God for what has happened to him. Would he be justified in feeling angry with the deity? To answer this question he has to examine the nature of his feelings. Is his emotion of anger a rational emotion? Is there a satisfactory process of explanation which extends from his idea of the cause of his anger to the emotion itself? Or is that process illustrated by imaginative and confused ideas which are based on nothing solid in reason? Once Job examines the explanation of what has befallen him, he might conclude that focusing upon a particular person is a mistake. He might wonder why God would be bothered with the fate of a particular individual like Job, and if he followed Spinoza's line on anthropomorphic language, he would reject the idea that God acts like a human being, only more so. Job might come to think that no one particular cause led to his present sufferings, but a whole host of confused imaginations and associations make it seem that the contrary is the case, and he might come to see that it is an error to be angry at a putative cause which cannot rationally be shown to be the actual cause of his sufferings. This realisation does not, alas, cure Job of his problems, but it means that he is at least left with the active utilisation of his own thinking capacities and does not have to regard himself as suffering due to the intervention of some external and all-powerful external cause.

Job is not, of course, relieved of his problems through a rational awareness of the reasons for his suffering. For one thing, he does not know what the causes of his suffering are, if he insists in looking for some non-contingent explanation. If he does not lay his problems at the door of his creator, then he might come to see them as events in the world which just do from time to time take place, sometimes affecting individuals and sometimes affecting whole communities. Adopting such an attitude does not necessarily make him feel better. What it does do, though, is put him more in control of his feelings, and emancipate him from the depression and frustration of being dominated by his emotions. We have to be clear here on the way in which Spinoza organises his moral vocabulary, doing away entirely with the customary interpretation of ethical expressions. When Job feels angry about the way in which he takes himself to being treated by God, his anger is sadness together with the thought of an external cause, in this case God. This emotion is 'bad' in the sense that it gets in the way of the process of clear thought, especially by dominating Job's thinking and getting him to concentrate upon just one sort of explanation. It is easy to see how on Spinoza's account the experiencing of an emotion like distress affects our ability to act. Essence is identified with *conatus*, so that the definition of a thing is identified with its power to act, either by itself or with other things. Once we experience the essence of an emotion like distress, we are subjecting our *conatus* to an ability to act in certain (less rational) directions and an inability to act in certain (more rational) directions.

One of the virtues which Job seems to epitomise is that of humility, but this is clearly a notion for which Spinoza has little respect. It is

a sadness which arises from the fact that a man considers his own lack of power. Moreover, insofar as a man knows himself by true reason, it is supposed that he understands his own essence, i.e. his own power. So if a man, when considering himself, perceives some lack of power of his, this is not because he understands himself, but because his power of acting is restrained. (*E*, IV, P53).

The humble person becomes passive in the face of his problems, and forebears from applying his intellect to a proper understanding of his situation. We have seen why he might argue that humility is a defect in our freedom, but not why it is wrong. If I reconcile myself to life as say, a non-sex symbol, I am limiting my activity in some way (not dressing carefully, not being expectant of female admiration and so on) and doubtless this is restrictive, but it does not strike one as wrong. We can see what is wrong with humility if we examine Spinoza's definitions of good and evil from *Ethics*, IV:

Definition 1: By good I shall understand what we certainly know to be useful to us.

Definition 2: By evil, however, I shall understand what we certainly know prevents us from being masters of some good.

What is good benefits us, and what benefits us preserves us, and 'We know nothing to be certainly good or evil, except what really leads to understanding or what can prevent us from understanding' (*E*, IV, P27). Job's humility is at fault because it prevents him from attaining a good, something which would be useful to him. This can only be a proper appreciation of the reasons for the situation in which he finds himself, which he erroneously blames on God. Job's emotions get in the way of an appropriate understanding of his situation.

What would Job discover if he could more adequately grasp what has happened to him? He would discover that what happened had to happen. God would not think about an individual like Job and decide to test him, since that would imply a lack in God. Why should God need to find out about Job's steadfastness? Surely he knows Job's character in the first place without any speculation about how far it could cope with difficulties. Why would God need to know this? Since God is infinite and includes everything, he is in the world and the world is in him. If God allows evil to occur in the world, this is equivalent to asserting that he expresses himself in an evil manner, which is hardly what we would want to say from a religious perspective. Once we perceive the world from the point of view of how it always has been and how it always will be, *sub specie aeternitatis*, we have to jettison our ordinary moral language in favour of higher intellectual categories of thought. This is clearly characterised by Spinoza as suggested by Genesis 3 where the fall from the garden coincides with the discovery of the distinction between good and evil. This inferior way of thinking goes hand-in-hand with an orientation which is *sub specie boni*, specifically human, finite, limited and uncritical.

This might seem to be a rather heroic strategy, since there just do seem as a matter of fact to be awful things happening in the world. Are we to say that they just seem to be awful, but when looked at in the appropriate Panglossian manner their awfulness dissipates and their role in the model of a perfect world becomes evident? Spinoza would argue that Job's nature or essence is the same as what he actually is. If he comes to suffer, then it is a part of his nature to suffer, and for him to wonder why he suffers, as opposed to someone else, is to ask why he is Job rather than someone else, which is a peculiar question. Everyone possesses his or her own individual nature which is different and unique. We are all specific ways of manifesting the divine character. Now, we might wonder like Job why the innocent suffer and the guilty flourish, and we might expect that on the whole decent people should benefit from their meritorious behaviour and thinking. This is to make the invalid assumption that we can group people together in general categories such that they are all appropriately describable in common ways. This assumption is invalid because we are all individuals, and as such what happens to us is the exemplification of our individual natures, beyond which no more universal conclusions may be drawn. Indeed, the desire to reach such conclusions is itself evidence of confused thinking in that it takes away from the reality that ultimately the only substance is God.

This is not to say that God is unable to differentiate between good and evil people. It is true that God should not be regarded as a judge who punishes the evil and rewards the virtuous. Virtuous people express the divine substance in more profound and integrated ways than do evil people. The latter do not share in divine perfection and in the love of God. But these degrees of perfection are not degrees of good and evil; rather, they are degrees of reality and express the divine substance more adequately and with greater understanding. Job should not be surprised that his virtuous past does not guarantee a pleasant present and future. The rewards of a virtuous life are there in the virtuous life itself, and provide no justification for expecting anything else in addition. Once we fall into the trap of expecting God to intervene in our everyday lives, we imply that he is like us, helping the virtuous and punishing the wicked.

So who is responsible for the evil in the world? The question is put very directly by Willem van Blijenbergh in a correspondence with Spinoza. He argues that God should be seen as the cause of the soul and the activities of the soul, so that:

> it also seems to follow necessarily, either that there is no evil in the soul's motion or will, or else that God himself does that evil immediately ... For example, Adam's soul wants to eat the forbidden fruit. According to the proposition above, that will of Adam happens through God's influence – not only that Adam wills, but that he wills in this way ... So either Adam's forbidden act is no evil in itself, insofar as God not only moved his will, but also moved it in such a way, or else God himself seems to do what we call evil. (Letter 18; *Coll. Wks*, i, p. 356)

In his reply Spinoza sees exactly what point his correspondent is trying to make. Adam's decision to eat the forbidden fruit is part of Adam's essence, and as such it is a perfection. There is a problem, then, in calling what Adam does a sin, since a sin is a sign of imperfection. It would seem to follow that Adam's action was not evil. There is a difficulty too in the notion of Adam's action not being willed by God. To say that God does not want him to act in the way he does suggests that the deity is imperfect, since events take place regardless of his will, and also involves an illegitimate anthropomorphic interpretation of God. It treats God as though he were like us, in having wishes and ambitions, and personal relationships with his creatures. Spinoza thus manages to reach the conclusion that Adam's decision is not evil, and nor is it in opposition to God's will.

This might seem to be an extraordinary argument. Not only is Adam's decision taken traditionally to be evil, it is the basis of the human condition in which so much subsequent evil flourishes. Spinoza is arguing here that we have to see evil from two points of view, our point of view and God's. As far as we are concerned, we might think of Adam coming to a different decision, which is equivalent to his having a different essence (being a different person, in effect), because we see him as deviating from the path which he ought to follow. This is because we fail to realise that the way in which the world is organised is the way in which it has to be organised. God, naturally, does not suffer from such a partial view:

The prohibition to Adam, then, consisted only in this: God revealed to Adam that eating of that tree caused death, just as he also reveals to us through the natural intellect that poison is deadly to us. And if you ask for what purpose he revealed it to him, I answer: to make him that much more perfect in knowledge. So to ask God why he did not also give him a more perfect will is as absurd as to ask him why he did not give the circle all the properties of a sphere. (Letter 19; *Coll. Wks.*, I, p. 360)

And while it is true to say that God is the cause of everything, it does not follow that the things which he causes are all the same. As he puts it, 'For though a mouse depends on God as much as an angel does, and sadness as much as joy, a mouse cannot on that account be a kind of angel, nor sadness a kind of joy' (Letter 23; *Coll. Wks.*, I, p. 389). So although the unpleasant features of the world originate in God along with the more helpful events, this is not to say that there is no difference between them. There is a difference, but it is not a matter of thinking how a different arrangement of the world would have brought about a different distribution of good and evil. If we are going to make sense of the phenomenon of evil, the first place to look is at ourselves, since it is from our point of view that evil is defined.

When we look at ourselves, we first of all have to look at our attitude

It's from our vantage point that events are considered evil

to what goes on in the world. There are two ways of accounting for what goes on, a mechanistic way and a logical way. The former is part of the chain of causation and finite, while the latter moves from the substance through an attribute to a series of infinite modes until it emerges in the form of a particular thing. These infinite modes consist of natural laws, which latter represent the power and necessity of God through the attributes. There can be no doubt but that for Spinoza causes necessitate the activities of finite things. The important thing here is to distinguish between the causes of a natural law and the causes of those things which are governed by that law. When Job falls ill, for example, what happens is that he is affected by the system of laws in the world of extension which assigns a law of infection to the world as a whole. These laws determine what happens to him, in terms of the more proximate causes and their more distant general principles. Although these proximate causes are finite, they are nonetheless necessary when considered *sub specie aeternitatis*, since they inhere in God's modes and are as eternal as God himself. Change occurs as specific essences become converted into concrete things, but in so far as the changing things are part of the system of nature they are infinite. The essence of the finite things have God as their ontological basis and are as eternal as he is.

For Spinoza the relationship between what we do and what led up to that action is not contingent. Everything has its own essence, and that essence is identical to its causal history. These individual essences exist in God and share in his eternity. They are equivalent to the causal processes which lead to or away from them, and so the notion of a different possible world is vacuous for Spinoza. The issue of why there is unmerited evil, or evil at all, in the world is not an issue for him. We have to understand that what comes about is a result of well-defined causal influences which actualise individual things and make them interact in different ways. If we are puzzled by what we find in the world we should investigate ourselves rather than the external world, since the grounds for the confusion and the classification of events as evil lie with us. What such investigation involves is not a peering inwards at some self-subsistent soul; rather, it is a scientific study of both internal *and* external phenomena which explain how we work. There is no point in wondering why God allows evil since this is to engage upon a woefully misguided anthropomorphic project. Our source in God is a source in an impersonal substance, and the causal influences which bear upon us and indeed make us what we are

are precisely that, causal influences without any plan or purpose or concern for our welfare. Peering into ourselves to try to investigate the real self is a waste of time. If we want to know more about ourselves we should look outside of our soul at the whole battery of sciences which explain how we become what we do. This investigation is an entirely causal operation, eschewing the notion of privileged self-knowledge or teleological inferences from the intentions of a creative deity.

Spinoza distinguishes between two sorts of investigation here, between *ratio* and *scientia intuitiva*. The former is a scientific study of the causal processes which lead in general to the construction of individual essences. Intuitive knowledge comes later, and is direct awareness of individual essences in one grasp. This perspicuous grasp of myself is at the same time an awareness of how I exist in God at the same time as God exists and is represented in me. This understanding is supposed to bring with it great joy as a result of my rational grasp of the way in which I exist in God and God exists through me, but an interesting feature of it is that it provides us with no additional information. It is rather a way in which scientific information can be organised to present a picture of the totality, and it is a path which only a few can successfully undertake. Although we are finite and mortal, the essences which constitute us are not, and our concentration upon the necessary and eternal essences brings with it no promise of immortality for ourselves as people. After our death there is no existing individual to keep on thinking, and so thinking about eternal things does not preserve us, nor any part of us. During this life we can come into contact with eternal things, and enjoy a special kind of happiness as a result, but we cannot as a result expect any eternal reward. Whatever reward exists in this form of thinking exists in this life and no further. The eternal essences will persist after we have departed, but their continuing existence will be of no benefit to us. The traditional religious idea that we shall be rewarded in the next life for our behaviour in this life has no place in Spinoza's philosophy.

It will come as no surprise that Spinoza's account of providence is similarly unusual. Like Maimonides he distinguishes between a general and a special providence. General providence is the way in which what exists is produced and maintained in existence as part of the natural system. Special providence is represented by the *conatus*, by the attempt of every individual thing to preserve its existence by itself, separately from the system of nature (*Short Treatise*, ch. v). Spinoza puts all the emphasis upon these individual things:

God then is the cause of, and providence over, particular things only. If particular things had to conform to some other nature, then they could not conform to their own and consequently could not be what they truly are. For example, if God had made all human beings like Adam before the fall, then indeed he would only have created Adam, and no Paul nor Peter; but no, it is just perfection in God, that he gives to all things, from the greatest to the least, their essence, or, to express it better, that he has all things perfectly in himself. (*Short Treatise*, ch. VI pp. 50–1)

Spinoza seems to agree with Maimonides that only individual things have real existence (*GP*, Bk. III, ch. 18; Pines, pp. 474–6). When it comes to analysing concepts like good and evil, Spinoza has then to conclude that they exist only in so far as they relate to comparisons which we make between things. Good and evil do not exist in nature. They only exist in so far as they are part of the essences of individuals (*Short Treatise*, ch. 10) and 'in nature there is no good and no evil' (*Short Treatise*, ch. IV p. 75). The question as to why there is evil in the world, then, is not really an issue for Spinoza. Our opinion that there is evil is based upon our imagination and a comparison of things which is often arbitrary. Really things just are as they are necessarily, and when we apply terms like 'good' and 'evil' to them we are reflecting on how they relate to our present interests and ambitions.

This is not to say that Spinoza thinks that there is no difference between good and evil. As we have seen in his replies to van Blijenbergh, there is taken to be a real distinction between the good and the evil man. They are the same in that they both depend upon God and realise their role in the world through their actions. The wicked person, though, has no grasp of his dependence upon the deity nor of how reality is organised. He just acts on the basis of his passions. The good person, by contrast, understands his position in the universe, his dependence upon God and the necessary nature of his actions. The idea that he plays an essential part in the workings of the world gives him a sense of pleasure and happiness. This happiness is not a reward for his virtue, it is rather part of virtue itself. The virtuous person does not seek to control his passions in order to receive the reward of happiness later – he is not after deferred gratification. His happiness arises along with his knowledge of God and his role in the world, and that happiness in itself serves to control his passions, thus playing a part in creating a more perfect human nature which has as its main aim the knowledge and love of God. The difference between a virtuous and a wicked person lies in the difference between their natures. It is not a matter of a difference based upon the distinct routes which they take in order to achieve happiness. These distinct routes themselves follow from the difference in their natures. We should not think of God as a supernatural judge who rewards the good and punishes the wicked. The rewards and punishments appropriate to good and wicked actions necessarily accompany those actions themselves. It is important to see that according to Spinoza there is a close relationship between evil and error. The evil person fails to perfect himself due to a deficiency in knowledge and understanding, a deficiency which no doubt has its causal antecedents, yet which nonetheless expresses a series of cognitive mistakes made by the unfortunate agent.

Like his medieval predecessors, Spinoza is in no doubt of the relative status of intellectual and practical knowledge. The former is far more significant than the latter. Some interpreters see his argument here as going in the direction of a general asceticism, whereby he is taken to suggest controlling the passions and reducing one's desires in order to magnify the role of the intellect in our lives. This is mistaken. He does indeed argue that it is helpful for the passions to be controlled and for that part of our lives which is not directly under the control of the intellect to be limited as far as possible, but this comes about along with the progressive development of our intellectual awareness, not as something to be aimed at *per se*. We should seek to behave well because this is on the route to greater personal perfection, it makes us more real and in control of ourselves, yet it is not possible to aim at virtue as an end. Virtue arises, if it does, as a concomitant of something else, the growth of our intellectual powers and an awareness of our relationship with the deity. This is not an awareness of a personal God, which would be to corrupt the relationship from an intellectual form of love to something far more personal, but rather of a principle which we incorporate and express. Evil arises when we assess actions as falling below the standards of the most completely real human nature. But evil is not part of that nature and has no essential reality. It just represents a judgment which we make from a particular point of view, and God cannot be the cause of evil. He cannot be the cause of what is inessential, he cannot express what does not really exist, and so wondering what role evil has in the universe should lead us to look at ourselves and not at the deity.

The Book of Job might be seen as fitting quite nicely into this scheme. It is true that Job, whom Maimonides points out is not described as wise, wonders why unmerited suffering takes place in a world created by a benevolent God. Job is thinking at this point of his relationship to a personal God, a deity who is properly concerned with the actions of his creatures and with the just arrangement of rewards and punishments. This is a level of thought for which Spinoza has no time, based as it is upon what he would regard as superstition and imagination. Yet it is interesting to see how later on in the Book the story develops. God's silence suggests that from the point of view of the deity the sort of argument which Job puts forward is entirely inappropriate as a means of acquiring an accurate view of the relationship between God and his creation. When God does eventually respond it is in terms of a poem describing nature, and that description is replete with the implication of God's power arising through natural processes. That reply, if it is a reply, satisfies Job. He comes to see, perhaps, that the way in which he phrased his question is misguided. There is no scope for a satisfactory answer to the problem of undeserved suffering if that problem is directed towards a personal God. There is an answer to the question if it is understood that the evil in the world arises out of our determination to interpret aspects of that world as evil, so that the direction in which we should look for a solution is not towards God but towards ourselves. If we want to know how divine providence arises we have to look at nature and its organisation, since this is the arena in which individual things acquire their reality and characteristics, and it is the only place we can go for examples of how God is related to us. At the end of the Book of Job we are told that he is rewarded for his steadfastness by the return, and even increase, of his material possessions. This can be taken as a metaphorical expression of the idea that once he comes to realise the significance of nature as an answer to his original question, now suitably reformulated, the problem disappears. A Spinozistic reading of the Book of Job sees Job as developing into a wise person through coming to understand how misplaced his original question was.

Why does Job's newly acquired wisdom free him from evil? This is because he comes to realise that what he took to be evil seemed to be evil due to his confused apprehension of what was happening. The wise individual appreciates that the things which happen to him as a result of external influences are necessary and must be accepted. There is no point in wondering whether one might be in a better position than one finds oneself in if things cannot possibly be other than they are. If we do wish that things could have turned out

Spinoza suggests that we must accept that which happens

differently we are not being rational. Spinoza operates with a simple dichotomy here. Either we accept that what happens has to happen with the consequence that it is irrational to wish for alternatives, or we have a crude understanding of morality and religion in accordance with which our moral decisions look prudential. Along these lines he distinguishes sharply between what he regards as the philosophical understanding of morality and the ordinary understanding. Most people believe that they are free in so far as they can act unhindered to realise their passions. As a result they interpret religion and morality as just such a hindrance, for which they deserve a reward in the next life if they allow their desires to be thwarted by religious and moral considerations. It is the thought of future rewards and punishments which controls their behaviour, nothing more, and Spinoza argues quite convincingly that this will not do. He has set up a rather extreme contrast here, and one might wonder whether it would be possible for someone to act well just out of moral considerations and with no hope of any practical personal reward or punishment. This is immediately ruled out by him given his definitions of good and evil. These are related to the individual's seeking to realise his goals, or being thwarted in that pursuit, and there can be no rational moral activity on that account which escapes what he sees as the necessary structure of reality.

There are certainly some very useful aspects of Spinoza's approach. Take, for example, the very famous proposition 67 of *Ethics*, IV – 'A free man thinks of nothing less than of death, and his wisdom is a meditation on life, not on death.' This might seem to be a moving spiritual observation, or sheer nonsense. It is just the sort of comment which raises the hackles of commentators such as Jonathan Bennett (*A Study of Spinoza's Ethics*, p. 324). Yet it is an interesting claim which shows how Spinoza's view of evil fits into his general position. Most people would call death an evil, perhaps even the worst evil, and do everything in their power to resist it. It is certainly true that death may appear evil since it frustrates the continuance of our activities. On the other hand, it is an inevitable aspect of life, of the sort of lives of finite creatures such as ourselves, and regarding it as evil is to commit a crime against rationality. If we did not die, then we could not live in the way in which we do live, and so death is something which the free individual should confront calmly, like all those other aspects of the world which could not have been other than they are. Since life and death are inextricably connected, thinking of one involves thinking of the other. There is a tendency for us to act and to think as if our lives are going to continue forever. Death may well be a prospect we try to ignore or fail to connect with our lives, and it is important that we grasp the inevitable conclusion of mortality. That does not mean that we should be miserable, or contemplate skulls or adopt an ascetic lifestyle. None of these conclusions follow from Spinoza's statement. What he means is that if we are able to view calmly the fact that we are going to die, then we shall understand far better the nature of our lives. It is senseless to regret what cannot be altered, and since death cannot be altered the wise person does not try to hide its existence from himself or pretend that it is a temporary stage to another form of life. What he accomplishes through his analysis is an awareness of the significance of death which has implications for the rest of his life.

Spinoza thinks it is important to consider why death is regarded as an evil. Death is the apparent termination of our efforts and appetites, and most people regard that series of dispositions as the most important part of themselves. That is, when I think of being dead I may regret no longer being able to drink a cup of coffee in the morning and similar activities which are completely bound up with being human and finite. The way in which we think about death reveals a great deal about our conception of life. Death should not be regarded as an evil, according to Spinoza. Most people would describe death as an evil, indeed, as the paradigmatic evil, but they are mistaken in this belief. What we regard as evil is only a privation, a partial mode of God which expresses no essence. In so far as things are evil, they are also unreal. There is certainly nothing unreal about death, and so the conclusion is that it cannot be an evil. Why not? Death is not an evil for two reasons. It cannot be altered and so is an essential aspect of us. In addition, our negative attitude towards death is something which is easily explained and can be dissipated by a reorientation in our thinking. As Spinoza puts it, 'insofar as we understand the causes of sadness, it ceases to be a passion, i.e. to that extent it ceases to be sadness. And so, insofar as we understand God to be the cause of sadness, we rejoice' (*E*, v P18s). Spinoza accepts quite readily that fear is a most powerful emotion, especially when combined with superstition in adverse conditions, but it is an emotion which we are obliged to counter. The adult who fears death is like the child who cowers in bed frightened of the bogeyman. While it is acceptable for a child to feel that emotion for at least part of his life, a rational adult is unable to provide the same excuse. Fear of death arises out of an inability or disinclination to understand the role of death in our lives.

Spinoza on many occasions argues that there is no point in

regretting what cannot be other than it is. The world has to take the direction which in fact it does take, and calling some aspects of it evil does no more than reflect what we regard as our interests. Now, it is certainly true that it is not rational to set ourselves tasks which we cannot realise, and nor can we be morally obliged to carry out impossible actions. Yet there is no need for our emotional life to be constrained entirely by the way in which the world is, even if it has to be like that. I may regret that I am unable to live to 150. What Spinoza would suggest is that I should seek to deconstruct my regret here so that the purely subjective aspects of it are seen as being based upon an inaccurate version of reality. I should appreciate that the length of my life is not the most important aspect of me, and I should rather concentrate upon aspects of the quality rather than the quantity of that life. I should also appreciate that I can do nothing about extending my life beyond its natural range, and it is a waste of mental effort to regret this state of affairs. I should try to convert my regret into a positive attitude towards the arrangement of nature, since then I will be in a position to take charge of my affairs and retain some autonomy and control over what remains of my life. That is not to say that the evil and suffering which are parts of my life have to be welcomed, but they have to be accepted as parts of my life, understood and interpreted as things which had to take place.

Spinoza is not arguing that we have to accept what life throws at us. On the contrary, we should not be passive recipients of evil and suffering, surrounding these aspects of our lives with personalised and superstitious paraphernalia. We should confront and then transform these apparently negative features of life into something more positive and acceptable. He is not advocating a general stoicism to the travails of the world. Such an attitude would be no improvement on that of a personalised deity trying to help us deal with our problems. Stoicism may involve a stubborn but resigned acceptance of the way in which nature pushes us around. This is far from the attitude which Spinoza thinks we should try to cultivate. We have to realise that we are parts of the natural world and cannot consider ourselves as any different from anything else in that world. The idea that a personal God is concerned for our welfare is just one way in which we seek to differentiate ourselves from the rest of nature. If what takes place in the world takes place because of divine will and purpose, we might expect to be able to escape from the pattern of natural events at least occasionally. This is not even the case for prophecy:

As to the particular laws of nature by which the communications took place, I confess my ignorance. I might indeed say, as others do, that they took place by the power of God; but this would be mere trifling ... Everything takes place by the power of God. Nature herself is the power of God under another name, and our ignorance of the power of God is co-extensive with our ignorance of nature. (*Tractatus Theologico-Politicus*, ch. 1; Delahunty, p. 171)

There is no point in looking anywhere outside nature for a solution to the problem of evil. If we are to seek a solution anywhere, it must be within ourselves. We should consider the sorts of things we call evil, and decide how reasonable that description is. If we conclude that our description is unduly affected by our limited point of view, then we must abandon it and replace it with a broader and more accurate description which eschews moral categories.

It is important to see the link between Spinoza's attack upon anthropomorphic language and his view of evil. If we are to form an accurate view of God we must abandon the sort of language we use about items of our experience. We must abandon the traditional religious notion of revelation and of any justification of religious law which is not limited to the social sphere. The only direction in which we can look if we seek guidance as to how to behave is the natural world, and so we need a theory of good and evil which is based upon a picture of the natural world. This is what Spinoza provides. Yet its central premiss seems dubious. This is that things cannot be other than they are. Such a principle of plenitude was very popular in the medieval world of Islamic and Jewish philosophy (Leaman: *Introduction*, pp. 32–4; *Moses Maimonides*, p. 57; *Averroes*, pp. 29–36), and is based upon an Aristotelian argument which identifies the actual with the necessary. Spinoza gives the principle a causal rather than a teleological interpretation, and yet the implications are not dissimilar. They suggest that the way in which the world is represents the way it has to be. That means that it is not rational to wish it to be different. Why not? Even if I accept that I have to suffer toothache now, because in the past I consumed an inordinate number of sweets, can I not rationally wish the present reality were different? Might I not imagine myself inhabiting a world in which one could eat sweets to the extent that one wished without suffering the consequences? Spinoza would reply that such thought-experiments are possible but they do not tell us anything about us apart from our ability to form such pictures in our mind. An accurate notion of a person is ineluctably caught up in the pattern of natural reality, and to wish that it were otherwise is to operate with a different concept of a person than that which is appropriate. If we really understand what sort of beings we are we shall come to appreciate that everything is organised in a determined way, and if we are rational we have to accept this and work from it in our mode of applying moral categories to the world.

Yet Spinoza goes on to argue that once we realise what part we play in the world we cannot regret what occurs, and we cannot think that evil really exists. Once we understand the situation we are in we are free, and once we are free we are not confronted by evil, since evil is what prevents us from realising our ends. An advantage of this view is that it acknowledges that freedom is more than merely indulging our desires. Those desires have themselves to be freely acquired. This is a point which Spinoza makes time and time again. To a degree it is true that if we are able to understand why something happens we are in a more powerful position than if we do not grasp its cause. It does not follow that we can no longer regard what is happening as negative and in opposition to our interests. This does follow if we accept Spinoza's premises, but there is no need to do this. There is a central difficulty in those premises. We are told to try to view the situation *sub specie aeternitatis*, and if we do so the role of the apparently evil event in our lives will be explained. Yet as finite creatures our ability to think in this way is bound to be sketchy, and we will be left with having to assert that the event under consideration fits into a global strategy, but we cannot know how. We may ascribe this strategy to God or to nature, or to both, and we are inevitably left in the embarrassing position of not being able to describe precisely how the event fits into the whole. We just have to assume that it does. We may well think that as we come to know more and more about the event we will be able to fit it into the general organisation of the world, but as finite creatures there is only so far that we can go. If we can never hope to come to any final understanding of the event, given our finitude, then we must give up any ambition to understand it completely, and with such an admission we are obliged to accept that we can continue to regard it as evil. If we could only understand it completely we could, if Spinoza is right, see why it is not really evil, but we will never be able to reach this state of affairs. So Spinoza is not really able to argue against the reality of evil as an aspect of our lives.

Like Maimonides, Spinoza thinks that the importance of evil diminishes as we progressively understand more about the situation giving rise to the problem. Like Maimonides, the question as to why there is undeserved suffering in the world is really a question to be directed not at God but to ourselves. Their route to God, the *via negativa*, makes this inevitable. If we can say nothing positive about God, if our language can only be ascribed completely equivocally to him, then we can draw no implications from his existence with respect to phenomena which we describe as evil. If we can say nothing about God beyond the sorts of things which Spinoza and Maimonides allow then we cannot frame the traditional problem of theodicy at all. This is what makes their approach so interesting. It might be thought to be highly heterodox and irreligious to suggest that there is no point in looking to God to solve the problem of undeserved suffering. Another reply might well be that the sort of response to suffering available from a personal and describable deity could only be banal. The idea that God can solve our problems, especially those problems which we do not deserve to have, detracts enormously from the apparently arbitrary character of life. God would be so obvious a part of our lives were he to intervene in this way as to transform him into a sort of 'Superman'. This is not how we should approach the deity. The deity is someone we have to discover in ourselves and in our world, and, as many theologians have pointed out, there must be some epistemic distance between him and his creatures. It might be thought that Spinoza rather overdoes the distance when he identifies God with nature, taking Maimonides' argument to its logical conclusion and doing away with the notion of God as a subject entirely. Yet what they both end up arguing is that the notion of God as a redeemer of humanity is far too comfortable a notion to be accepted in its traditional religious form. God can save us, but only through our own actions, and we have to struggle and fight to work out how to operate salvation. In many ways this is a far more demanding religious notion than the traditional one. It implies that we have to discover a sense of God within ourselves and must be able to use that sense to cope with the evils of the contingent world. This is very far from the cosy platitudes of traditional religion, but perhaps much closer to the real meaning of religion itself. We shall see how this task is analysed and developed in subsequent Jewish thought on this issue.

The important point to make here is that the argument which Spinoza produces to criticise the rationality of regret and repentance works quite independently of religion. When he says, 'Repentance is not a virtue, i.e. it does not arise from reason. Rather, he who repents what he did is twice miserable, i.e. impotent' (*E*, IV P54), he is arguing that there are two aspects to evil in the world. There is the actual occurrence of what we call evil, and then there is our later attitude to it. When we are involved in evil action we go awry, whether we realise it then or not, and this is unaffected by our feelings at the time. That is, for Spinoza, we might be enjoying ourselves, but in so far as we are behaving contrary to our nature, to how we should behave, we are miserable. Later, when we think about what we did and feel sorry about it, we are miserable again, although this time we might actually feel miserable. Both occasions share the feature that they provide evidence of impotence, of not being in control of ourselves and drifting into certain sorts of behaviour and feelings. Now, it seems rather strange that Spinoza so fiercely rules out the feeling of sadness at a past event. We can appreciate that such an attitude might seem to replicate the earlier event, and reason involves the possession of adequate ideas about how things actually are. The earlier event represents a mistake, and thinking about it now runs the risk of inducing us to concentrate upon something which is an error.

This might seem to be a peculiar argument. After all, does not repentance and regret motivate us to behave better in the future? This would be a common understanding of the position, and religion often invites its adherents to think about their previous wrongdoings as a means of avoiding such action in the future. Spinoza will not fall for this, and he is right not to do so. It may be that regretting a previous event will make it less likely for me to repeat it, but it may make no difference. There is enormous scope here for self-deception. Lewis Carroll points this out in *Alice Through the Looking-Glass*:

'I like the Walrus best,' said Alice: 'because you see he was a *little* sorry for the poor oysters.'
'He ate more than the Carpenter, though,' said Tweedledee. 'You see he held his handkerchief in front, so that the Carpenter couldn't count how many he took ...' (p. 73)

The Walrus certainly regretted his actions, indeed, he seems to regret them at the same time as he performs them. But his feelings about what he does have no effect upon his behaviour, and Spinoza would say that it would be highly inappropriate to hope that a particular feeling which we might or might not have could play an important part in governing our lives in a rational manner. We must look elsewhere if we are to find the appropriate attitude to adopt towards what we consider evil.

Yet it might be just as bad to dissociate ourselves from what we did in the past by failing to regret it. We might then be saying that the person we were in the past is a different person from the person we are now, and this casting off of responsibility for what would ordinarily be reckoned to be part of our lives and character could also be an exercise in self-deception. On the other hand, such an individual could say that what was done in the past was done by her, and even done quite openly and intentionally by her, and yet was no longer part of her. She may feel completely free of it and so have no need to regret it. It might be said that if she is really to appreciate the significance of what she did in the past, she must regret it now. The Spinozistic response could well be that the emotions surrounding regret and repentance are not helpful if we are to understand what was wrong about the previous action. They cloud our judgment and affect the rational basis of our attitude to that action. Spinoza recommends attempting to view the event from the perspective of eternity, something which we necessarily find problematic, but it has useful implications for our practical lives. There is a tendency to think of Spinoza's account as too abstract, as though he is so eager to emphasise the importance of the *sub specie aeternitatis* view that he is unable to understand properly what the world looks like *sub specie boni*. This is very far from the case, and we shall show that Spinoza presents a very powerful argument for the conclusion that regret is pointless.

The ideal he has in mind here is the case of someone committing some sort of wrong action and later on acknowledging that he did the action, that he intended to do the action, that he should not have done so and that it no longer has any important connection with him. This separating of oneself from the action is a vital part of understanding it. It enables us to analyse it calmly and objectively, and makes it less likely for us to perform it again, if we are to be guided by our rational thinking. Now, this might sound rather strange. It sounds rather like the sort of thing which people often say after a funeral when they are tucking into the sandwiches and drinks: 'Life must go on.' Indeed it must, and it would be wrong, in most cases, for grief to so disturb one that the normal functioning of life comes to a grinding halt. On the other hand, we normally expect some display of grief if we are to count a person as genuinely upset by the loss. If we do not see grief we might think that he did not really care about the dead person, or that he has internalised his feelings in an undesirable way, feelings which will eventually come to the surface in the form of depression and other types of overt behaviour. But are we latching on to any important conceptual points when we make these sorts of observations, or are we just assuming from the start that regret and repentance are a necessary condition of accepting the evil of a previous event? Spinoza would argue that it is not necessary to suffer now to prove that we understand that a previous event was wrong or evil, and that such suffering in fact prevents us to a degree from understanding what was wrong with that event. A concentration upon our present feelings may hide from us the real nature of the previous event to which those feelings are related.

As we have seen, there is a lot to be said for Spinoza's approach here, especially when we consider the account of regret which we find in the Book of Job. Job is confused, angry, defiant, aggressive and noisy in his protestations of innocence, and both Spinoza and Maimonides would point to these features as preventing Job from understanding what has happened to him and what is happening to him now. Job keeps on wondering what he did wrong in the past, whereas he should be asking what he is doing now and how he is going to cope with his present difficulties. The adherent of the rationality of regret would claim that failing to regret the past is to try to separate oneself illegitimately from that past. When we look at Job, though, we can see that his present grief makes him concentrate upon the past in the wrong sort of way. He is so determined to understand what happened in the past that he cannot understand what is happening to him at the time of his complaints. Since his present emotional state makes him see the past in a particular way, he is unable to see it calmly and accurately. This leads him to ask the wrong questions about his suffering and so hides from him the answer which he is ostensibly seeking. Job is an excellent example of what goes wrong when we allow ourselves to be controlled by our feelings. It would have been far better had Job considered his situation objectively, and then he would not have felt that he had been picked out for special and discriminatory treatment.

The trouble with relying on the emotions, according to Spinoza, is that this is a route to loss of freedom and power. We tend to enslave ourselves to our feelings and we are no longer able to act on the basis of reason. We are only really in charge of what we do when we act on the basis of reason, since otherwise we are at the mercy of variable and arbitrary emotions. We can accept the sort of point which Spinoza makes here without at the same time having to accept that it is possible to understand an event objectively, given our finitude. That is, we may try to understand an event as objectively as possible, but it is always going to be difficult for us, as members of the world of generation and corruption, to know that we have categorised that event properly *sub specie aeternitatis*. Spinoza is calling on us to accept that there is such a view even though we are unable to grasp it, or grasp it entirely, on a particular occasion. In some ways this is like the traditional religious teaching on providence, that the world is organised for the best by God and were we only able to understand how, our difficulties in seeing his justice operating in the world would be ended. Yet Spinoza's account of objectivity is not quite as mysterious as this, since he is appealing to a distinction between objectivity and subjectivity which is quite familiar to us, albeit not always easy to make precise in particular cases. Spinoza insists that we take up an active stance in seeking to cope with the evil and suffering which confronts us, and he suggests that to understand these phenomena we look no further than within ourselves and within our world. No other solution is available to us.

CHAPTER 7

Mendelssohn

Moses Mendelssohn was born in Germany in 1729 and like Spinoza received a traditional Jewish education, to which was added liberal doses of Maimonides. Like Spinoza, he achieved a high level of secular education and produced philosophical and literary work which had a very wide circulation among readers of all faiths. Mendelssohn was an important figure in the German Enlightenment, although not an uncritical member of that movement. He advocated that the Jewish community acquire German, abandon Yiddish and enter as far as possible into the civil life of German society. This was not to be at the cost of religion, though, which he maintained as vitally important. Mendelssohn had a dual role to perform. In the first place he had to persuade the Germans that the Jews were capable of performing an acceptable role within Germany, and that the restrictions which lay upon them should be removed. He tried to accomplish this by producing work in German prose of an excellent standard and by entering into a whole range of intellectual debates where one's religious provenance was irrelevant. He hoped in this way to demonstrate to German society that it was possible to combine Jewishness with the ordinary civil and intellectual virtues of German life. On the other hand, he had to persuade the Jewish community to reconcile its religion with ordinary civil life, to learn the secular language of German and to enter into the concerns of the modern European.

One of the routes to this emancipation of the Jewish community was taken by Mendelssohn to be the translation of the Bible into German, a task which he performed in an exceptionally interesting way. As we shall see, the nature of his translation reflects his belief that Judaism is not so much a revealed religion but a revealed system of legislation, which has rationality at its basis. In some ways Mendelssohn's project is shared by all religious and ethnic communities which live within a different culture and people. The aim is to reconcile faith with modernity, and the danger is that with the acquisition of modernity will come an abandonment of faith, something with which Mendelssohn was very familiar from his experience of the practice of Jews in Germany. The difficulty of Mendelssohn's project is that it involves addressing two entirely different audiences at the same time with different pieces of advice. The Germans were not to think of the Jews as a benighted and backward community separate from society, while the Jews were to become ordinary citizens of the Jewish faith. Yet at the time he was working the Jews were very much distinct from German society and there was little scope for their immediate acculturation as Germans. What is interesting about the project is its Enlightenment basis in the emancipatory nature of knowledge. If only the Germans knew what Judaism was all about, they would appreciate that it forms an acceptable basis to life as a German citizen. If only the Jews knew what civil society was all about, they would appreciate that it is an acceptable context within which to live a Jewish life. By the time of his death in 1786 both audiences had moved some way to agreeing with him.

Mendelssohn quite self-consciously represented many of the leading principles of the Enlightenment, both in his writings and in his person. He was much impressed with the works of Locke, Leibniz and Wolff, and took them to be arguing in favour of a natural religion in which philosophy would help us find the rational route to happiness. Explaining the existence of evil in the world is clearly going to be an issue which the Enlightenment has to confront, and it is there right from the start of Mendelssohn's work. His doubts concerning providence are interestingly different from those of his predecessors. He asks whether it would not be better for us were the world to be more predictable. Are not the number of chance events which occur inimical to our greatest happiness (*MM*, p. 33)? This rather unusual way of posing the problem arose from the accounts of providence often provided in the eighteenth century. This offered as evidence of God's freedom of action the existence of unexpected events in the world. This has the potentially rather awkward consequence for us that it makes the world a harder rather than an easier place to inhabit. The more we know about how things are going to turn out, the better able we are to plan accordingly and the more efficiently we can organise our lives. If existence is replete with miraculous happenings then we are frequently going to be at a loss as to how to behave, which will work to our disadvantage.

To understand this difficulty we have to distinguish between what God knows and what we can know. Although some events occur for no apparent reason from our point of view, they are entirely contingent; the situation is very different from the point of view of their divine creator. He does not just produce events like rabbits out of a hat, but the train of events follows a particular order and purpose. What that order and purpose is may not be obvious to finite beings such as ourselves, but God suffers from no such obstacle and what appears to be contingent is from the divine point of view really necessary. The apparently contingent event fulfils an important role as part of the best of all possible worlds. We can know that God must create such a world, at the same time as we do not know exactly how what he has created is part of such a world. To insist that nothing unexpected should happen to us is to ask to be admitted to the details of God's creation, something which is impossible for finite creatures such as ourselves.

Mendelssohn follows the familiar path of trying to marry philosophical and theological statements. On many occasions he referred with approval to what he took to be Maimonides' central strategy, the reconciliation of philosophy with the opinions of the rabbinic authorities. For example, familiar passages from the Talmud inform us that 'Everything God does, he does for the good' (*Berachot* 60b), and 'A person is obliged to bless God for bad things even as he blesses him for the good' (*Berachot* 9:5). Why? To see what the rabbis are supposed to have had in mind we must divide evils up into two kinds, moral and natural. Most evils are moral, brought about through our own weakness of will and selfishness. Some evils are indeed natural, but these are comparatively trivial, and where they are serious (like the phenomenon of death, for instance), they relate to our nature as human beings and cannot really be questioned. Everything which exists has a part to play in the perfect whole and everything strives to realise itself. One might expect that in the best of all possible worlds this would result in everything succeeding in achieving its potential, but this would go against the fact that we are happier if we are in a position to make free decisions, some of which go awry and bring about evil consequences. There is also the almost aesthetic principle that the best world is the one with the most variety, and the Leibnizian model is of different creatures attaining different levels of development at different times, thus incorporating infinite variety in a finite realm of existence. Mendelssohn was even prepared to interpret this principle in personal terms, when dealing with the untimely death at eleven months of his first child. The death of a child seems to be one of the most difficult events to explain within a divinely controlled universe, and Mendelssohn writes very movingly about this event:

The innocent child did not live in vain ... Her mind made astonishing progress in that short period. From a little animal that cried and slept she developed into a budding intelligent creature. One could see the blossoming of the passions like the sprouting of young grass when it pierces the hard crust of the earth in spring. She showed pity, hatred, love, admiration. She understood the language of those talking to her, and tried to make her own thoughts known to others. (*MM* p. 137)

Would the world not be a better place, one might ask, if tiny children did not die of natural ailments? Not according to Mendelssohn. Although we must ask such a question when in the grip of our emotions, we must also realise when able to think rationally that the organisation of the world as a whole is the most perfect order conceivable.

Mendelssohn accepts that this is difficult to prove. He points out in his theological writings that the more we observe order and regularity in the world, the less need have we of a belief in God's power. The only phenomena which seem to work as evidence of divine influence are the very occasional miracles, which suspend the usual rules of nature, and these by definition are rare. Yet once we examine the system of natural laws we are led, he argues, to observe the divine purpose within even the most prosaic and minute happenings. He refers approvingly to the way in which Lessing in his *Nathan the Wise* presents the idea of the vacuity of seeking God's hand in miracles when it can be observed in everything around us. It is well known that Mendelssohn had a powerful personal belief in providence, and in some of his writings he demonstrates the basis to this. He even manages to place Voltaire, whose *Candide* pokes cruel fun at the Leibnizian belief in the perfection of the world, within the realm of providence. Voltaire employed the talents with which providence had supplied him to attack providence, whereas Lessing did the same to try to vindicate providence. Lessing apparently wanted to show how the sorts of evil which *Candide* used to suggest that evil cannot be explained could after all be brought under the notion of providence. In the end, according to Mendelssohn, he despaired of the task as a poetic composition, and wrote *Nathan the Wise* instead, 'which, in its high seriousness of purpose, its wisdom and usefulness, stands in about the same relation to *Candide* as does heaven to hell or as do the ways of the Tempter to the ways of God' (*Morgenstunden* p. 71).

This play by Lessing embodies something of the Enlightenment ideal conception of religion. People of different faiths, here Judaism, Christianity and Islam, follow different practices but they all believe in the same God, and there is no qualitative distinction which can be made between their differing practices. The best approach to differences is tolerance, and the rational believer has no problems in accepting that there are people who follow different approaches to God from his own. Indeed, as Mendelssohn points out on many occasions, diversity of belief is not something to be regretted, but is itself a result of divine providence. He suggests with wry amusement that Voltaire excited less criticism with his witty critique of providence than did Lessing with his defence of providence. After all, one might expect that an author who sets out to establish the role of God in every aspect of the world's design would find his play acceptable to the religious and political authorities of the time. What Lessing's contemporaries found obnoxious in the play was clearly the Enlightenment interpretation of religion, as a rational enterprise pursued in different ways by different groups of people. In particular, the favourable representations of both Jews and Muslims did not strike much of a chord in a Europe which still regarded itself as defensively Christian.

One can see why *Nathan the Wise* annoyed people, and why Mendelssohn liked it. But why did he think it was primarily about the role of providence? It seems to be because of the way in which the play emphasises that it is the duty of everyone to fulfil his or her own individual destiny, and the diversity of these individual destinies is itself part of a pre-established harmony which exhibits maximum perfection. Mendelssohn's stout defence of Lessing even extended to the issue of the latter's so-called 'Spinozism', which so shocked the philosophical world of the Enlightenment. After Lessing's death it was alleged that he had declared his adherence to Spinoza, and indeed there is evidence to suggest that he was not unattracted to that thinker, which was regarded as equivalent to declaring oneself to be an atheist. One of the aspects of Spinozism which attracted Lessing was Spinoza himself and his lifestyle, which seemed to be based upon an extraordinary faith in the role of reason in the lives of human beings, but Lessing was also clearly given to defending people under attack by orthodoxy. While Mendelssohn is no adherent of Spinoza's philosophy he thought that enough of the pantheism could be used to form part of a rational conception of religion for Lessing's belief in Spinozism to be vindicated, and that in any case much of the basis of Leibniz's thought is to be found in Spinoza. Whether Mendelssohn is right in this view is highly debatable, but it is worth pointing out here that the Enlightenment view of Spinoza is very different from the philosophy of the man himself. Spinozism was taken to be identical with a refined form of pantheism, and this is acceptable so long as it leaves room for an individual God with power over the world. Of course, those thinkers like Jacobi who attacked both Lessing and Spinoza argued that religion could not be based upon reason, and that any attempt to do so results in atheism. The debate was not really about Spinoza at all, but rather about the role of God in the world. Any system of philosophy which placed total reliance upon reason runs the risk of excluding God from any meaningful role in the world, and that was the challenge thrown at the Enlightenment thinkers by their opponents.

This broader issue is not our concern here, but we are interested in the connection between the notion of providence and reason in Mendelssohn's thought. He is quite clear reason rules out a large number of traditional interpretations of evil. For example, the idea that when an unreasonable person commits an evil act he must eventually suffer a penalty set by God goes against both religion and reason. The only point that divine punishment has is to benefit the sinner, to improve him or at least encourage such improvement. The idea of a vengeful God, or a God who seeks to ensure that the mistakes we make in this life are aggravated by sufferings in another life, is very far from Mendelssohn's thinking. Mendelssohn claims that Judaism is with him here, and we might doubt that, but what he has in mind is a refined natural religion which underpins Judaism and which is common to a number of different faiths. The virtuous Jew and the virtuous Christian both follow the same demands of reason, although the procedural rules which they follow are different. They express the demands of rational religion differently, but it is the same thing which is being done in both cases, and the idea that God would reward them differently just because of the differences in expression is ridiculous. It is equivalent to God rewarding and punishing people on the basis of the colour of the socks which they choose to put on.

What the opponents of the Enlightenment suspected about this doctrine is that it leaves very little scope for God to do anything. That is what is really behind the controversy over Spinozism. If the world is organised in accordance with the rules of pre-established harmony, if there is a link between efficient and formal causes, if the diversity of the world is to the (ultimate) advantage of everything in it, then what role is there for divine action? It might be said that only God has sufficient wisdom and power to set the whole process going. Only he knows how to construct such a system which is at the same time complex and simple, complex in its detail and diversity and yet simple in its direction. One wonders how rational this belief itself is, or how similar it is to a feeling about the extent of the divine presence in the world. Take the death of Mendelssohn's child at eleven months, for example. He argues that she had achieved a degree of development during that period of life which served to support the view that she had developed in so far as she could have, given the requirements of the best of all possible worlds. Had she died earlier or later the world would not have been as perfect as it could otherwise be, and this would detract from its overall perfection. But what evidence is there for the truth of this proposition? We might well accept the distinction between natural and moral evil, and allow that there must be scope in the world for human beings to do terrible things to each other if they want to, so that occasionally children will be killed by adults or have their lives recklessly put at risk by them. Apart from this moral evil, though, there are many cases such as those of children just dying of natural causes, and one might wonder whether the world would not be a rather better place if all such events did not take place at all.

Mendelssohn is quite right to reject the view of divine punishment and reward as equivalent to providence. After all, as he points out, divine threats and blandishments would affect the will, while the intellect is interested only in questions of truth or falsity (*Jerusalem*, p. 62). Although the will obviously has a part to play in disposing us to seek the truth and avoid the false it would be improper for much of our motivation to behave well to come from the will. We should be able to recognise how we ought to behave through the use of our reason, perhaps not totally but certainly to a large extent. This is quite clearly part of the Enlightenment project, and is particularly important for Mendelssohn who not only had to make the Enlightenment case for religion in general, but also had to answer the frequent criticisms of Judaism in particular as a legalistic and rigid doctrine. He argues that Judaism is at least in no worse a position as compared with other religions in terms of its structure and rationality, and that his religion accepts that everyone in the world is capable of achieving happiness without the aid of a particular supernatural revelation, even a Jewish one. As he points out, it would be extraordinary if the great majority of human beings who lived at the wrong time or in the wrong place for the revelation were consequently to be denied happiness. Human reason is sufficient to establish the eternal truths which form the basis of happiness.

Does this mean that happiness is only possible where people are able to grasp these truths? This does seem to be his view, but it is tempered by the argument that even simple and uncomplicated people can experience these truths in their observation of nature, and providence arranges it so that everyone, whatever his or her intellectual ability, can become aware of such truths, and even where people arise who challenge them, there are also other people who defend them. This description of providence stands against the view of his friend Lessing and other Enlightenment thinkers, especially those critical of revealed religion, who see the development of history as a process of growth whereby earlier and more primitive (i.e. religious) ideas are aspects of childhood to be rejected later when more adult. Mendelssohn suggests by contrast that it is not the role of providence to ensure the uniform progress of humanity, and there is no reason to expect everyone to follow the same developmental pattern. His argument here is based upon experience, since he claims that when we observe the workings of the world we can see a big discrepancy between the ways in which different people achieve their ends. If 'Providence never misses its goal', then 'Whatever actually happens must have been its design from the beginning, or part of it' (*Jerusalem*, p. 96). Our experience does indeed suggest that different individuals and cultures develop in different ways and it is a mistake to insist upon just one model of improvement and progress. As Mendelssohn points out, there is often evidence of progress and then of regress and although providence is supposed to be in charge of everything which happens, it does not insist upon uniformity. On the contrary, the very variety of the way in which progress takes place is part of providence, and it would be deficient if there was uniform progress.

There are clearly some very attractive aspects of Mendelssohn's thesis here. The idea that it is possible for anyone to acquire an understanding of how she ought to live without the benefit of revelation is obviously important in a world where revelation is spread about in a rather limited manner. The idea that God could hardly threaten his creatures with punishments for sin as a way to incline them to believe in the truth of virtue is also interesting, and points towards some sort of distinction, as in Maimonides, between the languages of ethics and reason. Mendelssohn accepts that there is a role for punishment as a political device, but clearly differentiates between the punishment and the justification of the actions which the punishment is designed to support. I may do something because if I do not I shall be punished, yet this does not in itself justify my action on any other than prudential grounds. Mendelssohn suggests that

many a man does not dare to enjoy the benefits bestowed by providence in the here and now for fear of losing an equal portion in the hereafter, and many a man has become a bad citizen on earth in the hope of thereby becoming a better citizen of heaven. (*Jerusalem*, p. 40)

If we continually think of ourselves as under divine judgment, with the prospect of rewards and punishments in the offing, we may come to miss out on how we should conduct ourselves in this life with respect to the pleasures which are on offer. Mendelssohn is quite clear in presenting a view of providence which is cashed in terms of this life. For him, it is no answer to apparently undeserved suffering that the individual will be rewarded by providence in the next life. He puts a great deal of emphasis upon what can be observed to be the case. Although he obviously had a strong belief in a sort of afterlife, this is not a realm which is going to balance deserts with rewards and punishments. For one thing, although the threat of punishment might incline us to behave ourselves in this life, once we are dead the punishment has no purpose except as a means of revenge, which is not how he saw divine punishment at all. Also, if our motive for virtuous action is fear of punishment, then our motive is misplaced. The prospect of punishment might get us on to the right path, but if that is all that keeps us on it, we are far from acting with the appropriate motive.

The main difficulty with Mendelssohn's account of providence is its lack of evidence. He asks us to observe the world in support of his thesis that providence is everywhere, and any apparent difficulty in observing it is attributed to a limitation in our grasp of the facts, possibly due to our finitude. Such limitations do not, of course, affect God. We can certainly observe some instances of what might be called providence in the world, and there are some remarkable examples of natural events which seem not to be in our interests but which on a closer look turn out to be very helpful after all. Despite these points, there is no actual evidence for the existence of a general providence. On the contrary, there seems to be a good deal of evidence against the existence of such providence. Insisting throughout that providence is universal seems rather akin to a mystical belief that everything is designed for the best despite the contrary evidence. We might admire the fortitude which Mendelssohn himself displayed in the face of tragic events, but even on his own criteria he is unable to present a strong argument for his view.

It might be argued, of course, that looking for evidence of providence is a waste of time, since if it was so evident that it could not be doubted then there would be little role for faith, and if there is some evidence of it we are at least encouraged to make the mental leap to religious belief as a result. If there were no evidence of providence at all then it would be a heroic effort of faith to assert the influence of God on the world. An interesting feature of Mendelssohn's approach is that he is rather embarrassed by the existence of faith. Given his commitment to rationality, any form of faith which is going to be respectable must be rational, and if it is to be rational it must accord with a fair-minded view of the world. Hence the importance of the suggestion that if we look at the world in the right sort of way we shall observe it to be imbued with providence. It is certainly true that it is rational to construct a picture of a general providence out of the particular instances of providence which we can observe, and which would require some theory as to why what is apparently counter-evidence is not in fact to be assessed as such at all. Mendelssohn does precisely this. The problem with this sort of approach is that it is inevitable that what is being presented is a rather weak proof. Surely Mendelssohn would want to say more than just that we can look at the world in a particular kind of way. He seems to want to go further, to argue that this is the way in which we are obliged to look at the world, since this is the way in which the world is. Yet this just seems to be wrong. The world can just as easily, if not more easily, be seen as lacking in providence. Mendelssohn wants to say more than that we can view the world from a particular aspect, but he is too aware of the problems in saying anything stronger to try to present any very solid arguments in this direction.

Yet he has indicated an interesting problem here. If the presence of God is to make a difference to how the world is, then it must be possible to say something significant about how the character of that world is affected by God. The trouble with Mendelssohn's God is that he seems to be very distant from his creatures. He has set up a mechanism for their benefit, and left them to get on with it. The mechanism seems to be a very weak one, with little evidence that it works universally and plenty of evidence that it breaks down on many occasions. This highlights the Enlightenment problem in understanding our relationship with God. If that relationship is to be based upon rationality and not upon faith, then there should be evidence for the influence of God in our world. If the relationship is based on faith, this does not really matter, since we may believe in such influence despite the apparent evidence. If we have a combination of rationality and faith, which might seem to be an appropriate combination, we end up in an incredibly weak intellectual position. For in this case we look for evidence, or appear to look for evidence, and we accept what we can find, but we also discount contrary evidence on the grounds that it falls under the category of faith. It is rather like someone who is suffering welcoming an interruption in her pain as an example of providence, and then accepting the resumption of the pain as part of a divine plan which, if we could only see it as a whole, would be observable as the very best way of organising the world. Mendelssohn's problems here bring out some of the main difficulties with the Enlightenment project, and they set the agenda for much of the consequent discussion in Jewish philosophy on this issue. With the construction of modernity came a belief in the rationality of the world, and God's role was as a consequence put under severe question. If God is to have a role, then given the demands of rationality there must be evidence of that role, and the idea of a distant God who is still an appropriate object of religious devotion seems vacuous unless there is such evidence. But it is of the very nature of modernity to question the existence of anything outside of the world and society as an explanation for what is within it. Subsequent Jewish philosophers are as a result often driven to emphasise explanations of evil and suffering in terms more of faith than of rationality, to a certain extent perhaps as a result of observing the Enlightenment project grinding to a halt in the hands of Mendelssohn.

CHAPTER 8

Cohen

Once we get to Hermann Cohen (1842–1918) we see one of the successes of Mendelssohn's project. Cohen was an important interpreter of Kant and founded the Marburg school of interpretation, which had as its adherents a large body of the Kant scholars in Germany and further afield. He was working at a time when Jews were becoming very thoroughly assimilated into German society, often at the expense of their religion. Unsurprisingly, Cohen regards religion from a Kantian viewpoint, and in his books on Jewish topics he interprets the Bible as largely a practical guide to action. As a socialist, he has a rather optimistic view of history and he sees the development of Judaism as a revolt against idolatry and all that goes with it. What goes with it is a particularity which stands in the way of progress and enlightenment, and Judaism represents the journey into the light of improvement and the taking up of moral and intellectual burdens as free agents. This is not to say that Judaism is the only such route, but historically it played a vital part in the construction of modernity, according to Cohen. Like Maimonides, he spends a lot of time discussing the purpose of particular religious rituals and biblical passages, with the emphasis generally being on their practical value in the formation of a worthwhile lifestyle.

Hermann Cohen followed Mendelssohn in trying to demonstrate the rationality of Judaism, and also tried to demonstrate its compatibility with Kant's philosophy. The basis of religion is taken to be not revelation as such, but rather the way in which revelation presupposes a notion of moral perfection, a means for the agent to express his autonomy despite the vagaries of the world. He then regards the Book of Job as an illustration of the way in which the individual's own grasp of his moral standing is independent of his position in the world in fact. One of the particularly interesting aspects of Cohen's account of evil and suffering is his concentration upon economic factors. For him, the main feature of human suffering is not death but poverty. This explains why the prophets spend so much time railing against the poverty of the community, clearly something which attracted a socialist like Cohen. But he has put his finger on an important point here. When we think of suffering we tend to think of dramatic events such as death and illness, yet a far more pervasive form of suffering is to be found in the poverty of much of humanity. Religion is not an institution which is designed to bring about a miraculous lifting of essential aspects of humanity such as death, but it can be used to alleviate the suffering through poverty of the population. Judaism insists upon the universal application of economic and social justice, and the ritual aspects of the religion are based upon this insistence. There are other rational religions, and no religion embodies perfectly the idea of universality. The prophets reminded their audience that they have a responsibility for the welfare of society as a whole, a responsibility which they can come to appreciate if they think rationally about the nature of themselves as autonomous moral beings.

Much of Cohen's magisterial *Religion of Reason out of the Sources of Judaism* is devoted to the problem of suffering and the concept of sin. The Day of Atonement is said to be the most important festival in the Jewish calendar because of its emphasis upon sin and punishment. Punishment represents suffering which is part and parcel of human life, and its purpose is to lead to our redemption in so far as we recognise it as an essential aspect of our self-development. The suffering of the Jewish people in particular has a special meaning. The most important contribution of Judaism to human culture is the doctrine of monotheism, the idea that there is just one God for everyone at every time and in every place. Along with this idea goes universalism, which Cohen thinks the prophets embodied, whereby all nations will become progressively more unified and rational. The survival of the Jewish people represents the survival of the idea of a common humanity. Hence Cohen's antagonism towards Zionism. Were a Jewish state to be founded, the Jewish people would fail to represent so clearly the idea of a community dedicated in a special way to the worship of one God. Through their suffering the Jews represent pure monotheism and trust in God, since without a state there is no alternative but to hope in a future based upon the unity of humanity and an end to inter-ethnic strife. Paradoxically, the very separateness of the Jews symbolises the importance of the unity of humanity, and the role of Jewish suffering is to play a vital part in the discovery by everyone of that humanity, without which there can be no progress in history.

In one's own case suffering may well be the consequence of sin, and we can know this since we know what we have been doing and what thoughts we have. In the case of others, though, it is inappropriate to blame people who suffer on account of sins which they must have committed. Conversely, we may hope that God will forgive us for our sins when we have repented, but it would be wrong to think that he must do so. Suffering and punishment play an important part in our self-development and cannot be abrogated by divine fiat. Cohen uses this point to congratulate Maimonides on calling Job a prophet, which we have seen was very much the language of Islamic philosophy about him. He is a prophet because his suffering is a form of prophecy (*Religion of Reason*, p. 227). This is because it is part of the moral system and very far from being a defect. Job's friends were misguided when they tried to persuade him that he should search for the sin which lay at the basis of his suffering. Job was there to teach that suffering has a role in God's strategy for salvation. The suffering is there to help others, and it is trivialised if it is regarded as a punishment for earlier sins. Job is nonetheless in an ambiguous position, since as a prophet he suffers for others but as an individual he can use that suffering to develop into a better moral agent. This might seem to be a strange notion. One can see how suffering may help the individual to take stock of his life and the way in which he lives, but Cohen is making a stronger claim here, namely, that suffering is an irreducible aspect of such thinking. Suffering appears to be a necessary condition of individual self-consciousness. Again, we can see how it might contribute to such self-consciousness, but is it really a necessary condition? Some kinds of suffering are so severe that they seem to prevent the individual from doing any rational thinking at all, and surely there is a possibility of acquiring such self-consciousness without suffering. Cohen wishes to distinguish his position from that of religions which make suffering their final end as opposed to a means to an end. The only appropriate end, he argues, is morality itself, which he identifies with redemption and the relationship between God and humanity. Ascetics wrongly think that suffering has a purpose through the satisfaction to be derived from it in itself. One of the interesting aspects of Cohen's view is that he reverses the traditional attitude to the suffering of people, whereby such suffering is a threat to their wellbeing and very existence. In the case of the Jews it is their suffering which preserves them and which permits them to carry out their role in pushing along the progress of history. Were it not for the suffering, this could not happen at all.

This is an interesting and difficult idea which requires more consideration. Not only does Cohen argue that it is the suffering of the Jews which sets them off on their world mission, he even goes so far as to deny that there is any tragedy in this suffering, since it is not primarily constitutive of the decline of a nation but rather of the growth of an idea. The idea is monotheism and universalism which the Jews are taken to represent, and he identifies these notions with self-consciousness. Certainly it is the case that other communities have suffered in the past and will suffer in the future, but the difference between their suffering and the suffering of the Jews is that their suffering is evidence of their decline, while Jewish suffering is evidence of progress in the direction of its world mission. It is only when we are conscious of ourselves as morally autonomous beings, as capable of legislating for ourselves in terms of universal and rational criteria, that we can adopt an appropriate attitude to God. He compares this to the case of a person accepting punishment from a human judge coming to see how valuable that punishment is in making him understand the nature of his sin and reconciling himself to a mature attitude not only to the judge but to civil justice as a whole (*Religion of Reason*, pp. 234–5). Through that punishment the individual discovers who he is and what part he can play in society. He continues:

so those who professed monotheism had to recognize and acknowledge suffering as God's providence, ordained for the purpose of their self-sanctification, their education to the maturity of the I in its correlation with God. Israel's suffering symbolically expresses the reconciliation of man with God. (*Religion of Reason*, pp. 234–5)

So suffering must take place for self-sanctification or redemption to be possible. But when will this happy state of affairs occur? If not for a long time, how can we justify the thousands of years of suffering which lead up to it? Cohen tries to get around this problem by arguing that redemption and suffering are interwoven, so that whenever there is one there must also be the other. At every stage of suffering we are changing in potentially positive directions, we are becoming more aware of ourselves and more free. This freedom represents the end of suffering.

Why is suffering so important a part of our lives? According to Cohen, it marks the turning-point at which religion emerges from ethics (*Religion of Reason*, p. 18). Once I observe suffering, especially the suffering of other people, I have to start questioning the point of the suffering and start examining the significance of the interests of the other. Although I may not be in a position to answer the question as to why there is suffering, the point of asking that question is not to receive a theoretically satisfactory answer, but rather to orientate myself practically towards my fellow creatures. As Cohen puts it, 'In suffering, a dazzling light suddenly makes me see the dark spots in the sun of life' (*Religion of Reason*, p. 19). I recognise the importance of others when I recognise the significance of their suffering, and I can even come to have concern for my own suffering which is more than mere sentimentality once I have attempted to understand the suffering of others. There is no need for me to think that every instance of suffering which I undergo is as a result of some prior sin, and this is even more surely the case with others, for whom I have no evidence of the nature of their past behaviour upon which to apply such a judgment. Morality implies treating the interests of others on a par with my own interests and acting in line with universally rational principles, on the Kantian notion of ethics which Cohen so enthusiastically accepts, and it is only possible if I come to see myself as a member of a world consisting of moral agents who have a right to act and interests worth preserving. It seems clear that for Cohen there is no theodicy which will explain the suffering of individuals. Since we are human and finite we can suffer and will die, and if we arrange our social affairs in selfish and unjust ways then there will be a great deal of suffering in the world, primarily through the form of human poverty. God is not so much an individual who can be expected to redress such injustice as a principle of morality which we can approach. Suffering actually helps us to approach this principle by showing us how we should think of ourselves and at the same time how we should relate to others.

This is his analysis of the suffering of individuals, but he provides a different account of the suffering of the Jewish people as a whole. He comes to change his mind on the description of this suffering, which he later on agrees is tragic despite its progressive mission, although it is very different from the suffering of other nations. He argues that 'the freely assumed suffering declares the historical dignity of the sufferer' (*Religion of Reason*, p. 284). We might wonder about this description, since it might be thought that Jews, neither as individuals nor as a group, have made a conscious decision to take up this role. Cohen compares the role of the Jewish people in history and their suffering with the fasting which Jews accept on the Day of Atonement to help redeem their misdeeds. That fasting and the repentance which goes along with it is suffering which has been freely accepted, and so is the suffering which arises due to the Jewish people's uncompromising commitment to monotheism. Is this commitment consciously made? In some sense it is, in that it is always open to Jews to convert and forsake their religion, although this was often no escape from persecution. Not only must the Jews voluntarily accept their suffering, but they must also do this knowingly, according to Cohen. If they just do it because of habit or without any understanding of its purpose then they are not taking up the sort of attitude to their suffering which is appropriate. There is a difficulty here, which is that it is quite clear that most Jews do not accept such a role for their suffering, despite the sort of interpretation which Cohen applies to the prophets, and part of the purpose of his work is to help make the community understand the sort of attitude they should adopt to suffering.

World history has a messianic goal, and this is brought about when all humanity is reconciled with God. The Jewish community is 'the sacrificial victim who exposes himself to suffering because of his knowledge of the irreplaceable value of this suffering for the historical welfare of mankind' (*Religion of Reason*, p. 286). Even though it would be difficult to argue that most, or even any, members of that community were conscious of that role, and willing to accept it, Cohen might well be able to argue that these attitudes are implicit in the practices and law of the religion. Laws do after all reflect attitudes which need not be consciously experienced by those concerned with living in accordance with such laws. Cohen might be able to argue that to the extent that the Jewish community lived a separate life from other religious groups and practised some Jewish religious rules, it might be doing enough to play the role which Cohen describes. In fact, what would be of chief importance would not be the behaviour of the Jewish community but the attitude which the non-Jewish world had towards it. If the rest of the world regarded the Jews as uncompromisingly monotheistic in belief and so separate from other faiths then the Jews are able to play out their historical role regardless of their actual conscious beliefs or the role which they are directly interested in choosing to play.

There are some intriguing features to this approach. Perhaps the most immediately noticeable is the lack of discussion of death. For Cohen, death is no problem at all for theodicy. We just are creatures who die, we are finite and must expect to die, and no special problem arises through death. Nor is there any afterlife during which our existence will in some way continue. The notion of immortality refers to the wider context of our actions, and the idea of the Messianic age is to be interpreted as a period of harmony and universal co-operation. This is interesting, especially because for many believers death is a difficult issue for religious philosophy. This is not so much the fact that people die, which is fairly acceptable given the nature of finite creatures, but more the fact that they die at different times and in different ways, some of which make one wonder at the justice with which the world is arranged. The notion of suffering is identified with poverty, which places it firmly within the human realm of redress, but which might be felt to exclude the most difficult and also most interesting issues for a theodicy. The notion of the Jewish people playing the role of the scapegoat throughout history seems to involve a view of history which is essentially optimistic, in that it is always moving in the direction of progress and away from idolatry. Cohen seems to have a view of history which is closer to that provided by Lessing than by Mendelssohn, for the latter was sceptical about the idea of a steady progress from earlier stages of ignorance to later stages of enlightenment. It might be thought that Cohen's view of history is over-intellectualistic, structured as it is in terms of increasingly universal and rational concepts. There seems to be no scope for the occasional plunge into barbarism with which we are well acquainted and which even Mendelssohn seems to allow. On the other hand, an attractive feature of Cohen's account is that it provides some explanation for the phenomenon of antisemitism without a Jewish presence which has arisen since the end of the Holocaust. An intriguing feature of such cases where Jews are blamed for problems but where there is a tiny Jewish community is that Jews are taken to be a symbol of something which the population as a whole wish to reject. If Cohen is correct in thinking that the Jews represent universality and rationality, then it is precisely these notions which are being attacked through the form of attacks upon Jews, and the absence of actual Jews to attack is irrelevant. What is important is the *idea* which the Jews are taken to embody, and that idea has strength even though there is little physical Jewish identity to incorporate it. What Cohen provides is not really a theodicy at all, though, since it is clear from his account that there is really no personal God, nor a God who intervenes in the world. He provides a reinterpretation of religious language to suggest that the language we use about God is more appropriately understood as dealing with morality and the perfection of individual autonomy.

CHAPTER 9

Buber

Martin Buber (1878–1965) and Franz Rosenzweig (1886–1929) translated the Bible into German yet again, in an attempt at producing a version which would reflect the language of the time. By then, of course, German was the mother tongue of the Jews of Germany, and not only Yiddish but Hebrew were only a distant memory. Rosenzweig died before the translation was completed and Buber finished it himself, ironically when there was no longer a Jewish culture in Germany to revive. The Enlightenment project seemed to fail in the twentieth century, and not only as a result of the Holocaust. Even before this event Buber and Rosenzweig had become critical of the identification of Judaism with reason, arguing instead that this ignores the vital part which revelation and religious experience plays in Jewish life. Their approach to Jewish philosophy seeks to bring back the personal into respectable metaphysics. The long apologetic process of reconciling reason and revelation had come to a dramatic end in this century. There is much in religion which is not neatly encapsulated in terms of what might be regarded as the principles of scientific rationality, and this part of religion should be acknowledged and respected too. One of the goals of Buber's philosophy is to give due weight to the fact of religious experience. This is not to suggest that it is not possible to apply philosophy to such experience – clearly this is possible in his view – but it is a warning against regarding such experience as merely the raw data for philosophical arguments. Experience goes much further than that, it has a depth and a complexity of its own, and although the philosopher can explore these categories what will result will be a better grasp of the experience itself, not a dispassionate theory which has the experience as its object.

What has become clear by now is that the issue of suffering in Jewish philosophy has a close connection with the issue of the relationship between God and his creation. Perhaps one of the most concentrated approaches to this relationship was undertaken by Martin Buber in his account of the I–It and I–Thou relationships. These represent the two types of relationship which I can have with something other than me. I am in an I–It relationship when I use the other or when I regard it with an attitude of objective detachment. What Buber has in mind are the sorts of ways in which Kant argues we treat people as means to ends, generally our ends, which results in our failing to treat them as ends-in-themselves, but rather as objects. I am interested in the other person only in so far as he is of use to me for a particular purpose. This is not necessarily wrong of me, and there are surely many contexts in which it would be inappropriate to treat other people in any other way. If I am standing up in front of a class of unruly pupils in a school, my attitude towards them may well not be an attitude to them so much as individuals but as individuals falling under a general category, in this case a problem of classroom management. When I am wondering how to manage them, I am not directing my attention to them so much as persons, but rather I am looking for a general category of behaviour which can be modified (I hope) in specific ways. It does not matter who the individual pupils are. As far as I am concerned, they are problems who need to be solved. This has an impact upon my own status as a subject. Anyone standing where I am standing in front of the class would have the same problem as I am having, and the precise individual who is standing in front of the class is irrelevant.

The I–Thou nexus is exactly the reverse. The other is an end-in-himself, and I am an end-in-himself for the other, so we get a relationship of mutuality. This can be illustrated nicely by returning to the example of teaching. There is a form of didactic teaching in which the teacher addresses the pupils, where it does not matter who the teachers or who the pupils are. By contrast, there is a form of teaching which takes on the character of a conversation or dialogue, whereby both the teachers and the pupils influence each other through the educational process. This I–Thou relationship does not have to be limited to relationships between people. I can regard inanimate objects as a *Thou,* and see them as responding to my attitude to them, with the result they have an effect upon me. The I–Thou relationship cannot be abstract, while the I–It relationship has to be abstract. In the classroom-management example I am just someone trying to control a class; anyone could be in my position, and any children could be in front of the teacher. Yet when a conversation and dialogue is established between people they themselves enter uniquely into the relationship. The relationship is about *them*, and were the relationship to be about anyone else it would be a different relationship.

The difficulty which Buber has in establishing this distinction is in showing that it is a distinction of kind and not of degree. After all, there are relationships which seem more I–It than I–Thou, and yet which have some aspects of both kinds of relationship. Although there are clear instances of both relationships, there are many examples which are unclear, which suggests that the distinction is less useful than might be thought. One shrewd way around this difficulty is to suggest, as Buber does, that the distinction is based upon the character of the subject of experience, so that the I of the I–Thou relationship only emerges as the sort of subject it is through its participation in the relationship with the Thou. In a sense, then, the I of the I–Thou relationship is constructed through that relationship, and develops in accordance with its battery of such relationships. This is not to say that there is anything wrong with the I–It relationship, but it is important to recognise, according to Buber, that the latter relationship cannot hope to encapsulate the whole of reality. The sort of relationship which the I enjoys with the Thou is incapable of systematisation, objectivity or abstraction, and yet it is nonetheless significant. Indeed, in some ways it is more important than I–It knowledge since it makes manifest the richness which is capable of being experienced in the world of relationships.

We should expect at this stage that Buber would say that the I–Thou relationship with God is religion, and he does make this move, but not before dissociating that relationship from any accusation of sentimentalism. In a genuinely I–Thou relationship with the deity there is no use of images, no mystical insistence upon the dissolution of the subject, but a readiness to meet God in some way, and for him to respond to us. God must be available at least sometimes for a relationship based upon dialogue, and were he not to be thus involved in a relationship of mutual interest there could not be a religion based upon addressing and listening to God. This creates a huge problem, though, because it inevitably means that religion will have to dissociate itself from the mass of law and system which it generally involves. This panoply of abstract legislation cannot be part of the meeting between subjects which is so important a part of the I–Thou

How Does Buber describe evil? As a turning away from God. What does he mean for natural evil

relationship. He seems to regard the genuine I–Thou relationship upon which religion rests as in constant danger of deteriorating into an I–It relationship as our commitment to the individuality of the dialogue's partners wanes, hence the creation of systematic theology and religious law.

Like so many of his Jewish predecessors, Buber concentrates upon the internal aspect of evil, as compared with the evil which comes to us from the influence of others or of external forces. The contrast between good and evil arises only because it can be experienced personally by us. Evil is opposition to God using the power which has been given to human beings to do evil, and good is the turning towards the deity. The notion of turning is important here, because Buber describes evil as a lack or loss of direction, and its contrary is thus a rediscovery of direction, the direction towards God. Evil is in many ways the dominance in our lives of the I–It relation, while good is the replacement of much of this relation with the I–Thou. As Buber puts the point:

Evil becomes known only as it is experienced

no evil in the Abstract

> Good and evil, then, cannot be a pair of opposites like right and left or above and beneath. 'Good' is the movement in the direction of home, 'evil' is the aimless whirl of human potentialities without which nothing can be achieved and by which, if they take no direction but remain trapped in themselves, everything goes awry. (*Between Man and Man*, p. 78)

It is not difficult to see why Buber stresses the link between evil and lack of direction, since his whole philosophical machinery is based upon the notion of dialogue, which is intrinsically a relational notion. If no or inappropriate dialogue takes place, then there is a consequent loss in direction, and the sorts of target which we ought to be hitting are unavailable to us.

Evil is a loss of direction

We are taken to know, in some sense, that we ought to be directing our lives in particular ways towards others, and especially towards God. We are guilty if we avoid entering into a dialogue with God, and as a consequence with other persons and the world. Failing to acknowledge the evil within ourselves, which Buber regards as the failure to develop a mature conscience, is precisely to remain with ourselves and reject the move towards others, in particular God. It is in terms of this theory that Buber interprets the familiar biblical stories of Adam and Eve and Cain and Abel. The former pair do not consciously choose evil as opposed to good, but they wish to experience the possibility of action which is available to them. Similarly, Cain does not really know what he is doing when he kills his brother, but he uses his imagination to set before himself a variety of alternative actions, and just drifts into one as compared with another. Buber makes much the same point as Maimonides here. Imagination as the faculty which makes possible the setting before oneself of alternatives is intimately involved in the creation of the human notions of good and evil. For Maimonides the only way to escape from the chaotic realm of evil is to pursue the truth in its theoretical form, while Buber urges us to direct ourselves towards a proper relationship with another, and in consequence with ourselves. Two stages are involved in becoming evil. In the first one sinks haphazardly into inauthentic actions and intentions, while in the second one directly decides to act in wrong ways, acknowledging the intention as one's own and deciding to act upon it. Although Buber claims that there is a problem in reconciling human evil with divine perfection, and says that 'The abyss which is opened by this question advances still more uncannily than the abyss of Job's question into the darkness of the divine mystery' (*Good and Evil*, p. 51), there does not seem to be much of a difficulty here. Evil exists because we are able to experience and use our imagination to develop possible courses of action which take account of no other interests than those we have in acting.

Buber makes a very interesting distinction between sin and wickedness. Basically, the former represents what happens when we fall into confusion and lack of direction, while we become wicked when we start to allow our actions to cement a character which is disposed to go in the wrong direction. This is hinted at in the biblical passages in which characters are said to have 'hardened their hearts'. This comes about through a strong self-affirmation by the individual which cuts her off from dialogue both with God and the rest of the world. She is forming a character which is based upon her own wants and interests, and is not open to influences from either without or within which might challenge that character. This results in a personality intent upon using others as means to one's end, and believing that the ends justify the means.

It is a constant theme in Buber's work that the character of the means irretrievably influences the nature of the end. His analysis of contemporary Western society is rather similar to that of the early Marx, emphasising as it does alienation and the collapse of organic life in real communities in modern industrial society. This has the effect of converting what seems to be dialogue into nothing more than monologue. Much of what passes for conversation is really a desire by people to dominate each other, impress others and apply pressure in difficult situations. It is hardly surprising that in such an environment so many people should develop personalities which draw them away from confronting themselves and others in favour of an attempt at controlling the world and themselves by a refusal to acknowledge the significance of the other as a person.

How do we escape from the tentacles of this ever-present possibility of a descent into evil? Buber often refers to the image which Kafka presents of the world as a meaningless realm of existence which possesses a judge or creator, and yet this powerful individual has no interest in what goes on in the world. Once we have got into Buber's way of expressing himself it comes as no surprise to learn that the route to salvation lies in dialogue, this time between us and God. In some ways it seems to be something of an automatic process, in that if we approach God in the right sort of way we are rewarded by meeting him, and yet we are also told sometimes that the effect of the meeting is often unpredictable and puzzling. It is not just a matter of repentance and carrying out the various ceremonial acts which are available to us, but a complete transformation of the human personality is required and, since we all differ, the way in which this redemption will be able to take place differs between individuals. Otherwise the uniqueness of the I–Thou relationship which we have to try to establish will be threatened. The same imagination which can lead us into sin can help us transcend evil, since we can use it to harness our thinking in the appropriate direction. That is, understanding the very specific reasons we might have to reject genuine dialogue with others should characterise the strategy we pursue to ensure genuine dialogue eventually takes place. By contrast with Maimonides, this is not just an intellectual process. We have to use the concrete situations in which we find ourselves to develop an appropriate attitude to the other, one in which we are open to external influence and prepared to acknowledge the presence of God.

Buber is very determined to get over the point that when we approach God we must beware of being satisfied with a combination of subjective feelings. The whole point about referring to loving God in terms of fearing him is to bring out the uncomfortable nature of the relationship between human beings and God, the mystery and incomprehensibility of the relationship. Moving away from evil does not mean moving away from other creatures. On the contrary, one gets closer to God by loving particular individuals, and this is not a generalised affection for the whole of creation but a highly concrete relationship with just a few individuals. Avoiding evil, then, cannot involve ascetic practices or isolation, but rather ordinary action with the right motives and attitudes. Buber wishes to dissociate his approach from that of pantheists, sometimes associated with Spinoza. It is not that the world is already a holy place, it is only capable of so becoming if it is treated as such by the subject. This is what Buber found so moving in (his interpretation of) Hasidism, the transformation of quite ordinary actions into religious actions by their infusion with concepts which sanctifies them. This sanctification is a very practical business, involving not just intentions but at the same time actions in an indissoluble whole. The redemptive actions in which we can participate are not essentially grand and occasional events, but everyday actions which can take place at every and any moment. The coming of the Messiah, then, is not a future event, but an event which can take place to a degree at any time, and which indeed must take place at any time during which God is present.

It seems, then, that for Buber as for so many of his predecessors the Book of Job is more about finding a role for God in the universe as opposed to finding an explanation for the evil in the world which we can reconcile with the existence of the deity. Job can find meaning in what has happened to him through his attempts at establishing a relationship with God, a genuinely personal relationship of the type Buber advocates. The fact that God may be silent or apparently absent from the situation in which Job finds himself does not invalidate the relationship which Job tries to get going. Job comes to understand that if he is to learn from his predicament he cannot wait for God to do something to help him. On the contrary, he must himself seek to approach God in such a way as to transform both Job's understanding and experience of his life. So in an important sense his friends are right in constantly drawing his attention to himself, his past and his present thoughts, in looking for an explanation of his sufferings. His sufferings come to an end once he realises that the path to salvation lies in establishing an authentically I–Thou relationship with the deity and transforming his attitude to the world. It is far from clear what Job has to do to escape from his dilemma, but that is what makes the dilemma a dilemma. Only Job can discover what he has to do, since there is only an individual solution to this particular problem, and Job will have to find it himself.

In his commentary on Psalm 73 Buber seems to argue that what Job needs to acquire is a pure heart. The Psalm starts off by saying 'Surely God is good to Israel, to the pure in heart.' Yet the evidence is that things go rather badly with the remnant of Israel who carry out their religious obligations, and God does not appear to be particularly generous to them. Buber suggests that only those who are not pure in heart could draw such a conclusion. The pure in heart experience God's goodness, but this does not take the form of a reward. The wicked are precisely the opposite, they deliberately cultivate impurity of heart. The pure in heart do grieve at what they see as the relative prosperity and success of the wicked, and they do wonder how God allows such a state of affairs to persist. Now, the Psalmist does not follow Job's path and so goes on to accuse God of directly bringing about an unjust state of affairs. He feels the conflict between good and evil in the universe and yet is not led into despair and doubt. In his experience of the conflict he receives a revelation of the continual presence of God. This is not a report of an experience, since it is impossible to feel the presence of God continually. Buber uses the charming example of a father taking the hand of his small child in order to lead him through the dark, where the purpose is not only to guide but to communicate his presence to the child. The father is trying to get over that he is continually with the child. As Buber comments, 'He has led his son out of darkness into the light, and now he can walk in the light. He is not relieved of taking and directing his own steps' (*Right and Wrong*, p. 43). The child has to take his own decisions and go in his own direction, but he will be supported by the continuing presence of his father.

How is this support to be identified in the lives of people? One way is by the interpretation of death. According to Buber, the pure in heart see their death as the fulfilment of their existence. They will escape *Sheol*, the realm of unconsciousness and inactivity (Eccl. 9:10). This does not mean that they will receive a reward after death. What Buber is suggesting here is that the way in which we perceive death is irretrievably tied up with the way in which we regard life. When the wicked die they 'have in the end a direct experience of their non-being' (*Right and Wrong*, p. 46). This presumably is because they have through their lives cut themselves off from a meaningful relationship with their fellow beings and with God. When life itself comes to an end so does everything which has any significance to the wicked person. What he values is entirely constituted by his life, and when that life comes to an end his world is entirely terminated. The wicked are far from God and being, while those who are not wicked can come close to him. This does not mean that they go to a traditional heaven in which they are rewarded for their behaviour in this life. Yet the nature of their death is marked by the character of their lives. As Buber puts it, 'The time of the world disappears before eternity, but existing man dies into eternity as into the perfect existence' (*Right and Wrong*, p. 50). After we are dead we will not experience anything, since there is no longer anything around which can do the experiencing and which is part of us. Yet if we are not wicked and if we appreciate that our lives are connected with other lives and with other aspects of the history of the world we will not see death as an overwhelming evil. It will appear to be an acceptable feature of the nature of our lives as finite human beings.

For Buber the basis of the distinction between good and evil lies in reality. He sees the expulsion from the Garden of Eden as an expulsion from divine reality into a world where we are 'at the mercy of the knowledge of good and evil' (*Images of Good and Evil*, p. 92) without being able to transcend the contrast. Our imagination throws up images for our attention which distract us and play havoc with our ability to organise our lives. The situation is not entirely hopeless, though. Each individual has the opportunity to set about to recapture proximity to reality, and the Talmudic doctrine of the *yetser ha-ra*ᶜ, the evil urge, is identified by him with imagery and is a necessary cohabitant with the good urge in the process of human striving. The evil urge is taken to be more important than the good urge, and when God looks down on creation and says that it is 'very good' this is a reference to the significance of the evil urge in our lives (Gen. 1:31). Buber refers here to the Midrashic story whereby Cain responds to God's rebuke by claiming that it was God himself who provided the evil impulse for human beings. Cain is wrong to make such a response, since the evil impulse is only evil if it is used thus by human beings. We should unite the evil impulse with the good. The former represents passion, while the latter is what Buber calls 'pure direction' (*Images of Good and Evil*, p. 97) which has God as its unconditional end.

The wicked are those who are entirely at the mercy of their passions. Sinners are able at least on some occasions, perhaps only on one occasion, to stand back from their passions and feel the presence of something which stands above them. Attitudes to death are an important indication of where one figures on such a scale. For the wicked death is a terrible thing because it extinguishes the passions, and nothing of any importance for them can continue once the passions are finished. The wicked are dominated by their imaginations, and they cannot use those imaginations in constructive ways to work out a route to God, to reality. This notion of evil is an interesting one. Evil is identified with lack of relationship to reality, to being. As with Spinoza, the individual who regards evil as the frustration of her desires is deluded. As with Spinoza, the way in which we characterise our death is a part, and a crucial part, of the way in which we regard our lives, and our orientation towards death is at the same time an orientation towards life. If we want to discover the source of evil we have then to look at ourselves and at our tendency to be attracted by actions which reflect inauthentic being.

This might seem to be a rather unsatisfactory answer, in that it does not tell us very much. Buber's point would be that God does not tell us very much about how we should behave, since it is up to us to feel his presence and act accordingly. Evil comes about when we seek to deny that presence and act on the basis of that denial. This theory can perhaps be clarified if we look at the issue of the appropriate translation of what has been called the Great Tautology of Exodus 3:14. This is the passage which describes God's self-description as being to Moses on Mount Moriah. The message which Moses is supposed to transmit to the Jews is that God is equivalent to being, and there has been an enormous amount of discussion about the precise meaning of this passage. Maimonides used it to defend his theory of the *via negativa* as a route, and indeed the only possible route, to the deity. If all that can be said about the deity is that he is being, then we must clearly be careful in our ascriptions of more definite and positive qualities to him. One of the main differences between God and us for Maimonides is that God is a necessary being, while our being is entirely consequential on the existence of something else, ultimately, of God. So God's qualities, whatever they are, are essential aspects of him, they follow from his being. Our qualities by contrast are merely contingent aspects of ourselves. We could do various things and have certain thoughts, but God is entirely circumscribed in his activity by what he is. This is not an aspect of his imperfection. On the contrary, the fact that we can do some things and wonder whether to do others is a sign of our imperfection, since our actions are linked only loosely and accidentally to our essences. Although Maimonides suggests that we can talk about God's actions, albeit not about his qualities, it would be wrong to suggest that we can work from our understanding of these actions to an understanding of his qualities. God is not like us, and he does not act in the way in which we act, with particular aims and intentions. We hope to achieve certain ends through our action, and sometimes we succeed. God acts in a perfect way, his actions are expressions of his essence, and he acts entirely dispassionately. We may then ascribe the system of nature to the organisation of God, and we may call that system benevolent, but if we want to call God benevolent we must realise that if he is benevolent then he is benevolent in an entirely different manner from the sort of benevolence with which we are familiar.

Maimonides sees the Great Tautology as an indication that God is to be identified with being and nothing else, and so our understanding of the relationship between God and the world must be explicated in purely formal terms. What terms are these? For many Jewish philosophers they relate to the transcendent characteristics of God. For example, in his very important translation of the Bible into German Mendelssohn presents Exodus 3:14 as:

Gott sprach zu Mosche: Ich bin das Wesen, welches ewig ist. Er sprach nämlich: so sollst du zu den Kindern Jisraels sprechen: 'Das ewige Wesen, welches sich nennt: ich bin ewig, hat mich zu euch gesendet.' (cited Rosenzweig, *GS*, III, p. 804)

God said to Moses, 'I am the being which is eternal'. He said that this means, 'This is what you should say to the children of Israel: "The eternal being, which calls itself "I am eternal" has sent me to you.'

In his discussion of this translation Rosenzweig congratulates Mendelssohn for capturing, or attempting to capture, in one phrase God's providence, eternity and necessary existence. Yet identifying God with eternal being can be something of an evasion. Buber translates God's proper name as 'He-is-there' (*Images of Good and Evil*, p. 67) and Rosenzweig translates the entire passage in this way:

Gott aber sprach zu Mosche:	And God said to Moses:
Ich werde dasein, als der ich dasein werde	I shall be present, as I shall be present
Und sprach:	And he said:
So sollst du zu den Söhnen Jisraels sprechen	You should say to the children of Israel
ICH BIN DA schickt mich zu euch. (*GS*, III, p. 804).	I AM PRESENT sent me to you.

The emphasis which Rosenzweig wishes to bring out here is not on the everlasting being of God but on his eternal presentness, his being present for us and with us now and in the future. Mendelssohn was intent to represent the Jewish God as amenable to deistic sensibilities, so that the commandments are little more than symbolic gestures which reflect the eternal principles of reason. Throughout his work he argues for the identification of Judaism with central principles of rationality. Yet Rosenzweig by contrast points to revelation. In this way he sought to bring back the personal God into Judaism. The identification of God with being is a gesture in the direction of a personal revelation, one which took place in the past and which is constantly replicated today and in the future.

For Rosenzweig, Job represents the man who prays and has faith, the man who deals successfully with the false logical friends by the strategy of entering into dialogue with God. These friends are the sort of people who say 'Why should there not be a God – so long as He does not bother Himself with what men are doing on earth' (*Right and Wrong*, p. 18). Both Buber and Rosenzweig stress the way in which we relate to God, and denounce aspects of how we might interpret that relationship as too distant. The discussion of God's name at Exodus 3:14 is very useful here, because we appear to be told very little, or indeed nothing, in this passage. Since tautologies tell us nothing, this is hardly surprising. But this tautology tells us a lot through telling us nothing. It tells us that if we are to understand the nature of God and his relationship with us we have to look at ourselves and our lives. We are supposed to abandon the comforting traditions of unthinking faith and seek to establish a real relationship with being or God. This is a difficult undertaking. It involves a serious investigation of our attitudes to ourselves, to others and to what lies beyond us. Traditional religion might be regarded as a technique for hiding the necessity for such radical thinking, and it cannot be enough in itself to set us in the right direction. The notion of feeling the presence of God is not primarily a subjective notion. It involves changing our lives and our attitudes to a whole category of apparently mundane events. We cannot say of evil that it is something imposed upon us from without, something which we must try to avert through prayer and good fortune. Evil is very much part of us and of our role in the world, and we have to appreciate this before we can try to overturn it and move in more positive directions. We cannot divorce the notion of evil from the notion of God, and if we are to be clearer on the former we must at the same time know what to say about the latter.

As we have seen throughout the argument in this book, the question

we must recognize that evil is very much a part of us and our role in the world of evil in Jewish philosophy is not simply a matter of reconciling a good God with nasty events in the universe. It is a process by which God becomes more real to his adherents. The idea that the problem of evil is that of reconciling a distant God with present travails is itself a problem, since on Mount Moriah God revealed his 'Gegenwärtigsein, das Für-euch- und Bei-euch-dasein und -daseinwerden' – 'His being-present for you and with you, now and in the future' (*GS*, III, p. 806). That is why he only said 'Ehyeh asher ehyeh' – 'I am who (or that) I am', since he wants to indicate that the important aspect about him which is to be grasped is his presence, not the precise nature of his being. That precise nature is something which we have to construct out of our experience of the events of the world, including the evil, and from the nature of our understanding of the revelation in the Bible. If we could know God's nature by attending to the world as in the Enlightenment view put forward by Mendelssohn we would be in a position to consign the deity to some distant role in our world, a role which would demand a rather banal interpretation of his connection with the evil in the universe. We might take Mendelssohn's line and suggest that were the ultimate pattern of reality to be revealed to us then we should see how benevolent the design of that reality in fact is. What is banal is not so much this 'solution', although it is bad enough, but the demand for such an explanation.

Why did Maimonides argue that there is no possibility of acquiring the final apprehension or ultimate description (*nihāya*) of God? Negative theology is all that we can pursue, since the divine attributes are completely equivocal with respect to the language we use to describe that with which we are familiar. When it comes to talking about God, something which we must do, silence is the most appropriate vehicle of meaning (*GP*, Bk. 1, ch. 59). As he goes on to say:

The most apt phrase concerning this subject is the dictum occurring in the Psalms, Silence is praise to Thee, which interpreted signifies: silence with regard to You is praise. This is a most perfectly put phrase regarding this matter ... silence and limiting oneself to the apprehensions of the intellects are more appropriate – just as the perfect ones have enjoined when they said: Commune with your own heart upon your bed, and be still. Selah. (*GP*, Bk. 1, ch. 59; Pines pp. 139–40)

It should be recalled that for Maimonides if something is the object of knowledge then it must be the object of *ilm al-yaqīn*, certain knowledge. Having a vague idea of x is not a route to knowledge of x, and this is even more the case when x is the deity, since our lack of a clear idea is not due to contingent features of the epistemic relationship between ourselves and God, but is part and parcel of that relationship. Yet at the very same time as Maimonides denies us any possibility of objective knowledge of God he insists upon the importance in our seeking to come as close as possible to acting in the way in which God acts, which we can to a degree follow from our observation of the world. Were it a relatively simple matter to determine God's role in the world, then it would be an easy matter to delineate his influence over our lives. We could 'read off' his influence from our observations of the world, just as a geographer can read off the existence of natural features by looking at a map. All that the geographer has to do is to understand the map, and he or she then knows all that needs to be known about the terrain. The situation is very different for us. We may understand the physical features of the map very well without being able to come to any firm conclusions about the precise nature of the plan behind it. This is where Job goes awry. He expects God's role in the world to be that of a powerful and considerate father, yet were he to be wise he would have understood that the way in which God organises the world is *sui generis*. It has nothing to do with the methods of kind fathers as we understand them. The language concerning the divine attributes is not metaphorical or analogical, but completely equivocal. We have very little to help us on our journey to discern God's role in the world, since we have very little to help us discern what God is like.

This approach to the notion of God is influential in the analysis presented by Buber and Rosenzweig. They also see the significance of the declaration from the thorn bush – 'ehyeh asher ehyeh' – as giving only the most skimpy details of the precise attributes of the deity. What is important about the speech is that it reveals that the universe, which to all appearances is unconcerned about the lives of the creatures living in it, is a place where one can be addressed by a Thou and where one has the choice as to whether we respond to such a contact. It seems to Job that God has hidden his face, that there is no justice, that although God has created the world, he is not concerned to save his faithful followers in it. What is important about the answer which Job receives is not that it is the right answer to his questions – and it is certainly not what could be regarded as the right answer in an obvious sense – but that he does get a response. God enters into a dialogue with Job. What is impressive about Job is that he does not rely upon prior revelation to achieve an understanding of God. Job understands that there is a need for existing and continuing communication with the deity, as Exodus 3:14 suggests. It is no good trying to answer our present queries by referring to a revelation which took place in the distant past, since we have to experience that revelation now if it is to have value in our lives. In a sense, that is the difference between Job and his friends. They talk about the past, about Job's actions and the covenant with God, while Job is talking about the present, about the impact of God upon the world now and what that impact means for us. His friends represent the banalities of formal religion, while Job's enquiries form part of the construction of a living faith. This comes out nicely when one considers the sort of reply which God gives Job. God answers Job's questions with yet more questions (which is often seen as evidence that God is Jewish!) in such a way as to provide no answer at all. For Job's friends this would be entirely unsatisfactory, since they expect of religion that there is a neat set of rules and axioms which can be applied to every situation and which can be filed away in one's mind as constituting the religious part of one's life. Job wants to be part of a vivid and continuing relationship with God, and he will not be satisfied with the normal religious platitudes. He insists on contact with God. If God could answer all his questions that contact would not be worth having. Buber's Job knows that the evil in the world is the result of the way in which human beings make decisions and live their lives, and it is no good appealing to God to answer as to why this is so. We have to look at ourselves if we are going to solve the problem of evil, and the contact with God can only help us work out how to solve our own problems. No supernatural nanny is available to perform this task for us.

In her novel *Latecomers* Anita Brookner describes the character of one of the main protagonists, Hartmann, a self-subsistent and comfortable individual:

The idea of God, for example, he rejected as derogating from his own serene existence. To the proposition, 'I am that I am', Hartmann, if he ever thought about it, would have replied, '*Et moi?*', not meaning any disrespect, but rather acknowledging a simple division of activities in which paths would never cross. (*Latecomers*, p. 6)

The individual who does not acknowledge the significance of God, like Hartmann, solves whatever problems occur to him concerning the existence of evil on a humanistic or case-by-case basis. Buber would argue that there is not a great deal of difference between

Hartmann and Job's friends, since the latter also fail to acknowledge the signficance of God in the world. They employ religious formulae to describe God's relationship with the world which have no life in them. In terms of their current lives the declaration 'I am that I am' represents a past and finished event. As with Hartmann, this declaration represents something which does not have anything to do with them now. God's utterance can be seen as pointing to the great freedom which his creatures have in relating to him. There is a Jewish traditional story of a river called the Sambatyon which is so pious that it stops flowing on the Sabbath. Rosenzweig remarks that if the Sambatyon rather than the Main flowed through Frankfurt, the whole Frankfurt Jewish community would be faithful Sabbath observers. Yet this would be of no satisfaction to God. God makes life difficult for us by concealing the nature of his actions. We are obliged to employ our capacity for freedom to take up an appropriate understanding of our relationship with God. There is no scope for expecting God to sort out our problems for us just like that. God tells us so little about himself because he wants us to work out by ourselves how we are to approach him and what sort of questions we can put to him. Job's questions about the existence of evil and suffering are clearly inappropriate, which is why God does not answer them. Buber and Rosenzweig suggest that instead of looking towards God for answers, we should look at ourselves within the context of establishing contact with God. The conclusion is that evil is a problem for us, not for God, and it is useless to look to the deity for an escape route from our troubles.

The interesting question, although not one for which Buber furnishes an answer, is why the experience of the proximity of God is expected to satisfy someone like Job. Evil is the situation in which God is regarded as entirely distant and 'Other', completely beyond the sufferer. So Job is answered by references to God's creation of the world, which is far from being an assertion of his power by contrast with human weakness and ignorance. God's creation signifies his attempt at communication with his creatures, since creation is paradigmatically a communicative act. Had God felt no need to communicate, he would have had no need to create, since it is only through creation that anything came into existence with which he could communicate. The sufferer exists in a state of tragic isolation, feeling abandoned by God, and the creation story is effective in Job precisely because it shows the sufferer that God is not absent, but is available and present despite the suffering. Buber makes the interesting remark (*Prophetic Faith*, p. 197) that Job is in the the company of the prophets, given his attempt to come to know God. This is an unusual comment, and to understand it we have to return to his analysis of Exodus 3:14, where God says 'I am who I am.' This revelation is basically a personal address, it is an attempt at establishing a relationship with a group of people who acknowledge the meaning of that relationship. This is not the same as listening to someone address us in the street, for in that case there may be no doubt as to what the message is. In the case of God's attempt at communication, it is up to us to decide what he has said, and what that means. It is very much the role of the prophet, according to Buber, to point out to the community that God is there, not as a remote figure from the past, but as an ever-present aspect of the here and now. The apparent emptiness of the tautology of Exodus 3.14 reveals all that we need to know if we are to respond to God, namely, that he is present and is available for contact. If God were to say more about himself, perhaps by providing a detailed description or list of laws and rules for his followers to obey, then he would no longer be freely available to us. We should have to respond to him, and we should have little choice as to how we did so. It is the difference between having someone banging on one's door to be admitted, perhaps with a suitcase full of goods to be sold, and hearing no noise at all from the door, but deciding nonetheless to pull it open to see if there is anyone there. Should someone be there, one can then decide whether to acknowledge the individual, and whether to accept anything from him or her. This is Buber's paradigm of free acceptance of the presence of God, and it is something which he regards as far preferable to the ordinary religious account of the relationship between the creator and his creatures.

Quite naturally, this sort of strategy leads to an entirely different view of evil than that prevalent in earlier Jewish philosophy. Buber and Rosenzweig helped to create what the latter called *das neue Denken*, the New Thinking, which represents an existential turn against traditional metaphysics. What is true, on this approach, is not so much facts or necessary truths, but rather what can be confirmed through human activity. Human life is full of possibilities and ambiguities which can be grasped and transformed through one's free creative decision. The past is not so much a series of determined facts as something to be acted upon and altered. There is no escape from this situation, and looking to a permanent set of instructions is to misunderstand our role in the world. We are who we are because of the necessity of taking the risk of working out for ourselves how we should behave and what is there to support our decisions. As Buber himself puts it:

the dialogical leads inevitably to Job's question to God. Yes, that it does, and God praises 'His servant' (Job 42.7). My God will not allow to become silent in the mouth of His creature the complaint about the great injustice in the world, and when in an unchanged world His creature yet finds peace, only because God has again granted him His nearness, he confirms Him. Peace, I say; but that is a peace compatible with the fight for justice in the world. ('Replies to my critics', p. 713)

The important point which Buber makes here is that Job finds peace in an unchanged world. Nothing happens to bring his immediate sufferings to an end, but what changes is Job's attitude. He changes by feeling God's presence. At no time did Job doubt God's existence or power, but he regarded him as distant and unconcerned with his wellbeing. Once he perceives that God is near to him, he is comforted. Job's friends blame him for questioning divine justice, and for even setting out to extract an answer from God. Yet Buber argues that he was entirely justified in acting as he did, since it is appropriate for Job to try to work out what relationship exists between him and his creator. If Job were really to be patient, and to be satisfied with the banalities of traditional religion, as are his friends, then he would not be the impressive individual which he turns out to be. He would in effect replace the tautology of Exodus 3:14 with a detailed and delimited list of God's duties *vis-à-vis* his creatures, which is indeed how he starts off, in the form of a plaintiff trying to enforce a contract, a covenant in fact between humanity and its creator. Job transcends this legalistic understanding of God through his efforts at coming into contact with him, through his understanding that it was for Job to respond to the challenge which God established through creation, the challenge of responding to him and acknowledging his presence.

One might think that a long distance has been travelled from an account of the religious justification of evil within the context of Judaism. But this is not really the case. As we have already seen, there is quite a tradition of the question of the meaning of evil and suffering being thrown back at the questioner, so that the latter has to work out what this meaning could be. What is perhaps worth noticing in Buber's account is that the material out of which Job constructs his understanding of the point of evil is highly indeterminate. One might wonder whether there is anything which constrains him to interpret his relationship with God in one way rather than another, or whether there is a specifically Jewish character to such interpretation. We find in the stories of the Hasidim which so fascinated Buber an account of a kind of pantheistic mysticism which represents a variety of authentic and interesting kinds of relationship, but the precise nature of the relationship which we are to form between us and the deity, the relationship which will encompass and explain the phenomena of evil and suffering, this is entirely up to us. There are many indications how this relationship should not be characterised, but very few positive instructions, as one would expect given the existential tendency of Buber's thought. Myths, stories and legends are entirely appropriate material out of which to define a relationship with the deity, since they provide us with examples of such relationships which we can examine, accept or reject in our projections of ways of connecting with God.

Buber takes the *via negativa* and the God of Exodus 3:14 to their logical conclusion in his analysis of the sort of relationship which we can have with God. This relationship should be a relationship to a Thou, in the rather pompous English translation of *Du*, and so we cannot surround it with the ordinary religious language in which the concepts of evil and suffering appear. We cannot look for an answer to the problems associated with those concepts which is going to be anything more than the discovery that we can enter into a relationship with the deity, a relationship which can lead to practical consequences if we behave in particular ways as a result of the relationship, but not a relationship which should be expected to be of advantage to us in any other way. The relationship is reciprocal in that both we and God come together, but all that God provides is his presence. It is up to us to make use of that presence in directing our lives in ways which will fight evil and suffering. We find in religious and other forms of literature indications as to how we might go about this, but these are only indications and it is very much up to us to decide how our practice in struggling against suffering reflects the awareness of the divine presence. We cannot evade our responsibility by appealing to a set of religious norms and customs which will tell us exactly how we should act. It is just because only a *via negativa* is available to take us towards God that we are left very much to decide for ourselves how we are to embody the presence of God in *praxis*. According to Buber, Job counts among the prophets because this is the teaching at which he arrives, and which he communicates through his Book. There is then no one answer to the problems of evil and suffering. We have both to enter into a relationship with God and work out for ourselves how to challenge these malign forces in our world.

It is through a relationship with God, that we can work out for ourselves how to deal with the forces of evil.

Buber frees God from responsibility in evil, as he emphasizes the need for humans to enter into a relationship with God and discern the meaning in that relationship for how they confront evil.

CHAPTER 10

The Holocaust

As we have seen, there is a well-developed discussion in Jewish philosophy about the role of evil and suffering in a world created by God. This discussion received new impetus after the Holocaust, but the nature of the topic changed. Many philosophers argued that the Holocaust was not just a more recent disaster to be classified along with previous disasters affecting the Jewish people. The Holocaust was often taken to be a unique event, requiring very different approaches as compared with preceding tragedies. This leads to the suggestion that only a radically different form of explanation for that evil will do. The Holocaust is taken to represent a break in history, in the sense that the hermeneutical categories which were employed up to that event no longer function afterwards. This claim will be considered here, together with the implication that only an entirely new way of expressing oneself will do in the changed situation of post-Holocaust existence. More traditional approaches to accounting for the evil of the Holocaust have also been pursued by some thinkers, and it is useful to relate these to the earlier tradition of Jewish philosophy in this area.

There are two huge difficulties in analysing the topic of the Holocaust. One is trying to write dispassionately about such horrifying and comparatively recent events. In addition, many writers who themselves suffered directly during the Holocaust write movingly about it, yet with more emphasis upon finding an emotional *modus vivendi* within Judaism than with really providing arguments as to how to classify the event. A good example of this approach is to be found in the work of Elie Wiesel, who is largely responsible for the creation of the term 'Holocaust' as a conceptual category. His work is replete with questions regarding God's responsibility for the sufferings of the Jews during the Holocaust, and the appropriate reaction on the part of the sufferers. Wiesel makes it clear that in his view an omnipotent God could have prevented the Holocaust, and that God is omnipotent. So why did he allow it to happen? Wiesel does not answer this question, but restricts himself to the not unconnected question as to the appropriate Jewish response. This seems to be to refuse to abandon Judaism despite the guilt of God. Yet since God is taken to be guilty of great crimes against the Jewish people it is difficult to see why they should continue to pray to him or follow his laws. Of course, it is wrong to see Wiesel's work as an analytical attempt at grasping the Holocaust, but we shall see that the feeling that the Holocaust justifies paradoxical and radical positions is quite widely shared by other writers on the issue.

Wiesel argues that God lets down the Jews through allowing the Holocaust to occur, and yet that the Jews should continue to adhere to their faith. Richard Rubenstein agrees on God's guilt, but differs on the appropriate reaction to it. As he suggests:

How can Jews believe in an omnipotent, beneficent God after Auschwitz? Traditional Jewish theology maintains that God is the ultimate, omnipotent actor in historical drama. It has interpreted every major catastrophe in Jewish history as God's punishment of a sinful Israel. I fail to see how this position can be maintained without regarding Hitler and the SS as instruments of God's will ... To see any purpose in the death camps, the traditional believer is forced to regard the most demonic, anti-human explosion of all history as a meaningful expression of God's purposes. (*After Auschwitz*, p. 153)

It is worth quoting Rubenstein here since he represents so much of the post-Holocaust tradition. Yet he is of course entirely wrong in his account of the treatment of disasters in Jewish thought. Were every catastrophe to have been regarded as merely punishment of a sinful community then it really would not be worth studying the system of thought which produced such simplistic suggestions. Even if we could justify the suffering of those directly guilty of backsliding, there are enormous difficulties in explaining the suffering of the entirely innocent. In previous disasters, as in the Holocaust, not only the evil members of the Jewish community suffered. Indeed, one might even suggest that they were usually more successful in escaping suffering than their more gullible and virtuous peers. What can justify the murder of Jewish (or any other) babies, for example? If Jewish thought had argued that it was carried out to punish a sinful community then it would be difficult to justify seriously considering it. Yet as we have seen, there is a tradition of sophisticated discussion in Jewish thought about the role of God in the sufferings of his creation.

Is God guilty? If so, what is God guilty of?

Although the discussion here has not concentrated upon theology, but rather on philosophy, it would be wrong to regard theology as unaffected by the philosophical debate, and many of the philosophers were theologians also.

Since Rubenstein has a simplistic view of God's role in history, he is obviously going to have to make dramatic decisions about how Jews should interpret that role in the face of the Holocaust. As he says:

> If I believed in God as the omnipotent author of the historical drama and Israel as His Chosen People, I had to accept ... that it was God's will that Hitler committed six million Jews to slaughter. I could not possibly believe in such a God nor could I believe in Israel as the chosen people of God after Auschwitz. (*After Auschwitz*, p. 46)

This leads to the conclusion that God must be rejected and the meaninglessness of life acknowledged. There is no divine purpose to the course of events and we live in a world which is indifferent to us. It is no good after Auschwitz believing in the comforting transcendental myths of the past, that a good and powerful deity was looking after us. The fact of Auschwitz rules out such ideas forever. If we are to find meaning in the world it is meaning which we ourselves will have to create out of our experience of life. One might think that he is then going to conclude that there is no point in maintaining a Jewish identity, but he actually suggests Jewish values can and should be maintained if reinterpreted in the light of post-Holocaust values. The traditional rules of ritual still have a role to play due to their powerful psychological symbolism, and the Jewish tradition is a useful starting point for the radical thinking about what value one can perceive in the world through our personal creation of such value. What is required is a form of Judaism without God, and consequently without the notion that the Jews have a special relationship with such a deity. In his earlier work *After Auschwitz* Rubenstein suggests that the return of many Jews to the land of Israel signified a move to become closer to nature and an end to the attempt at transcending our physical nature through a traditional belief in a transcendent God. In his more recent work, *Approaches to Auschwitz* in particular, he seems to adhere to a notion of God, but within a mystical and immanent sense which is far removed from the traditional religious conception. After Auschwitz, he claims, whatever role we provide for God must be very different from that which seemed satisfactory previously.

Emil Fackenheim also argues that a complete revaluation of thought is required after the Holocaust, but with less radical conclusions than those provided by Rubenstein. The Holocaust is to be interpreted as an aspect of God's will, and the conclusion is that the Jewish people should survive. He calls this the 614th commandment (there are traditionally taken to be 613 commandments to be followed in Judaism), that Jews must not grant posthumous victories to Nazism. Although Jews may find it difficult to maintain their faith in God after the horrors of the Holocaust, to abandon that faith is to disparage the martyrdom of those who perished in the camps. To conclude that after the Holocaust the world is a meaningless place (Rubenstein's conclusion) is to side with Hitler, for whom all things are possible and acceptable because there are no transcendent rules of moral behaviour. Nonetheless, the Holocaust does mark a radical turning in human history which requires a *tikkun* or mending of the break. Fackenheim advocates a kind of muscular Judaism, by contrast with the passivity of previous generations. In the past martyrdom was a route to bearing witness to God and *kiddush ha-shem*, sanctification of the (divine) name. But such behaviour is senseless within the context of a policy of genocide. What makes sense during and after the Holocaust is active resistance to the policy of murder, formerly in opposition to the Nazis and now for the sake of the Jewish State.

Despite the practical aspects of his philosophy, Fackenheim fails to see any answer to traditional theological problems with respect to the Holocaust. It is not seen as a punishment for sins or with a purpose in some other way. Its enormity is taken to be represented by its complete absence of explanation and interpretation. Fackenheim considers other major disasters in Jewish history, like the destruction of both the First and Second Temples, and argues that they can be fitted into some cosmic plan wherein the divine purpose is visible. Although these were terrible events, and no doubt tested the faith of the participants and their descendants, they in the end served to unite God with both history and the Jewish people. Yet the Holocaust goes beyond such events in that it challenges the very notion of God's connection with the world. The appropriate conclusion for Fackenheim is not to sever that connection, but to use the sufferings of the Holocaust to reaffirm it. This might seem to be perverse, and there is a good deal of quite complicated philosophical discussion behind his view, but the basis of it really is that he sees Jews as having a rather simple choice. If one disagrees with Hitler one must believe in the Jewish God, and denying the existence of that God is to side with Hitler.

Does anything prevent Fackenheim's view from being perverse? One might well be both opposed to Hitler and, as a result of the experiences endured during the Holocaust, no longer a believer in the Jewish God. The Holocaust has proved to be a powerful emotional argument in modern times for Zionism, and Fackenheim follows the argument to suggest that the foundation of the State of Israel represents an extraordinary attempt to supersede the Holocaust. It represents the first time for almost two thousand years in which Jews have attempted to take responsibility for their own future in much the same way as other nationalities have done. For the first time in the past two millennia Jews were the majority in their own State and set about defending themselves against their enemies. Now, whatever one thinks of this sort of language, it has to be said that it provides no sort of religious justification for maintaining belief in God. The Holocaust was understood by many Jews to mean both that they should reject the idea of a God who intervenes in the world and accept the principle that they have to defend themselves. Many Zionists would argue precisely that the absence of a God implies the necessity to take one's future in one's own hands. Fackenheim suggests that God revealed himself in the Holocaust, but there seems to be little evidence of this even in Fackenheim's own writings (although what would count as evidence is obviously a difficult issue). The central difficulty he leaves us with is his insistence upon the Holocaust implying the necessity for the maintenance of faith. What seems to follow more surely from his arguments is the importance of the survival of a notion of Jewish identity, but this is very different from adherence to God, and in particular the rules and customs of the Jewish religion. In his account of the Holocaust Fackenheim himself points out how the Nazis were intent on genocide, not just on the destruction of religious Jews, and an appropriate response might be felt to be the survival of the community, not the religion as such.

Fackenheim calls the Holocaust a *novum* to emphasise its break with the past, and Arthur Cohen coins a similar expression. He borrows Rudolf Otto's notion of God's holiness as a *mysterium tremendum* to coin the notion of the Holocaust as a human *tremendum*. The concentration camps were a *tremendum* since they were based upon a celebration of death as opposed to life, in such a way as to emphasise the irrational and mysterious aspects of the world. Like his predecessors, Cohen doubts whether the Holocaust can be placed within any explanatory context whatsoever. He argues that any modern theology must embody the following principles: (a) the universe is a place which provides evidence both of God's presence and the existence of evil; (b) God really affects the world through his actions, and (c) he is the creator of the world. God is taken to have created the world in a moment of extreme love, and created human beings who could respond to him freely. Of course, the existence of such freedom frequently leads to cruel and irrational actions on the part of human beings, and the Holocaust is an example of such behaviour. To suggest that God could have prevented such events is to want him to intervene in the running of the world on our behalf, which would prevent us from exercising our freedom. God is seen as rather like the driving instructor who helps a person get through the driving test and then legally on to the roads by himself. If that person subsequently has an accident it would be wrong to blame the instructor. He provided adequate instruction, and it is up to the individual to use that instruction in whatever way he wishes. If he wishes to drive too fast or recklessly, then it is pointless to blame the instructor for not intervening. At some point we have to drive by ourselves and cannot expect someone else always to be at hand to help us.

God cannot be responsible for the Holocaust since he no longer does anything in the world. He has provided instructions as to how people ought to live and these are available to us. If we choose to ignore them then there will be painful consequences. There would be no merit in a world in which we had no choice concerning following or rejecting God's law, nor would God wish his love for his creation to be returned in an automatic and compulsory manner. During the Holocaust people exercised their freedom to behave immorally and without reference to the rules of behaviour which are available to everyone. God cannot be blamed for it. Were one to object that a benevolent God could hardly permit so many innocent people to suffer to such an extent as is represented in the Holocaust, Cohen would reply that God's benevolence is to be found in his creation of the world and the human beings in it. He need not have created anything at all. Cohen is clearly working here with the sort of Aristotelian God so beloved of the medieval thinkers like Maimonides and Halevi. The problem with such a God is that he is distant from the world as it is at the moment, and a whole range of traditional religious activities such as prayer fail to seem relevant. After all, if God is not going to intervene in the world, why ask him to? That is the form of much prayer, requesting God to do things on our behalf.

A more orthodox account of the Holocaust is provided by Eliezer

Berkovits. First, in his *Faith after the Holocaust* he emphasises the importance of the traditional notion of *kiddush ha-shem*, the maintenance of faith and its proclamation even in the most dire circumstances. This can take the form of martyrdom and a calm acceptance of one's fate. Although Fackenheim suggests that within the context of the Holocaust it is meaningless, there is some scope for arguing that the contrast between the rapacity and barbarism of the murderers and the piety and saintliness of the innocent victims can represent the presence of God. By contrast with many of his contemporaries, Berkovits argues that the Holocaust can be put firmly within an historical context, and it is only within such a context that it can reveal its theological implications. The only difference between the Holocaust and previous disasters lies in the size of the former, and there is little theological significance in size. The issues surrounding the death of just one innocent person are the same as in the case of six million. God allowed the Holocaust to take place, and the Holocaust is a huge moral outrage. How could it happen? Berkovits employs the traditional notion of God turning away from his creation (*hester panim*, hiding his face) to suggest that at some points in time God mysteriously hides himself. This is far from arbitrary, but makes possible the capacity of human beings to act freely. Were God to involve himself in the evil decisions of human beings he would create a world in which injustice was impossible, but morality would be impossible too. There would be no scope for independent human action. If God hides himself for ever, though, there would also be no scope for morality, since the world would be infused with absence of meaning. In that case, anything would be allowed.

So God has to perform a delicate balancing act. He has to be sufficiently absent to allow us to make our own decisions, and yet he has to be present on enough occasions to inform us of his plans for the world. Berkovits argues that the Jewish people itself is the continuing witness of God's intervention in the world. Its sufferings and yet survival is evidence both of God's hiddenness and intervention. That is why the Nazis were so intent on destroying the Jews, because they bear witness to the role of God in history, a role which they sought to supplant. So the Holocaust is just the most recent and most terrible of those many occasions upon which the Jewish people have been obliged to suffer in order to make God's reality manifest. A good example of the fluctuation between God hiding his face and revealing himself is the Holocaust followed by the creation of the state of Israel, with the result that 'we have seen a smile on the face of God. It is enough' (*Faith after the Holocaust*, p. 156).

The theologian Ignaz Maybaum comes to a similar conclusion, albeit from a very different starting-point. He also places the Holocaust within a comprehensible historical context and sees a special role for the suffering of the Jewish people. In his *The Face of God after Auschwitz* he argues that Hitler especially hated the Jews because they bear witness to the existence of God and the divine purpose of the world. The primary role of the Jewish people is to bring the gentiles to God, and the disasters which they have suffered are stages which have to be undergone for this process to be completed. Such destruction (*churban*) has the role of introducing a new historical period, one in which the nations are progressively brought nearer to God. The gentiles learn through the *churban*, and only through such cataclysmic events, how they should align themselves to God. The two preceding such disasters, the destruction of the First and Second Temples, resulted in the creation of the Jewish diaspora and the institution of the synagogue. The former helped mankind by dispersing the Jews to disseminate God's message among the nations. The latter brought about a purer form of worship, an abandoning of sacrifices and a realisation that God is everywhere. The third *churban*, the Holocaust, is designed to put the gentile world in direct touch with the Christ-like suffering of the Jewish people as vicarious atonement for the sins of the world. The Holocaust represents the end of the medieval world, with its dependence upon a narrow view of religion and community, and the introduction of the modern world based upon reason and modernity. Hitler, then, is God's servant in just the way that Nebuchadnezzar was in the past, and the six million Jews who were killed were innocent victims who died because of the sins of others. Maybaum points out that although one-third of the Jewish population was destroyed, the remaining two-thirds survived in spite of the Nazis, and the survivors should realise that they are supposed to persist in their attempt at the progressive transformation of society.

A number of interesting issues have arisen in this discussion. A theme which returns time and time again is the question of the uniqueness of the Holocaust. Was the Holocaust so different from what preceded it for an entirely new set of moral categories to be required for its analysis? There do not seem to be any good arguments for so classifying the Holocaust. Certainly it was an event of extra-ordinary cruelty, yet the Jewish people have suffered such events before, and may do so again in the future. Moreover, genocide is not restricted to attacks upon the Jews, and many other ethnic groups have had to endure quite horrendous attempts at liquidation. It is also worth pointing out that some groups of people have been destroyed for non-ethnic reasons, perhaps for political or economic reasons, and it appears to be invidious to classify such non-genocidal murder as less horrible than the equivalent number of genocidal murders. Murder is murder, and the murder involved in the Holocaust was of a huge dimension, so huge that it makes us wonder at its having happened at all. There is a tendency to think that if it is treated as just like any other kind of murder, albeit on a larger scale, one is being disrespectful to the victims and somewhat failing in delicacy. Quite a popular line is that adopted by Arthur Cohen when he claims that

The death camps are a reality which, by their very nature, obliterate thought and the human programme of thinking. We are dealing ... with something unmanageable and obdurate ... The death camps are unthinkable, but not unfelt. They constitute a traumatic event and, like all decisive trauma, they are suppressed but omnipresent, unrecognized but tyrannic, silted over by forgetfulness but never obliterated. (*The Tremendum*, pp. 1–2)

What is interesting is that all the writers who comment upon the indescribability of the Holocaust go on to produce lengthy descriptions and explanations of it. They all have different theories surrounding it, and argue over its appropriate contextualisation. Now, however horrible an event is, nothing prevents us from discussing it. As Cohen points out, a traumatic event may take some getting over, to put it mildly, yet one can try to analyse and describe the event, and is indeed presumably under some obligation to do so if the event is ever to be confronted. As the capacity for human destructiveness progressively increases it is to be expected that worse and worse events will take place, and it is very much the role of survivors to try to deal analytically with such events if we are to learn anything at all from them.

We should distinguish here between the sorts of things which philosophers say about disasters and the sorts of comments made by ministers of religion. Some philosophers are religious functionaries as well, which makes it sometimes difficult to distinguish between two sorts of statement. There are a number of moving and interesting comments which people make about the Holocaust which relate far more to a therapeutic role than to an explanatory one. A speech which sounds good in a synagogue may not impress philosophers, and vice versa. Much of the literature surrounding the Holocaust is directed to a religious congregation, and should perhaps not be expected to make serious analytical points. Of course, if it is true that the enormity of the Holocaust means that no serious analysis of the event can be carried out in the first place it would not matter. This is not the case, though, and the Holocaust is just as capable of being studied and understood as any other human phenomenon. There is no doubt that the Holocaust provides a potent emotional justification for many things in the world which Jews support, in particular the state of Israel. We must try to separate clearly the arguments and the rhetorical flourishes if we are to get closer to finding a philosophical explanation of the Holocaust.

What meaning does the martyrdom of the Jews in the Holocaust have? So far we have looked at some answers provided by Jewish thinkers, but before we return to the topic it might be useful to look at some Christian reactions to this problem. The Christian argument tends to be that a Christian analysis of the experience makes possible an understanding which the Jews are denied, since the latter are not prepared to take that extra step towards a belief in the Messianic status of Jesus. When we were looking at the Book of Job it will be recalled that some Christian writers see the ending as profoundly unsatisfactory and almost pointing towards a Christian solution. After all, Job is left acknowledging God's power and wisdom, and is rewarded by the return of even greater wealth and children, yet what seems to impress Job is the immense gap between the role of the suffering and contingent human being and the all-powerful and wise deity. The text can be seen as an attempt by Job to understand the nature of that gap, and in the end he is left to wonder at the contrast between the human and the divine. The personhood of Jesus Christ mediates between the two aspects of this radical division, and would have answered many of the questions which Job proferred. Similarly with the Holocaust. A frequent question which arises in the Jewish literature is, where was God in the Holocaust? God is supposed to look after the Jewish people, and here they were being subjected to the most dreadful tortures and destruction. A moving story by Elie Wiesel is made much of by some Christian theologians. A young man was being hanged by the Nazis in front of all the inmates of a concentration camp, and while he was thrashing about in protracted agony, an observer asked where God was. Wiesel heard an internal voice saying that he was hanging on the gallows up there in front of them all (*Night*, pp. 61–2). This is a highly suggestive comment for Christians.

After all, if God did not suffer at all he was indifferent to the pain of his creatures. He would have been so distant and superior to his creatures that the events in the world are of no direct interest to him emotionally. By sending his son to participate in the sufferings of the world, God acknowledges and identifies with those sufferings, and provides scope for eventual salvation through them.

Before we explore this suggestion further, it is important to accept that Wiesel's own conclusion was not a Christian one. He seems to have found the Holocaust a very challenging period for his faith, and no notion of a suffering God would have helped him. The interesting Christian suggestion is that much of the Jewish commentary on the Holocaust goes awry. That commentary asks why God allowed such a thing to happen, whereas the correct question is the one which Wiesel heard in the camp, namely, where is God? How far does God participate in the suffering of his creatures? The implication is that the only notion of a God worth having is of a God who can suffer, and in this respect the Jewish God falls down. He stands far above the fray, and it is hardly surprising that Jews wondered what he was up to during the Holocaust, since he seems to have preserved his distance throughout. The Christian solution is to point to the possibility of God actually joining in the suffering of his creatures, a very dubious notion from the point of view of Jewish thought. On both the Jewish and Christian view, God created the world, probably *ex nihilo*, and brought about everything which takes place in the world. We might argue that much of the world's character is not directly created by the deity, but only allowed to develop by his starting the process off, but it must be assumed that he has the power to intervene and prevent many of the things which actually do take place. Now, we know that many terrible events do take place in the world, terrible events which God could prevent, or at least limit, were he to think it desirable. If our notion of God is of a being who remains interested in the world but is determined not to intervene, not to prevent things happening which cause immense suffering, then we are left with a rather unattractive concept of the deity. After all, if I build a fire in my lounge and watch complacently as my infant child wanders towards it, I can hardly excuse myself for her subsequent burns by saying that I did not actually plunge her hand in the fire. It does not much matter whether I am watching her with mild interest or not concentrating upon her at all because my mind is taken up with abstract thought. If, on the other hand, I do not intervene but suffer with her, then at least I am involved in what goes on in the room, and I might have some sort of justification for allowing her to harm herself, like trying to encourage her independence and so on.

The parent who is completely detached from the wellbeing of his child is not to be praised, and nor is the deity who is entirely separate from his creation. Yet does the analogy really work to the advantage of the Christian case? Does the fact that an adult might suffer along with a child excuse preventable harm? There used to be a phrase which adults produced when thrashing their children to the effect that it hurt the thrasher more than the victim. This is supposed to be because the adult felt ashamed and humiliated at the crime of the child which necessitated the thrashing. But if the punishment itself is wrong, does the fact that the punisher also feels pain on its occasioning make any moral difference? It might if the punishment is morally appropriate, but then we get back to the traditional discussion of the purpose of the suffering of the apparently innocent. If their suffering is acceptable for some wider reason then the pain or lack of pain of God is an irrelevance. For example, if a parent quite justifiably allows his child to take certain risks, those risks do not increase in their justifiability if the parent shares in the pain of the child when she comes to grief. We might admire a parent who suffers along with the child more than the sort of parent who does not, but the fact of sharing suffering is not of primary moral significance. What is morally important is the justification of the suffering in the first place. This is precisely where the Jewish discussion is located.

This might appear to be a diversion. If God cannot participate in our suffering, whatever the rationale for that suffering, surely he is limited in his relationship with us. If we could choose as between a suffering God and an impassible God, we might prefer the former, since we might think that we would then be able to call on the succour of a deity who really knew what we were undergoing. If God is a perfect being, then does this not imply that he can share our feelings and sensations? Of course, there are enormous problems here in explaining how a non-corporeal deity can experience feelings, but the sending of Jesus is part of the attempted escape from such problems. To be comforted by a deity who can feel our pains with us seems preferable to dealing with a God who is far above such feelings. Now, we must be careful here in how we describe the comforting relationship. It is certainly true that many people who are experiencing a particular problem look for an interlocutor who can sympathise with

What are the
moral conundrums which
a theodicy must try to address

them precisely because she is capable of having shared that problem, or even has actually experienced that problem. Such people often say that one has to have experienced the problem before one can help others over it. This therapeutic model can be quite limiting, though. It suggests that a necessary condition of comforting someone is being able to share their problem, or even to have experienced it in the past, and this is surely not the case. The person who is undergoing particular feelings might welcome the intervention of others who are able to put those feelings within a broader context, and there need be no implication of their having shared that problem. If counsellors were trained to share their clients' problems when they came to work with them they would be emotional punchbags, which is precisely why they are encouraged to detach themselves from such problems. Only if they are detached can they provide clear and useful advice. This does not mean that they have to be totally detached, but sufficiently detached to be able to work efficiently with the client to resolve the problem, in so far as it can be resolved.

There are many times when we are in trouble where we would like someone to comfort us by entering into our troubles directly, by crying with us, perhaps, or telling us of a similar situation which affected them. An important aspect of this relationship is that the other person, the comforter, is not generally in a position to do anything directly about the problem. If I am ill and in pain, I may be comforted by someone talking to me about a similar illness which he had, but that is not the attitude which I expect to find in my doctor. I expect her to try to cure me and treat me efficiently. I hope that she is sympathetic to my plight, but I also hope that this will not interfere with my treatment. I hope that she will be able to preserve some distance between what I am suffering and what needs to be done to alleviate my condition. Were I to have a choice between a comforter who could share my distress and a technician who can end it, I think I should choose the latter. Of course, these alternatives are not mutually incompatible, but the significance of the distinction is that it points to the very different relationship we have to God as compared with other finite creatures. God is in a position at any time to bring about an end to our sufferings, and we should be entitled to expect more than just comfort from him. He can solve all our problems, and when we pray to him we often request him to do so. So God is not really in the position of a human being who can know about our problems but need not share them with us. The latter is often far less desirable as a companion than the person who can feel for us because he suffers with us. This is not an appropriate comparison to make when we are talking about God, though, since we can never forget that God can do far more than just listen and sympathise with our problems. He can solve them. It is due to the way in which he created the world that those problems arise in the first place. How can we approach God for comfort when he is able to remove the problem for which we wish to be comforted?

This is not to say that there is nothing to the idea of a God who can understand what his creatures are suffering, quite the reverse. The argument could be that God understands perfectly what it is for his creatures to suffer, but in a very different way from that which we employ. When it is said that God is present on the occasion of the boy on the gallows, the implication does not have to be that God actually suffers with him or through him. It could be that God understands what part that event has to play in the developing pattern of human history, and he could as a result of observing events of that type feel very sad at the cruelties which human beings can bring upon each other. Were he to intervene directly in history to prevent such apparently gratuitous suffering he would totally change the sort of relationship we have with him. This relationship is an essentially distant one. Even though some people feel the presence of God in their lives in much the same way as others feel the presence of their friends, only on a very naïve version of religion would one expect God to answer one's prayers in much the same way as our friends answer our requests. Most religious philosophers accept that God has allowed us a great deal of latitude in our organisation of our lives, and if things start to fall apart it is useless to expect him to come along and pick up the pieces. At least, it is useless to expect this to happen if by it we mean what we mean when we think of our friends helping us with our disasters. The world would be an entirely different place if God was prepared to intervene whenever the innocent are threatened by the wicked. Even when millions of entirely blameless people are killed in the most ruthless and cruel manner he is unable to intervene unless he is interested in changing radically the relationship he has with his creatures.

It was suggested earlier that one of the perils of the notion of a suffering God is that it identifies God too closely with ourselves and the sort of behaviour we might expect from each other. Yet there is something to be said for this identification. Can God really be said to care for us if he is prepared to do nothing to save us when he could quite easily do so? Even human beings sometimes behave in this way, and justify their inactivity in terms of valuable ends which it is hoped to realise. Although most parents care passionately for the welfare of their children, they may allow them to fall into traps if they think that this will be part of a useful learning experience. They may allow their children to come to harm if they place great value upon the autonomy of those children. Indeed, they may even justify their inactivity in terms of concepts such as love and concern, claiming that it takes greater love to allow one's child to come to grief rather than to prevent that sorry conclusion to follow from her actions. Children have to learn eventually that they must stand upon their own feet and take their own decisions about risks and possibilities, and only such a learning process can result in an autonomous and fully moral agent. Of course, as parents we are very much confined within the bounds of our finite knowledge, and may find it difficult to think about how a failure to intervene on our parts may improve the eventual moral status of our children in the future. This limitation is not a limitation for God, and he can quite easily be thought of as understanding how the present sufferings of his creatures might fit into some global arrangement for the improvement of the whole of creation. In much the same way that a parent may sigh at the wrong decisions which his child takes, God may sigh at the mess which human beings make of their lives. This notion can be encapsulated within the boundaries of a Jewish theology without much difficulty. There is no need, then, for the Christian idea of God becoming man in order to share our sufferings to be added to the Jewish notion of God in order to make sense of that suffering.

Yet the Christian approach to the Book of Job is interesting in that it stresses an important point. The God in the Book is a distant figure, and although he responds to Job's demands for attention towards the end of the Book, he does not appear to relate to Job as a person so much as an idea, an idea of an infinite and omnipotent creator. Although there is communication between God and Job, the latter is left in this world apparently alone while God is somewhere else entirely, and the distance between them remains as vast as ever. Christian interpreters often argue that this is a gap which needs to be filled, and, as we have seen, they filled it with the idea of God becoming man, of God actually participating in the mental and physical sufferings of his creatures. Now, we have looked at some criticisms of this suggestion, but it nonetheless makes a useful observation on the relationship between God and his creatures in many Jewish accounts. This relationship is quite a distant one, and this distance is a problem. If God is really conceived of as being very distant, then he might not seem to be available to do many of the things in which he might be expected to have an interest. As we have seen when examining some of the philosophical accounts of the presence of evil and suffering in the world, God seems to play the role of an absent parent, or of a technician who has set up a mechanism and then abandoned it, or even of someone who cannot react to anything on the earth because whatever happens to us is what we have brought upon us through our intellectual and moral efforts or through our frailties. Even after we have analysed the arguments in favour of these conceptions, it is still appropriate to wonder whether enough of the traditional God of religion survives to fulfil the sort of role which is appropriate to that subject.

This is a highly controversial and complex problem in the philosophy of religion, and it is not one which could possibly be settled here. But there are some relevant points which have emerged through this discussion of the theology of suffering. Job did not require God to suffer with him in order to feel that his challenge to God had been successful. What Job wanted was to feel that he was in contact with God, that God was capable of responding to him, and once he thought that he was in communication with God his quest was at an end. God had responded to his plea for attention precisely by attending to him. This is perhaps the minimum which a religion requires, or at least the three monotheistic religions with a root in Judaism might be expected to look for such a relationship. The dichotomy of the infinite and the finite, the omnipotent and the relatively powerful, the omniscient and the limited in knowledge, and similar contrasts between the divine and the contingent require mediation if the object of religion is to be more than a remote and largely irrelevant idea. Since the issues of evil and suffering are so closely linked to determining our relationship with God they are particularly useful in working out what form that relationship takes. Most of the Jewish philosophers we have considered would reject the notion of God becoming man and suffering with us because they would regard that approach as bringing God too close to humanity, and so demeaning the significance of the concept. Yet the accusation which they in turn have to rebut is that the concept of God which they construct in their philosophies is too distant a figure

What is the minimum that our theories require?

to take on the characteristics of a God who could make sense of our sufferings. This problem has perhaps been highlighted as a result of the Holocaust, but it was a theme of earlier disasters also. How we expect God to react to our sufferings represents how we want to think of God, what his relationship with us is going to be, and it is a particularly acute problem for Jewish philosophers who are already operating with a concept of a God who is quite distant from his creatures. They then have the problem of reconciling a distant deity with the demands of his followers that he make himself more present to them, a demand which given that distance is especially hard to satisfy. Perhaps that is why Job is so impressed to have got a response from God. Since he saw God as so distant from the world and from Job's problems he might not have expected to have had any reaction from the deity, and so when it comes he appreciates the significance of the event. Job certainly does not resolve the tension of a distant God and suffering humanity once and for all, since after his meeting with God he still has no answer to his questions concerning the justification of the suffering of the innocent.

Many Jewish thinkers who write about the Holocaust emphasise the essential difference between that event and other superficially similar disasters affecting other ethnic groups, or even the Jews in previous periods. A good deal of the argument surrounding the Holocaust deals with this issue, and the very concept of the Holocaust or *Shoah* is designed to point to the distinctiveness of the event. Since the event is taken to be unique, the ordinary forms of analysis will not apply to it, since these techniques are designed to cope with the normal events of the world, not the exceptional. To claim that the Holocaust is just one more disaster like previous disasters, and that it falls into the category of extreme persecutions of ethnic minorities is to misunderstand, it is claimed, the very special nature of the event. Now, whatever one might think of this sort of argument, it is worth pointing to its connection with the distant God of Jewish philosophy, or at least of the philosophers we have considered here. Perhaps an aspect of the Holocaust's uniqueness is the dramatic way in which it brought into focus the apparent distance of God from us. During the Holocaust God seemed to be distant not just from a portion of the Jewish people, as was the case in the past, but rather from the kernel of Jewish civilisation, which was almost entirely destroyed and totally displaced geographically. This is precisely the sort of event which one might expect a deity to prevent or ameliorate through his intervention, and yet there is no indication that he did. This is not to suggest that it is impossible to find religious explanations for the Holocaust – no end of these have been put forward – nor even that nothing good can be seen to have come out of it. Many would argue that the State of Israel is a valuable consequence of the disaster. Yet what the Holocaust did was to bring into stark focus the significance of the distance which separates God and his creation. It seemed to many thinkers that the distance was so great in much Jewish philosophy that it is impossible to ask why God did not prevent the Holocaust, since there is little room for God to prevent anything at all happening in the world.

The apparent inaction of God, together with the idea that he does not intervene in the world anyway, suggests that God is very far away indeed. If even the Holocaust does not elicit a response from the deity one might wonder what role the concept of God can still play within a religious philosophy. Jewish philosophers tend to work with a rather bare notion of God, and they have in the past spent considerable efforts in denuding it even more, to the extent that it seems difficult to explain how God could intervene in the world of generation and corruption at all, where by 'intervention' is meant something close to what we ordinarily mean by intervention. Then along came a disaster of such a magnitude that it seemed incomprehensible that a God could stand by and let it happen, but of course it is not incomprehensible, since previous generations of philosophers had expended much effort in explaining the difficulties in looking for divine intervention. Given the way in which the concept of our relationship with God had been developed, it would have been incomprehensible to have had to deal with an account which described divine intervention. In the same way that the Enlightenment project seems to have come to an end after the strategy of Mendelssohn's approach to evil faltered, so the Maimonidean project of purifying the notion of our relationship with God comes to seem insufficient after the Holocaust. It is precisely in such circumstances that we should expect to have a rationale for the suffering, together with an analysis of our relationship with God which permits us to understand what has taken place. In stressing the uniqueness of the Holocaust Jewish thinkers are implying that a new theology will need to be constructed to make sense of the event, since the existing conceptual materials are insufficient to do the job. This in part is what is behind the radical approaches which have been taken to elucidating the meaning of the Holocaust, and we must bear this in mind if we are going to be able to put the varying approaches to Holocaust theodicy in context.

So far we have looked at a variety of Jewish responses to the Holocaust, and to a Christian approach. The Jewish responses differ in their assessment of the theological significance of the Holocaust. Some argue that a complete reorientation of thought is required as a result of that traumatic event, while others try to fit it into the pattern of Jewish history. Perhaps the most radical approach is undertaken by Rubenstein, who seems to have abandoned traditional conceptions of the deity in favour of a deity who can be approached through mysticism, but who does not have the ordinary divine characteristics, such as power to influence the world. On this view God is the divine nothingness, and as such is the source of being and existence, since by nothingness he represents a superfluity of being. Death and destruction is just a return to this nothingness, from which life later emerges in a different form. In just such a way did the State of Israel emerge from the devastation of the Holocaust. What is interesting in this account, which has only been sketched here, is that the sort of God which survives is not the sort of God for whom evil and suffering is any sort of problem, because it is not even an issue. This God plays no part in history, has no power over the world and cannot be thought of as taking decisions and observing the activities of his creatures. The traditional God is dead in the sense that after the Holocaust he does not make any sense as a concept, and if we are to hold on to a theology at all we have to redesign God so that he can represent the very basic processes of growth and death. Although Rubenstein acknowledges that his conception of the deity is not restricted to Judaism, he does not conclude that Jews have no need for Judaism. On the contrary, we need to employ the customs and rituals of our faith in order to participate in even the restricted form of religion which he advocates. The ceremonies of religion have an important part to play in linking us with the rituals of life, and through those ceremonies we can come closer to the life-cycle and are better able to cope with crises and problems.

It is not clear what connection there is between this theory and the Holocaust. Rubenstein often writes in such a way as to suggest that it is the fact of the Holocaust which necessitates such a radical departure from traditional perspectives on God. Yet the 'death of God' theory is hardly original to him, and was very much current in Christian theology when he put together his work in this area. This is not the place to assess the merits of that approach as compared with more traditional accounts, but it is relevant to examine the value of Rubenstein's theology in dealing with evil. For him it is not a problem which arises at all. There is no personal God taking decisions about the direction of history, there is no effort on the part of the maker of the universe to balance good and evil, and so there is no point in wondering why God does not prevent harm to the innocent. God is not in that sort of business at all anyway. When we look at the Holocaust, he argues, we can see that the whole business of theodicy is futile. If God was even remotely involved in reconciling fates with deserts, the Holocaust would be an impossibility.

Even if we accept with Rubenstein that the hand of God cannot be observed in the Holocaust, are we obliged to go as far as he does in transforming the notion of God and religion? First, it is worth saying that the Holocaust is not the only terrible period in the history of the Jewish, or any other, people. Many instances of the slaughter of the innocent preceded it, and it was just as difficult then to perceive the role of God protecting the innocent and punishing the murderers. Although the magnitude of the deaths in the Holocaust certainly outweigh most earlier disasters, the principle that God does not step in to save innocent lives is one well known to everyone. The second comment which seems appropriate is to wonder whether God's apparent unwillingness to prevent evil really has to have the dramatic consequences which Rubenstein recommends. If Rubenstein is right, then the rationale for adherence to a religion is sociological rather than a matter of faith as we now understand it. We can use a religion to structure the way in which we participate in a community, but it has no deeper meaning than that. In the city of Liverpool most people support either Liverpool or Everton Football Club, and as a consequence regard themselves as members of specific communities, and such membership is taken very seriously. Many people support the team which was traditionally supported in their family, and as such they are linked to traditions in the past and also to the future, yet very little can be adduced in support of such solidarity apart from that tradition. If this is what Rubenstein means by religion, and he often does seem to mean this, then he is operating with a notion of religion which cannot ever *justify* anything. If it is impossible to find an acceptable explanation for the Holocaust within traditional religious language then we may be forced nearer to such a radical transformation of the concept of religion, but this would be very much of a last resort.

Arthur Cohen also argues that the events of the Holocaust imply that God does not participate in history. A benevolent God who observed the Holocaust and chose not to intervene is unacceptable unless another account of his relationship to the world can be formulated. Cohen takes the path of arguing that God's involvement in the world now is through his Law, not through direct action. Were God to intervene in human actions, however desirable such intervention might seem to those currently involved in those actions, he would leave no scope for human freedom. So to the accusation that God was silent during the Holocaust Cohen would respond that this is not true. God has set out for us a Law which we can follow or not, and if we choose to abandon the principles of justice we can wreak havoc in the world. These principles are available to human beings as a whole, and we would not be able to accept them freely unless we could at the same time reject them. Sadly, during the Holocaust many people disregarded God's teaching on how to behave, and the consequences are as one would expect. Blaming God for the Holocaust is like blaming the government for the fact that people get killed when they drive too fast and break the speed limit.

One of the advantages of Cohen's view is that it is clearly within the bounds of traditional Judaism, at least as compared with Rubenstein. Another advantage is the scepticism he applies to the notion of the State of Israel as a beneficial consequence of the Holocaust, a topic to which we shall return later. We have seen how earlier thinkers like Maimonides also tended to stress the idea that God's influence on the world was not so much the influence of a person but more the influence of a law. Only if this is true can we freely choose our actions and worship God with the appropriate attitude. This attitude is one of love, as opposed to expecting a reward or fearing a punishment. Yet one might wonder whether God should not have limited our ability for evil, in much the same way that some vehicles are limited in terms of the speed they can go. The state is limited in the paternalistic measures it can take to preserve the welfare of its citizens. The citizens of the liberal state want to be free to take their own decisions about how much they can drink, smoke and how they should behave. The liberal state normally intervenes when the freedom of some individuals impinges upon the freedom of others. If we want to drink ourselves to death we are normally allowed to do so, but if as a result of drunkenness I wander around the streets abusing people I may well get arrested. The rationale for this is that we should be free to take our own decisions about our own welfare, but once we come into conflict

What should be the limit of free will?

with the welfare of others then it is incumbent upon the state to intervene and to try to sort out the conflict of competing freedoms and benefits.

One might expect God to do something similar. The point that we are free to follow or not to follow his Law is an important one, but when our immoral behaviour affects the welfare of others we might expect him to intervene on behalf of those others. The child who is bludgeoned to death by his drunken father needs a protector, and we might expect God to take up that role. It might be said that if one were to misbehave and start to harm others, then the arrival of divine thunderbolts would radically affect one's capacity to misbehave, and ultimately our freedom would be curtailed. If we knew that once we went too far divine intervention would take place the whole character of our activity as autonomous creatures would have to alter. Yet it could be argued that it would be no bad thing for this to happen. How important is it that we be free to act in whatever way we wish? Perhaps the highest levels of moral behaviour can only be expected of people who are also capable of the worst depravities. If we know that we shall be prevented from sinking into the lowest depths by some external power our motivation to avoid such a fate would be different than if we know that nothing except ourselves prevents us from such immoral behaviour. A religious motive for one's action is certainly purer if it is not based upon fear of retribution, as is a social motive that I will not, for instance, steal because it is wrong as opposed to not stealing because I might be punished. Yet in society we do not expect everyone to seek to behave well. We expect some people to be tempted to misbehave, and we hope to discourage them by setting out penalties for such misbehaviour. This is especially the case when the welfare of innocent people is at issue. We might expect God to do more for the protection of such innocent people than just present a set of rules which should be followed for the benefit of everyone. There are certainly moral benefits to be found in life in a *laissez-faire* universe, but these are not obvious to those who undeservedly suffer at the hands of those who go in the wrong direction. The Holocaust seems to emphasise precisely this point. Would the world not be a better place if the deity were prepared on at least some occasions to step in directly in support of its innocent inhabitants who otherwise face suffering and death?

Berkovits and Maybaum argue by contrast that God does work through history and they seek to relate the Holocaust to the series of disasters which have occurred throughout Jewish history. God cannot involve himself too closely in helping the virtuous and punishing the wicked because this would inevitably result in the disappearance of human freedom. The Holocaust is not an arbitrary event of human depravity, though, because it fits into a pattern of anti-Jewish persecution and a rejection of the message which Jewish culture seeks to transmit to the world. One might find the historical account interesting and quite persuasive, and still wonder at the benevolence of a deity which requires so many innocent people to suffer to bring about a better eventual result. According to Maimonides, God works through history by helping us gradually to change our dispositions through following his Law. He could have changed our dispositions all at once, but he prefers to give us the opportunity to enter into the construction of our own characters, since only in that way can we freely seek to be virtuous (*Moses Maimonides*, pp. 141–3). This seems quite appropriate, yet when one considers the enormous cost of this working slowly through history one wonders at its justification. I may want my child to work out by herself why fire is dangerous, because this is likely to improve her understanding of it and respect for it. Yet I am unlikely to watch impassively while she crawls into a fire. This does seem to be very much what God has been doing throughout Jewish history, and if he is to be regarded as directing that history in some way he is open to the challenge to justify his behaviour.

Many of the writers we have considered are convinced that one justification for the Holocaust is the establishment of the State of Israel. The Holocaust is described as an entirely new event in the history of the world (although, of course, it is not) and a host of new terms – *novum*, *tremendum* and *churban* – are developed to describe it. One motivation behind this use of language is to prepare the way for another new notion, an independent state. Fackenheim suggests that this state is an aspect of *tikkun*, of a mending of the rupture in Jewish–Christian relations signified by the Holocaust. Although many Jews were killed, some survived and set up their own country in which they have taken their own responsibility for defence and welfare. This is indeed a new step in Jewish history, and the Holocaust has proved to be valuable emotional ammunition for the justification of the State of Israel. But it is difficult to explain rationally how Zionism follows from the Holocaust. Could the State not have been formed in a less traumatic atmosphere, and as a result of less horrendous events? Does the formation of the State guarantee the survival of the Jewish people?

If God does act in history one might have expected him to produce a Jewish state in a less chaotic and bloodthirsty manner. In any case, the existence of the State does indeed put the responsibility for their future in the hands of its citizens, yet it is far from obvious that that future will be secure, or that it will not be secular as opposed to religious. The creation of the State is an event of immense importance in Jewish history, and yet one might wonder how it relates to the slaughter of millions of people in another part of the world. One might even wonder how to reconcile the creation of the State with the inevitable injustice to the non-Jewish inhabitants of the region. Justifying the Holocaust in terms of its role in the creation of the State of Israel just will not do. It raises far more questions than it settles.

Yet the relationship between the Holocaust and the State of Israel is an interesting one. It brings out the paradoxical nature of much of the literature on the Holocaust. If God wanted to bring about the State of Israel, why did he use the Holocaust as a route along the way? If he wanted to benefit one group of Jews through the creation of the State, why did he allow another group to be subject to extraordinary persecution and death as a forerunner? This sort of paradoxical reasoning runs through the whole area, as when Wiesel says 'How I sympathized with Job! I did not deny God's existence, but I doubted His absolute justice' (*Night*, pp. 55–6). Yet if God is no longer just, if he is prepared to stand back and allow his people to be murdered, what point is there any longer in acknowledging his existence? This might seem to be a strange way of putting the question, since it is not usual to make existence dependent upon moral probity. In the case of God, though, we might say along with the medieval thinkers that God's attributes are part and parcel of his being, and that we cannot separate his existence from his essence. He does not just happen to have certain qualities. Rather, he has them by dint of what he is, and he would not be what he is without them. Even if we accept that God still exists without the moral qualities which we previously ascribed to him, the point of worshipping him would be lost. A God who is no longer to be worshipped is dead, perhaps not literally but in practice. Wiesel comments in his description of the boy on the gallows that at that point faith in God and God himself die with the boy, and with the deaths of all the other innocents in the Holocaust.

What makes Wiesel's works so interesting, and artistically effective, is that he maintains both that God is dead and that he is still alive. God is shown to have ignored the plight of his people, and at the same

Can one believe in an unjust god or a Job's injustice we don't understand?

time he is said to be caring. It is worth pointing here, as Wiesel does, to the similarity with Job, who also attacks the notion of a caring God while at the same time apparently hanging on to it. This is important, since once it is accepted that the way in which things are in the world means that we can no longer hold on to the notion of God, or at least the traditional God of religion, we get onto a new line of problems, and abandon those previously potent problems of reconciling the existence of God with evil. In most of Wiesel's literary works we have a conflict between the accusers of God describing the terrible things which God apparently permits, and the adherents of God urging submission, patience and trust. He often uses the device of the institution of a court of law at which God will be tried for what he permits to happen, where both the prosecutors and the defence lawyers argue eloquently for their clients. The traditional claim that the sufferings are *umipnei ḥata'einu*, punishments for sins, is quickly rejected as implausible, given the people who are suffering and their lifestyle. Wiesel himself seems to be on the side of the sufferers, claiming that submission to suffering is mistaken and that it robs us of integrity. It is an exercise in self-deception, in directing our accusations against ourselves as compared with God, against whom they ought to be directed. But this defiance is not at the same time a denial of God. A covenant still exists between the Jews and God, and if the latter does not choose to protect the Jews it is still possible for the Jews to hope for a renewal of the relationship and the agreement on more beneficial terms. Wiesel not only criticises the passive and absent God, he also criticises the apathetic acceptance of that situation by the Jews. It is a human task to relieve suffering and a Jewish task to do it in such a way as to bear witness to the principles which lie behind the covenant with God. It is important to take practical action to relieve the suffering of human beings, and this is the only route to perfection. By helping others who are suffering and by avoiding being imprisoned in one's own suffering (perhaps just two aspects of the same activity?) one works towards releasing the Messiah, or redeeming God through our actions. At the same time we have to appreciate that there is no point in looking for an answer to the conundrum of God's apparent inactivity during the Holocaust. This is a mystery which will never be resolved. Wiesel does not think that after the Holocaust Jews can ignore their religious obligations. They should continue with a Jewish lifestyle, and if their practical action to help others does not end up redeeming God, at least it will serve to redeem themselves.

Wiesel sees the relationship between God and the Jews as an eternal process of interrogation. In it 'there are quarrels and reconciliations, more quarrels and more reconciliations ... yet neither God nor the Jews ever gave up on the other' (*A Jew Today*, pp. 163–4). Through this

endless engagement with God we proved to Him that we are more patient than He, more compassionate too. In other words, we did not give up on Him either. For this is the essence of being Jewish: never to give up – never to yield to despair. (*A Jew Today*, p. 164)

Why not? Part of the answer would have to be that it would be wrong to yield to despair, since the actual reasons for God's apparent inactivity are unavailable to us. No neat answers are available to us which could explain God's actions during the Holocaust and previous disasters, and we must hope that if we still address ourselves to him we shall receive some response. In any case, the basis of this interrogation of God is to be practical, and we seek to show God how suffering should be relieved by relieving it ourselves. It does not really matter, then, whether God ever responds or not, since we act as though he were capable of responding, and our actions serve to relieve suffering, our own and that of others. A theme which runs through Wiesel is that it is not only in God that we should trust, but also in humanity as a whole. We might not just despair of God's capacity to relieve our suffering but also of the redemption of human beings. After all, the horrors of the Holocaust were actually carried out by human beings, not by demons, and it would be a natural conclusion to think that human beings were incapable of perfecting themselves as a whole. We should aspire to a state of affairs in which both human beings and God respond to our plea for justice, and yet we should at the same time be not too confident about this happening. In the past both God and humanity have let us down, and we should hope that one day they will impress us with their desire to behave well, but until that day comes we must actively set out to fashion our own fate in the best way possible.

One might wonder why Wiesel refuses to accept that God no longer exists, given the evidence of his apparent inactivity during the Holocaust and similar disasters affecting the Jewish people in the past. There is both a theoretical and a practical answer to this question. From a theoretical point of view we cannot know enough about God to know whether he acted during the Holocaust or not, or what the motives for his apparent inactivity were. So it is always possible for us to continue to adhere to a caring God despite the evidence to the contrary, provided that we do not use this as an excuse for doing nothing to help ourselves and those who suffer in the world. On a practical level, and this is clearly the level which Wiesel regards as more important, we must act as though God existed, and as though humanity could live in a civilised manner, since any other form of life is an escape into despair, from which there is no possible route to improvement or redemption even of our own lives, let alone God's. In some ways Wiesel is following a similar route to that suggested by Fackenheim. The evidence of the Holocaust works against the idea that the victims suffered because of their, or others', previous sins. So it is not possible to understand the phenomenon of the Holocaust in terms of such neat theological theories as that of just retribution. Yet it would also be a mistake to abandon the link between the events in the world and the God of the Jews. To abandon that link, to cease to live as Jews, would be to grant success to the project of extermination so enthusiastically adopted by Hitler and his followers. We can set out to oppose their strategy by continuing along a Jewish path, albeit with the refusal to see the sufferings of the community as divine retribution. We are to maintain our faith despite what happened, as opposed to the normal justification of faith, which is in terms of what God does for us.

Is this not rather perverse? If someone is continually nasty to me because they want me to be nasty to them in return it might be an interesting strategy on my part to contain myself and respond by being pleasant, knowing that this annoys them even more. Surely this is not the model with which Fackenheim is operating here. It would be inappropriate to the dignity of the whole relationship between us and the deity for us to seek to annoy God by going against what he expects us to do. Perhaps a better example would be where someone ignores me, and I nonetheless carry on trying to attract his or her attention. I do not know why I am being ignored, and I keep on trying to stop being ignored, yet I always seem to fail. It is possible that I am not being totally ignored, since some things happen which can be taken as evidence of a response, but there is no conclusive evidence either way, and whatever I do seems to produce no direct response. If a person were to act in this way with respect to her attitude to another person we might well call it perverse. There are contexts in which it would not be perverse, though, and these are worth discussing. For example, we might be trying to contact someone with a psychological problem or a physical condition which makes it difficult if not impossible to register any reaction on his or her part. We might spend ages talking to him to try to elicit a response. We might carry on even though we have no reason to think that he will ever respond, perhaps because we have it on medical advice that it will never happen. Such action is not perverse, but instead is rather praiseworthy. Even if the person we are trying to contact never responds, a whole host of other good things occurs. We try to help the afflicted. We set out to put the interests of someone else before our own interests. We are in a very difficult and discouraging situation where we have no realistic hope of success, and yet we continue to plug away in the attempt at helping another. This exemplifies what Wiesel means by the importance of not giving in to despair, since in this sort of case it does not really matter whether our attempts at communication are in the end effective. It would of course matter to us and to the object of our attentions, but the attempt does not lose its significance just because it does not have a successful conclusion. The success of the action lies very much in the action itself, and any positive result is desirable but incidental to the moral status of the enterprise itself.

There is a difference, though, between acknowledging the moral undesirability of despair and the rationality of not despairing. When we think in terms of our work with a particular non-responding individual, a time may well come when it would be unreasonable to continue. However optimistic we might be as to the possibilities of success, a point arrives when we are able to think only in terms of miracles as a possible route to success. Besides, there is a limit to the amount of attention which we should give to one person. There are others who also deserve our attention, and concentrating on one person beyond the point at which one might expect results is an inefficient use of one's time, time which could be spent helping many others. This sort of comparison does not really work in this case, since Wiesel would argue that through constantly seeking a response from God by our practical works we behave as we should, and if we fail to seek such a response there is a danger that we might be submerged by cynicism and passivity which would extend over to our practical life. Perhaps he is correct in thinking that it does not much matter whether we ever get an answer provided that our life remains open to such an answer. But once we move away from the practical level, we might well wonder how long it is reasonable to wait for a reply. Even if the existence or non-existence of such a reply is irrelevant to the character

we
seek
a reply
do not though our practices, but they ourselves

of our behaviour, we should perhaps be concerned about the truth of the proposition as to whether God is capable of providing us with an answer which could satisfy us. Many of Wiesel's plays and novels are based upon this issue. Is there anything which God could say in his favour, in his defence, which would help us understand how he behaved when he was in a position to save the Jews from destruction?

If we look at the rituals of Judaism it becomes noticeable that there is an emphasis upon the ways in which God has helped the Jews. There is the covenant, the flight from Egypt, the Temple and the Messiah. Judaism is an optimistic religion despite the many disasters, which are commemorated on the whole as minor fasts. The events of redemption are celebrated as major festivals such as the Passover, Tabernacles and Pentecost. Were it to be otherwise, Judaism would be a rather gloomy religion, since there is plenty in the history of the Jewish people to form the basis of a transformation from a religion emphasising redemption to one laying the stress upon suffering. Such a new religion would be perfectly feasible, but it would present no aspirations for God to enter history and help his people. In some ways it would not be a religion at all, only a martyrology, and it would make no recommendations for positive action for its adherents. This is not in itself a criticism of such a religion, since it might be thought to be the only honest conclusion to draw from Jewish history. The important point to make here, and it is implicit in Wiesel's work, is that it is not inevitable to seek such a transformation of the religion. There are arguments which explain the apparent absence of God during the Holocaust and similar disasters, and these call for a more sophisticated understanding of the relationship which exists between us and God. Such an understanding is part of the continuing critique of the notion of God as a loving father *simpliciter*. The apparently paradoxical connection between a guilty God and his faithful servants is not paradoxical at all, but a critique of the notion that God could be accused of guilt as can his creatures. When Job and Wiesel accuse God of allowing the innocent to suffer, they refuse to deny his existence. This is not just an exercise in intellectual or emotional laziness but a realisation that his relationship with us is very different from our relationships with each other.

One might still wonder whether, as a result of the Holocaust, it is worth holding on to the idea of a God who has concern for his creatures. This is not to say that one could deny the existence of someone whose existence is obvious in revenge for the lack of concern which that individual apparently displays. If there were no doubt about the existence of God, then we should be obliged to acknowledge his existence, however annoyed with his behaviour, or lack of behaviour, we might be. Yet this is hardly the case here. One of the important forms of evidence for many believers of the existence of God is to be found in the events of the world, and if the character of those events is contrary to fairness, then such believers come to find their religious adherence weakened. Even for more sophisticated believers the nature of what happens in our world is not unrelated to belief in the deity. This is because they may cash religiosity in terms of practical action on the part of human beings. If the important aspect of the religion is its ability to produce a stream of moral and political activities, then perhaps the existence of the deity himself is not so crucial. Indeed, many of the writers on the Holocaust do not have much to say about God, but a good deal to say about his creatures and how they should react to that event. Those thinkers such as Fackenheim and Wiesel who stress the importance of not abandoning one's faith despite the Holocaust do have a point, in that if one abandons one's faith there is no longer any special problem over the Holocaust. It is just a terrible event in a world of terrible events which is under the control of the human beings who live in it. The problem of the Holocaust is only a problem if one wants to hold on to a belief in God as well as an understanding of the events of the time, at least if the problem is to do with more than a causal explanation. Yet we might wonder what it means for God to exist for thinkers like Wiesel and Fackenheim, who emphasise the importance of maintaining adherence to Judaism while at the same time accepting that on a traditional view of Judaism God was in a position to intervene on behalf of the victims.

The answer to this question may seem obvious. God exists, but he does not necessarily directly intervene in the world on behalf of his creatures, so we need to create a more sophisticated model of the relationship between God and the world. God allows human beings to get into a mess if they pursue a wrong path, and if he were to step in all the time to rescue us from our difficulties he would be in the position of a sort of superior nanny, and so far too interventionist to maintain the sort of distance which is appropriate in a deity. Fackenheim's development of the 614th commandment, that the Jewish people should not offer Hitler any posthumous victory by disappearing through the throwing-off of their faith, is then not perverse, as we have

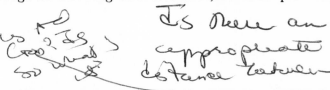

seen. It is based upon the idea that we cannot expect God to rescue his people from even enormous difficulties, and so involves a more sophisticated understanding of the nature of the covenant between the Jews and God, and of the nature of the relationship between God and humanity as a whole. Yet the question then quite naturally arises as to what difference it would make for us to talk in terms of God existing at all. This is a different question entirely than the question as to whether Jews should continue to act as Jews, since it is possible to follow a religious lifestyle without any especial commitment to a particular notion of a deity. One just goes through the normal customs and practices of the faith, yet without any particular acknowledgement of the character of the faith's deity. This has the advantage of allowing for a more appropriate distance between human beings and the deity, but it is an interesting question as to whether that distance is now rather too wide to be acceptable from a religious point of view.

Many people in Britain join Conservative clubs not because they are committed members of the Conservative Party, but because those clubs have good social facilities, and the members want to be able to play snooker or drink at a pleasant bar. They do have to join the Conservative Party to become members of the Conservative Club, and no doubt in doing so they have to undertake an adherence to the principles of the Conservative Party, yet it is surely quite possible that many of these people are not Conservatives, do not vote Conservative in elections nor align themselves with the principles of that Party. On the other hand, they would probably find it difficult to make even that token adherence to the Conservative Party if they were profound enemies of conservatism. As with any lifestyle, it is possible to share in it without any very strong beliefs about it, although if one had strongly negative beliefs about it this would present a problem. Is this like the post-Holocaust Jews adhering to Judaism yet without any strong belief in a personal god who is concerned with their affairs? After all, both Fackenheim and Wiesel do point out that the point of the Holocaust was not to kill those believing in the Jewish God, but rather those who were Jews. It was no escape for Jews to claim not to adhere to the practices of their religion, nor even to disbelieve in God. The point of the policy of the Nazis was to eliminate the Jewish race, and so to oppose that policy it might be sufficient to encourage the survival and indeed expansion of that community without paying any particular attention to the religious beliefs of the members of the community. One of the main arguments which Fackenheim and others have produced in favour of the uniqueness of the Holocaust is that it was not a pragmatic project serving some perceived prudential end, but an end in itself. As Fackenheim points out several times in his *To Mend the World*, Eichmann actually managed to get trains diverted to Auschwitz from the Russian front. So an appropriate response might be to reassert the survival of the Jewish people, which means that there should be some level of continuity of Jewish life within the different countries in which Jews live.

What is the nature of this life? Actually, it is quite minimal. As Fackenheim puts it:

> Back in 1951 Martin Buber did not ask about the children of Job, either the first or the second. He did ask, however, two related questions. How is a '"Jewish life" still possible after Auschwitz'? For this he substituted, as being 'more correct', how a 'life with God' is still possible 'in a time in which there is an Auschwitz'. To the first two of the three questions the same answer must be ventured: *there must be a possibility, for there is a reality*. The living children cannot – dare not attempt to – replace those who died; yet in writing a new page in Jewish history – *through* founding a new Jewish state but, note this well, not *in* it alone – they can, do, must take their place. Is a 'Jewish life' still possible? This too must be possible, for on that new page it is actual. But – the third question, Buber's 'correct' one – 'in a time in which there is an Auschwitz', can there still be a 'life with God'? (*The Jewish Bible after the Holocaust*, p. 94)

Fackenheim responds to this third question by pointing out that one might say that life with God was possible since it is actual, but he quite rightly rejects this line. His argument for this is that there are many ways of living which regard themselves as living with God, and how can we distinguish between the false and the genuine? He goes on to claim that a Jewish life 'with God' is possible in Israel, and he describes in some detail how Israel, like Mordecai, has the role of protecting the Jewish remnant, a task it can only perform through the hope of help from 'another place' (Esther 4:14). The interesting aspect of this response by Fackenheim is that it is clearly based upon practice. That is, life with God is possible and indeed real because of the activities which a part of the Jewish population carry out, and this is provided with some additional religious support by a reference to the Book of Esther. But we could return to his earlier response to Buber's question and wonder what privileges a Jewish sense of living with God over competing notions. In any case, it seems rather odd to claim that living with God involves hoping for divine help in order to preserve a remnant of the original community for whom no divine help came at all. Surely the implication cannot be that the latter community did not have the right attitude to its God, and as a consequence suffered the Holocaust. This would go entirely against Fackenheim's theory of the Holocaust.

So what is life with God? The important feature to be noticed is that it is the pursuit in a practical sense of moral and political objectives, where the connection between these ends and the deity is quite vague. To understand Fackenheim's point more clearly here we need to pay attention to his adaptation of Hegel. Fackenheim uses Hegel's account of modernity to argue that the Jews as a cultural force represent modernity, a feeling of *Selbstvergewisserung* (self-confidence) in the role of the modern individual in society. Once the Jews became emancipated and came to live within the cities of the gentiles, they threatened the old ways of thinking still surviving in those cities and came to represent the onset of modernity on the basis of the growth of technology, a cultural development immensely threatening to all those who feared the changes in thinking and lifestyle which modernity inevitably brought with it. As a form of self-assertion modernity met its temporary match in the denial of modernity by the Nazis, and in the attempt of the latter to use the technical apparatus of modernity to destroy the harbingers of modernity in Europe. In destroying the Jews they attempted to put aside at the same time the presence of the infinite and ethically transcending God whose existence is embodied in the witness of the Jewish community. Hence the necessity for a total annihilation of the Jewish people, and the setting up of a policy of complete destruction which bore no relation to the particular characteristics of individual members of the community. In the same ways that the Jews tried to transcend what was traditional in European society through modernity, through a total reinterpretation of European values and practices, so their opponents tried to transcend the Jews, quite literally in this case by wiping them out utterly. Hence the importance for Fackenheim of his 614th commandment, for the Jewish people to survive. To be destroyed, albeit via the more gentle means of assimilation as compared with the death camps, is in effect to be transcended by the forces of negativity and anti-modernity. If Hitler is not to be awarded a posthumous victory, he must not be allowed to have presided over a process which results eventually in the disappearance of the Jewish people. Given the dialectical way of thinking of which Fackenheim is so fond, this would mean that the ways of thinking represented by the Jews had finally been overcome and transcended by what is opposite and opposed to them.

Arthur Cohen makes a useful distinction here between ultimacy and finality. He suggests:

Finality and ultimacy differ crucially. Ultimacy entails the formal and configurational character of the real event, whereas finality describes its intention and its goal. It is one thing to speak of the *tremendum* as ultimate, quite another to affirm its finality. If final, *everything* is intended to evil and we must conclude that our affairs are run, if not by blind caprice, then most surely by a malign divinity. (*The Tremendum*, p. 49)

The final solution was not final, although it does represent the ultimate opposition of vast historical forces in an attempt at purging the challenge of modernity. The final solution represents a state of affairs in which anything is possible, in which the normal restraints of morality no longer have purchase, and where the familiar personal relationships between people are transcended by an impersonal methodology of destruction. Hence the argument that the Holocaust was an extraordinary event, not just because of its size, but because of its ambitions. It represents an attempt at diverting the course of history by ruthlessly extirpating the vanguard of historical progress, the Jews, without regard to any of the characteristics of that people as individual persons. That is why it is also important to stress that the majority of those concerned with carrying out the Holocaust were not psychopaths nor especially cruel. We need to take seriously the many instructions by its leading perpetrators to fight against pity and against the exclusion of some Jews on account of their individual characteristics. What was involved was a battle between two competing ideologies both of which were prepared to assert confidently that they represented the future. It was a battle in which no prisoners could be taken. As far as the Nazis were concerned, the only way to exterminate the challenge of modernity was to exterminate the Jewish people, not just in the sense of killing its members but by destroying the whole entity, the entire idea of the Jewish people. What was at issue, on the Hegelian analysis so favoured by Fackenheim, is a metaphysical conflict between two contrary principles in total dialectical struggle for transcendence, a struggle which is made even more severe by the fact that it is of the nature of such a meeting of ideas that neither can finally triumph over the other.

We do not have to share Fackenheim's Hegelian approach to

appreciate many of the points he makes. One advantage of his argument is that it does seem to express quite nicely what is so different about the Holocaust as compared with other persecutions of the Jews, apart from scale, of course. Cohen brings this out well with his distinction between finality and ultimacy also. If the final solution had really been final, then history would have come to an end, since one idea would have completely dominated over its contrary, and clearly this did not happen. But what did happen was in a sense ultimate in that it represents fully the power and influence of the forces of negativity, and has marked so severely and permanently the character of modern life despite the defeat of Nazism in Europe. Cohen is quite right to argue that a really final solution would exemplify a malign deity, although it must be said that it is difficult to know what role a personal God can play within the Hegelian dialectic. An ultimate *tremendum* provides evidence of a freedom to act among human beings, but not an entirely radical freedom completely without transcendental control. There can be little doubt but that the theology of the Holocaust is for many thinkers unconnected with the theodicies which preceded it, so that any understanding of the phenomena of evil and suffering will have to be on different lines from those acceptable in the past.

CHAPTER II

Back to the Bible

The Holocaust is not the only critical event in this century which has led to a re-examination of the principles of Jewish philosophy. The creation of the State of Israel has also proved to be important in this respect, and the implications of the State for the continuing status of the Jewish people are intriguing. Whatever the relationship between the Holocaust and the creation of the State of Israel may be, it is clearly an important question for those concerned with the topic of evil and suffering, and a broad range of responses will be discussed. In some ways the discussion in the second half of this century of the Holocaust has been rather unsatisfactory. Old solutions no longer seem to hold sway and new solutions are not persuasive. Perhaps we are still too close to the Holocaust to be able to view it calmly and rationally, and it is too early to place it within its historical context. One of the major contributions which this century has brought to the topic is to question the value of a purely philosophical approach. Can the philosophical aspects of the issue be divorced from everything else about it? Clearly they can if we are to adhere to the philosophical project initiated by Philo and ending with Hermann Cohen, but if we join the project established by Buber and Rosenzweig and pursued with some energy after the Holocaust we might doubt this possibility. Perhaps philosophy by itself will not help us understand the role of evil and suffering in Jewish history, and for such an understanding to emerge it will be necessary to combine philosophy with other approaches – poetry, drama, mysticism and so on – which leads us back to the Book of Job, where we started.

It is obviously a gross simplification to see the Bible as a philosophical treatise, and we can only admire the ways in which some commentators manage to impose a syllogistic structure on biblical prose. Sometimes it seems very forced, as with Gersonides' discussion of the

Book of Job, and yet there is a point to such an enterprise. It brings out the fact that the Bible is full of arguments as well as everything else which it contains, arguments which are designed to buttress and illuminate the spiritual message of the text. There certainly seems to be something of a development of the notion of suffering and evil in the text, which very early on gets to work on the role of the negative, or the apparently negative, in human life. The stories of Adam and Eve, the serpent, Cain, the Flood and the Tower of Babel portray suffering as due to the justified wrath of God. Human beings were provided with the opportunity to choose between good and evil, and since they went in the wrong direction, they were cursed and deservedly condemned to suffer for their errors. The whole notion of a covenant which is so important a theme in the Bible is based upon the idea that if we stick to our contract with God and behave correctly we shall be rewarded by his grace. On the other hand, if we go awry, as we all too often tend to do, he will punish us, either directly or through the agency of others, and we will suffer. We had the choice, and we received the warning, and since we chose wrongly we have to suffer the penalty.

This is far from being the only account of suffering in the Bible. It would be unfortunate for any religion to take the attitude that once one has sinned, there is no escape from divine punishment. There has to be some scope for hope and redemption, otherwise religion is just a matter of grim resignation to fate. When God punishes his creatures in the Bible, he often also succours them. For instance, when Adam and Eve are excluded from Eden they are thoughtfully provided with warm clothes. Although Cain was obliged to wander from place to place, a fugitive, his son built the first city, and the Flood was survived by Noah, his family and a collection of animals. The optimistic side of religion is perhaps nowhere so well contrasted with the negative as in the Psalms, whose author is both immensely depressed at the sufferings of his people and at the same time encouraged by the presence of God and his help. This is very much a feature of many of the prophets, who castigate the community and threaten it with dire punishment, often describing almost gloatingly the punishment which has already been exacted, and yet also expressing confidence in a vision of a new state of affairs in which God will redeem his people. A lot of things are going on in these books, but one interesting feature is that we are no longer operating on a simple reward–punishment level. The sufferings which befall Israel are indeed represented as a punishment, and the Jews are admonished by the prophets for their sins, and yet it is not clear that their redemption is attained through their moral improvement. Rather, God is represented as in control all the time, and he chooses to benefit his people after they have suffered, for what precise purpose we are not sure, as a manifestation of that power and authority which lies behind everything which happens. We may be confident of an eventual happy outcome, and of God bringing about such an outcome, but quite why it happens, or when it happens, is not something which we can explain.

We are told in the Book of Proverbs that 'No ill befalls the righteous, but the wicked are filled with trouble' (12:21). Without the benefit of thorough reinterpretation, this is patently false. The Book of Job explains why. The comforters of Job go completely awry. They assume that he must at some point have provided God with a good excuse for punishing him, since everyone commits sin on at least some occasion. Anyway, they argue, suffering has a powerful pragmatic function. It improves us and helps point us in the right direction. Job does not accept these suggestions, not because he is so arrogant that he refuses to consider the possibility that he might be guilty of sin, but because the existence of such sin would trivialise his suffering. Of course his life is not a perfect life, and it is true that suffering can improve our character. Yet Job's life is notable for its virtue, and it is pretty obvious that his sufferings do little to improve his moral standing. Job's friends are referring to rather simplistic interpretations of how the Bible explains suffering, especially the suffering of the (apparently) innocent. Job questions these interpretations, since they quite obviously do not square with his experience, but on the contrary they contradict his experience. What Job does not challenge is the power of God, and he does not even consider whether God exists or not. A whole range of problems would not be problems if the existence of God could be called into question by innocent suffering. Job's steadfast faith is rewarded at the end of the book by the return of his possessions, indeed, by their increase, which suggests that he is on the right lines. It is acceptable for us to wonder why we suffer when we have done no wrong, or at least no wrong which deserves such radical punishment as Job apparently receives, and we can query the justice with which God rules the world. We can even question the ability of God to know everything which takes place in that world. What we cannot question is the existence of God, since if we question that we do away with the whole problem.

Many commentators would say that it is this refusal to countenance the issue of God's existence which makes the Book of Job so unsatisfactory. For many people the problem of innocent suffering is precisely the problem of reconciling the existence of a God with facts about the world, where by 'God' is meant 'deity worth worshipping'. If an omnipotent and omniscient deity allows innocent suffering for no good end, then such a being is not a suitable object of devotion. He would be more like a malignant demon. These propositions reflect the feelings of many who have experienced suffering for no apparent end, and people commonly lose their faith when they undergo such suffering. That is, they lose their belief in any sort of God, not just in a benevolent deity. One can see the point of their change of attitude, since the issue of God's power is not perhaps the most important problem for those suffering unfairly. They want to know what the point is in having such a God if he does not prevent innocent suffering. I may continue to pay my union dues because I know that the union is strong enough to defend me if my employer decides to victimise me. If the union declines to intervene, I might well come to wonder why I bother to continue with the subscription. The whole meaning of the union in my life could thus become reduced. I could acknowledge that it is still there, but not in a helpful sense, or I could conclude that it is not really there anymore in anything but name. Failure to intervene is equivalent to failure to exist, a possibility which Job does not appear to accept.

This is one of the intriguing aspects of the Book of Job, the fact that in spite of his travails Job never questions God's existence. In the end he does not even seem to object to the way in which God treats him, since God is said to be so powerful and different from his creatures that any sort of conduct seems to be acceptable. Some have seen this as a weakness in the Book, since it might be thought that the existence of innocent suffering is a criterion of the non-existence of any sort of religious object of devotion. This is why some passages in the Bible seem rather simplistic, since with their emphasis upon the covenant, punishment and reward, and God's power over his creation they imply that the existence of God is very much tied in with the regulation of suffering along a moral plane of some sort. What we find in Job is a far more sophisticated doctrine, one which eschews the platitudes of traditional religion in so far as the justification of suffering is concerned. The issue of suffering and the question of God's existence have nothing to do with each other, according to Job. The neat solution that God rewards the innocent in the afterlife for what they suffer in this life is picked up only to be rapidly dropped. It is far from being a neat solution in any case, since the question would always arise as to why God would make someone suffer at all if that suffering was not deserved. To compensate the sufferer afterwards might be better than not to do anything at all, but it is far from the standard of behaviour which we could expect a deity to meet.

Job seems to see his faith as something to hold on to despite what God allows to be done to him. This argument has surfaced in this century in the form of Fackenheim's suggestion that the appropriate reaction to the Holocaust is to maintain one's faith despite everything which happened, since to do anything else would be to give Hitler a posthumous victory. There are marked similarities between this point and the situation of Job. After all, Job is being made to suffer in order to see whether his faith is malleable, and the steadfastness which he (eventually) displays represents his refusal to allow the test to upset his judgment. He defies God to allow anything to be done to him and will not accept that his suffering is meaningless and good grounds for challenging the role of God in his life. This notion of suffering being meaningless is important here. What permits Job to hold on to his faith is his assertion that what is happening to him has a meaning. Precisely what that meaning is may not be available to him, but that there is a meaning to what is happening to him is something of which he is convinced. In some ways this displays the strength of Job's position as compared with that of Fackenheim, since it is not clear from the latter's writings that the Holocaust really does have a meaning. Its very uniqueness seems to rob it of meaning, preventing it from being placed within a context which would explain it. For Fackenheim it is almost as though the maintenance of faith despite the Holocaust provides it with meaning, and the refusal or inability to hold on to one's faith as a result of those events robs the Holocaust of any possible meaning.

Job is convinced that his suffering has a meaning, although he is far from sure what that meaning actually is. Now, one might think that this is an inexcusable evasion of the issue, but there are some attractive features about this position. Perhaps the best thing about it is that it avoids a banal solution to the problem of suffering which talks about an afterlife and eventual rewards for the innocent and virtuous. Job does have some rather good arguments for being unable to say precisely why the suffering has taken place, since he refers on many occasions to the great distance which lies between us and our creator. Again, it would be banal if the reasons for God's decisions were to be transparent in his actions. Another useful point in Job's favour is that he concentrates upon the way in which the role of God impinges upon the life of the individual. Other biblical figures stress the link between God and the community, often with unfortunate consequences in so far as the notion of suffering is concerned. When we look at the words of the second Isaiah we can only regret that he had not shared the care with which Job spoke of the reasons for suffering. When the former speaks of the purpose of the Babylonian exile and the destruction of Jerusalem he suggests that patience before such suffering will result in return to Israel. Not only that, but the example of the Jews surviving their exile as a religious community and then returning to their land will be a potent symbol to other people of the power of the Jewish God. This is also a frequent theme of the Talmud, which has it that 'Whoever gladly bears the sufferings which happen to him brings salvation to the world' (*Bab. Taanith* 8a). In our own time a frequent argument is that the link between the Holocaust and the birth of the State of Israel is far from contingent. Without the enormous suffering endured by the Jewish people in the Holocaust there would perhaps have been no restoration of the promised land, and so in some ways the point of that suffering is the realisation of the Zionist dream, or at least part of it.

This sort of language has a use if we can make moral distinctions between the suffering of an individual and the suffering of a community, but we have to be careful how we make such a distinction. Some would argue that no such distinction can be made, because the suffering of a community is nothing over and above the suffering of the constituent parts of that community. In some ways this is true, but it is an over-simplification. There are all sorts of things which can affect communities over and above their effect upon the members of those communities. Thinkers like Maimonides, for example, talk at length about the role of religious law and history in binding the community together and creating an attitude which will be helpful to the future and to the wellbeing of the group. Maimonides argues that one of the main purposes of religious law is to weld the Jewish people together, to distinguish them from other religious groups and to enable them to think more accurately about the source of that law, that is, the nature of God. Much of Jewish history is explicable according to him in terms of the divine ability to understand the significance of being subtle in his treatment of groups. Why did it take forty years for the Jews to move from Egypt to Israel? One reason is that it took that long for the community to work its way out of Egyptian ways of thinking, helped here by the new laws, and to forge a sense of identity and solidarity. What better means to that end than to continue on a long journey of some danger and have to work together with other members of the community to survive? The introduction of new legislation is clearly easier if the community is cut off from its past and has to establish new rules in a novel and challenging framework of life. Had the Jews gone straight away to Israel they would have set up a quasi-Egyptian state, a state which was replete with customs and ideas of their previous lifestyle. God could naturally have immediately conveyed them to Israel, but he wanted to use human nature to change itself, by gradually encouraging the Jews to transform themselves into better and more distinct people. God could also have just changed the consciousness of the people, so that they immediately threw off their Egyptian ideas and adopted those notions of which he approves. This would have been to dissipate the possibility of free choice and merit in the ethical struggle which the Jews had subsequently to confront. In these ways what happens to the community is clearly distinct from what happens to individuals. Individuals may feel, and rightly feel, that they ought to behave in particular ways because of their social obligations. They may at the same time think that they individually have no need to behave in that way, since they personally do not have a problem in understanding what the purpose of the behaviour is.

What Maimonides is pointing to here is the way in which we relate to the religious law, and the importance of that attitude to the community. For example, the role of the commandment not to seethe a kid in its mother's milk may well be to counter an Egyptian custom with another specifically Jewish restriction (*Moses Maimonides*, pp. 136–8). If a community is used to eating a particular kind of food, then any change is likely to have a large effect upon the ethos of that community. Yet if the reason for this restriction is explained in purely pragmatic terms it might well come to be disobeyed or only occasionally obeyed. If individuals can take the line that they personally are not attracted to Egyptian customs, or their contemporary equivalent, then they might well decide not to bother with the restriction. If, on the other hand, they realise that the restriction has a divine basis and also that they may not have perfect knowledge of their own state of consciousness, they might be more likely to adhere to the law. A state of affairs whereby many people interpreted the restriction pragmatically would lead to a marked decline in its force and potentially in a similar decline in feelings of communal solidarity and separateness. Maimonides sees God as a kind of perfect social scientist who understands how groups bond and survive, and as a result specifies rules to make this possible. Particular individuals may come close, to a degree, to his thinking and may think themselves excluded as a result from the details of the law, yet they would be deluding themselves. They may understand, at least partially, their own minds, but they do not understand the role which such rules have in the formation and preservation of community, and if they act with only their individual goals as ends they will weaken the ties which link them with their co-religionists. As a result, the religion itself will be weakened. So even if they think they understand the point of the law, and even if they think the law does not really apply to them because their minds have already been changed as the law wishes, they must act in accordance with the law. They have responsibilities to the community as well to themselves, and God is best able in his legislation to understand how this is to be acknowledged in practical life.

If this sort of argument works then we can see how it might also be argued that the sufferings of the individual might redeem the community, and also how the sufferings of the community might improve the character of that community and result in greater perfection than could exist without such suffering. The Holocaust did, in a sense, lead to the State of Israel. The deaths of the martyrs at other times did, to a degree, inspire the rest of the community and strengthen their faith. To bring the scale of the discussion right down, a personal tragedy might bring a family closer together, and a community can establish new bonds and roots when a disaster affects a part of it. There are many contexts in which this all happens, and the role of martyrs is important in a whole range of religions, not only in Judaism. Clearly someone who is prepared to die for his or her religion is evidence of the seriousness with which they hold their views, and could well impress others. On the other hand, suffering may lead some people to distance themselves from a religion. Many Jews caught up in the Holocaust did not find their faith strengthened by the experience, but quite the contrary. They regarded the events of the Holocaust as indications of the absence of God and the vacuity of their previous religious commitment. Now, it cannot be denied that different people interpret suffering in different ways, for some as a prop to their faith and for others as an obstacle. But presumably those who argue for the link between suffering and the redemption of the community do not base the link on contingent facts about what those involved think is the meaning of the suffering. The nexus cannot be supposed to be contingent since such a relationship would vary with the individual, as it quite plainly does, and would, if successful in describing people's reactions, be based on nothing more than behaviour and accompanying emotions. When it is said that the return to Israel from the Babylonian exile and from the Holocaust were possible because of the prior suffering, that suffering has to be conceptually linked with the eventual outcome. The outcome did not as a matter of fact just follow the suffering, but the suffering must be at least a necessary condition of the outcome.

Whatever one's reading of history, such a thesis is surely implausible. Is it not possible to conceive of a state of affairs describable as the formation of the State of Israel without the Holocaust? It is certainly true that it would not have been the same state as that which emerged, since there is no doubt that the precise character of the State did borrow many of the features of the Holocaust. Yet to insist that exactly the same state must follow from different antecedents is to trivialise the argument, since whatever precedes a state of affairs may be taken to have an impact upon the nature of what it produces. Having just had a cup of tea, I am writing this page with a tea-sated attitude, and had I not had the tea, my feelings right now would be different, and so in a sense the absence of the tea would change the character of what in fact is now taking place. But surely far more than this is meant when it is argued that prior events characterise essential aspects of present and future events. The State of Israel would have been different without the Holocaust, perhaps very different, but there still surely could have been a state. The Holocaust does not even seem to have been a necessary condition of the State. Prior suffering, and the attitudes towards that suffering, certainly characterised both the return from Babylon and the State of Israel, but not so strongly that either event could not conceivably have taken place without it.

It might well be argued that the point is being missed completely here, since the link between the suffering and the effect is not meant to be a causal link at all, but rather a spiritual link. What this can be taken to mean is that the nature of the effect is only as it is because of the role which the prior suffering had in leading to it. That is, the meaning of the effect could not be as it is without the prior suffering and the role of that suffering in bringing about the effect. There is some scope for this argument, since the events in question are full of religious significance. The thesis could be that what is important is not just, say, the formation of a state designed specifically for Jews but the formation of a state which can serve as a refuge for Jews were they to need one, a refuge whose status is immeasurably influenced by the events of the Holocaust. From a secular point of view the formation of the State of Israel could be regarded as possibly following on from a whole range of different events, but from a religious point of view it fits into a notion of God's relationship with his people after their great suffering, and would not be the same at all without that context. This is not just the trivial point that it would be different in the sense that what led to it is different. Rather, it would be different because a basic constituent of its religious meaning would be absent. The implications of such an argument are interesting and important. It would explain why those caught up in the tragic events of the Holocaust might not understand what the point of their suffering is, since they, unlike the deity, are unable to view the world *sub specie aeternitatis*. Their suffering plays a part in the progress implicit in a divinely led human history, but they would not understand how this could be the case. It is only through their faith and steadfastness that they can advance the progress of the Jewish people, and of humanity as a whole, through witnessing the power and grace of God. As Halevi argues throughout the *Kuzari*, the main Jewish virtue is not saintliness or humility, but fidelity. Through the sufferings of individuals the welfare of the group as a whole is advanced, and the role of suffering is to benefit the community.

This seems an entirely reasonable notion, and of course it takes on a lot more strength when one considers the sorts of argument which Maimonides produced to show how the political consequences of religious legislation and history may be very distant from the beliefs and attitudes of the individual participants themselves. We tend to get tied up in our own concerns and fail to grasp the broader picture. There clearly can be an important distinction between self-consciousness and the consciousness of the community, and the former may transform the latter in ways which are far from perspicuous. The sorts of example which Maimonides produces are quite compelling, but it might be wondered whether this really works for suffering. We may choose to follow religious law, and may be satisfied with a fairly naïve rationale for that law. We are unlikely, unless we are martyrs, to choose suffering and then be satisfied with a particular interpretation of it. Judaism is not a religion which glorifies suffering, and the ordinary believer would do much in his or her power to avoid such negative experiences. In any case, many Jews who suffered during persecutions were not even in a position to choose, since they were children too young to know what being Jewish meant. How is their suffering supposed to contribute to eventual benefits to the community, and world, at large? The route along such an argument is well trodden, and yet one might wonder how easy it would be to reconcile with a benevolent deity. There is an important distinction to be made here between different kinds of sufferers which tends to get blurred by many writers, especially those who classify all those who are murdered by persecutors as having died for *kiddush ha-shem* (sanctification of the Name). They may all have been killed because they were Jewish, but their attitudes to their Jewishness need not all be the same. Some would not even regard themselves as Jewish, some would be assimilated into the host culture, others would even be too young to understand what they were. It seems rather inaccurate to give their deaths a meaning in religious terms which they themselves might deny, or fail to understand.

This is not to suggest that an event can have religious significance only if the participants are aware of it. There is no point in arguing for such a thesis, because it is obviously wrong. It is quite sensible to argue that particular disasters which befell the Jewish people led to states of affairs which were of great value to that community, or at least the survivors of the persecuted community. Indeed, the rationale for the persecution is not limited to ultimate benefits to the Jews, but is made more general in terms of the example of faithfulness in the face of adversity for the benefit of all mankind. Even though the notion of a causal connection between the suffering and the eventual outcome might seem suspect, it is not supposed to be a contingent relationship anyway, so it hardly matters whether it forms part of a convincing historical account or not. What is at issue is whether the subsequent events are essentially marked by the suffering, and it is not in general too difficult to argue thus. The difficulty, though, lies not in the connection between the suffering and the result of the suffering, but in the need for the suffering in the first place. It might seem that there is no difficulty in arguing for the necessity of the suffering once it is accepted both that the result is beneficial and also irretrievably formed by the suffering. If the relationship were merely contingent there would be no difficulty in wondering whether the result might be attainable by other, less unpleasant, means. Yet we have accepted that the connection tends to be made in terms of a necessary connection, and as such it is not possible to have the outcome without the suffering. That would seem to terminate the discussion, since there is no point in regretting the cause if it is an essential precondition of a worthwhile result.

Something about this argument might strike us as rather worrying. Is it really acceptable for innocent people to suffer in order to produce an ultimately beneficial result, a result which is not going to benefit the sufferers themselves? Once one thinks about this question it becomes obvious that there are ways in which such suffering is acceptable. For example, I may take part in highly dangerous experiments in order to help humanity at large, and I may perish as a consequence. This form of behaviour is what we should normally classify as supererogatory, as going above and beyond the call of duty. This sort of activity is not a good example for what went on during events such as the Holocaust, though. The participants in that tragedy had no choice about their acceptance or otherwise of suffering. They found themselves immersed in a hostile and deadly prison. Some of the literature surrounding the Holocaust, especially that produced by Wiesel, talks in rather Christological terms about the victims, as though they had chosen their tragic role for the benefit of the rest of humanity. This does seem wildly inaccurate. Jesus certainly does seem to have chosen the role which was thrust upon him, and he was aware of the wider context within which his suffering took place. He was one person, and his suffering was designed to redeem the world. The slaughter of the millions of Jews and others in the Holocaust was very different. Here we have huge numbers of confused people who die in an apparently futile way, with no expectation of rising subsequently from the dead, and the connection between their suffering and the formation of the State of Israel does not address the issue at all of why they suffered. To suggest that the State owes its particular form of existence to the suffering is one thing, and to argue that the formation of the state explains or justifies the suffering is quite another, and it is important to be clear on this distinction.

As we have seen, the question of the purpose of the suffering is something which comes up time and time again in the literature, and what lies behind this discussion is often not so much the issue of suffering itself but the question of our relationship with God. There is often a tendency to look for a God who shares the status of a kind father, and then wonder why so many terrible things happen despite his omnipotence. On the other hand, one might take the presence of suffering to be evidence of a different kind of deity, one which relates to the world in more subtle and indirect ways. This comes out nicely in some of the work of Levinas. He refers to a book which he read on the sufferings of the fighters in the Warsaw Ghetto and he comments:

The perspective of victims in a world in disorder, which is to say, in a world where the good does not triumph, is suffering. Suffering reveals a God who, renouncing all helpful manifestation, appeals to the full maturity of the integrally responsible man ... The suffering of the just for a justice which is without triumph is lived concretely as Judaism. Israel – historic and carnal – has become once again a religious category. (*Difficile liberté*, p. 102)

It is worth quoting this passage because it illustrates very well a number of interconnected points which have been running through the general discussion. To react to terrible disasters like the Holocaust or its predecessors as though they provided evidence of the death or non-existence of God is to react in a childlike sort of way. It is to reject the existence of God because he is not the sort of God which we should like him to be. It bears marked similarities to disowning a child when he or she commits some major crime. There was a practice in some Jewish communities for a funeral ceremony to be initiated when a child acted in a way which set him or her beyond the pale of acceptability, such as perhaps marrying out of their faith. The parents would act as though the child were dead, and would go through the mourning ritual to emphasise their present and continuing lack of involvement in the future lives of their offspring. In some ways this is also evidence of the childish refusal to confront the action and cope with it which is manifested by the believers who come to refuse to continue their belief because God has 'let them down' with the sort of things he has allowed to occur. Both the disowning of the child and the disowning of God fail, since the relationship between the individuals concerned persists despite their refusal to continue to acknowledge it. The parents pretend that the child is no longer their child, and yet nothing they can do can prevent their child from being their child.

It might be argued that there is not much difference between a God who hides his face and a God who is not there at all. Yet a God who hides his face gives his creatures the opportunity to take responsibility for the actions of themselves and the natural world, in so far as the latter is under their control. They may come to regard suffering as not something which arrives from without the world, nor as something which has as its point the redemption of some part of human experience, but as part and parcel of our experience of a topsy-turvy world in which there are good people and evil people, and where the former do not often manage to control the activities of the latter. Levinas suggests that living a Jewish life is trying to live virtuously without any guarantee that the virtuous life will be superior in material terms to the lifestyle of the vicious. Levinas would use this sort of argument to suggest that traumatic experiences such as the Holocaust do not throw doubt on religion, but on the contrary on the absence of religion, on humanism. Humanism is based upon the idea of a basic set of characteristics shared by all human beings, a notion which is supposed to collapse when confronted by the horrors of the Holocaust, when human beings acted in a way previously believed to be unimaginable. What the Holocaust demonstrated was the need to move towards a more sophisticated notion of the relationship between God and the world, a relationship which places far more reliance upon the ability of the world to go awry without the direct intervention of the deity. By contrast with the humanist who would talk in terms of a basic notion of human nature existing throughout history and acting as a foundation to the various historical changes which occur, we might think of history as revealing the necessity to reinterpret continually the relationship which God has with his world, and that reinterpretation might itself be part of history.

When we look at the Bible we find a variety of accounts of suffering and the role which God plays in the events of the world. Some of these accounts represent God as intervening directly to help people, and the most famous perhaps of these accounts in the *akedah*, the sending of the angel in the nick of time to prevent Abraham sacrificing his son Isaac to God in accordance with his original instructions. It is easy to represent this incident as a test, and the virtuous Abraham is rewarded by God when he passes his test. His faithfulness to God is proved, and God prevents any harm coming to him as a result. Yet this is very different from the many incidents of which we are aware, where pious and faithful individuals have apparently been put to the test, have passed it with flying colours and yet have not in any way avoided the sufferings which one might have expected God to remit.

One might say that the *akedah* incident is a moving example of how God might relate to the faithfulness of his followers, yet it certainly does not represent the only way in which that relationship can be expressed. Were it to be the case that God always intervened to help those deserving of help, our adherence to him would take on the nature of a prudential relationship. It would be a means to a particular beneficial end, and it might be thought that that entirely misrepresents the nature of the relationship. This brings us back to the parent disowning his child when he offends their religious principles. The parent expects the child will continue to behave in a certain way, and once this expectation is not fulfilled the parent refuses to acknowledge the child as his child. Yet there is more to the relationship between parents and children than the mutual fulfilment of expectations. A child who offends a parent is still the child of the parent. *That* relationship has not changed, although other aspects of the relationship may now be different. For a parent to insist that once the child has acted in a certain way he is no longer the child of the parent is to over-simplify the nature of the relationship between them. It might be argued that the individual who expects every example of the relationship between God and human beings to replicate the *akedah* story is guilty of similar over-simplification. Even if God hides his face, he is still there, and his links with his world persist even where he decides not to make them manifest. This is not to advocate the continuation of blind faith despite everything which life can throw at us, although there might be something to be said for such an attitude from a religious point of view, but rather for a more sophisticated understanding of the relationship between us and God. Just as the parent who has been offended by his child has to reassess his links with that child, so the believer who is astounded at what God permits to happen in the world has to reassess his relationship with God. He may decide that he does not want to have any further relationship with God, but that is very different from deciding that there *is* no further relationship. It may be that we do not have the ability to make decisions about that at all.

We might see these different accounts of the role of suffering as different ways of approaching the same phenomenon, with some accounts having privileged status as compared with others. Or they could all be aspects of the same thing, regarded from different points of view. Some might be seen as heavily flawed and to be replaced by others, and different interpreters would argue over which are to replace which others. There is certainly a whole variety of ways of approaching these texts. We have remarked on the strangeness of regarding the Bible as a system of arguments, very much the view in the Islamic world, and this is often not because there are no such arguments, but because there are too many of them. There are so many arguments presenting such a series of contrary positions that one is often at a loss to take them seriously as arguments. Some recent hermeneutic approaches are very impressed by the variety of readings which biblical texts can have, and one of the most fertile texts to take here is the Book of Job. Virtually anyone who reads this Book will wonder how to reconcile the different parts of it, and he will not be surprised at the speculation concerning different authors and traditions being combined in the same text. Although the way in which this book is taken pays more attention to its literary qualities than its demonstrative power in much modern interpretation, it is worth looking at some of the leading approaches to the Book in order to see whether there are important and interesting arguments which arise as a result of the work of the hermeneuticists, which are sadly unavailable to those more concerned with the philosophical aspects of the text.

One of the most interesting and challenging contributions to Job is Bruce Zuckerman's *Job the Silent*, which argues that the most relevant text to read with Job is *Bontsye the Silent*, a familiar Yiddish story in which an individual who has been unfortunate throughout his life and yet virtuous and patient dies and is greeted by a great fanfare in heaven. While on earth he was regarded as a very minor character, in heaven he is obviously designed for a leading role, and his simplicity persists to the end, when he is asked what it is that he would like and he gives a reply in terms of food and drink of a very simple nature. Most readers of this short and moving story have taken it to praise the simplicity of Bontsye. Here is an individual who has behaved well and was continually done out of his just deserts. Yet he did not complain, he settled into a humble and obscure existence of poverty and exploitation, and after his death received his eventual just reward. Even then he is so simple in nature that he cannot think of anything more exotic to request than a hot roll with fresh butter for breakfast every morning. Most readers take the story to be a delightful evocation of what it is to live a simple and virtuous life, and to contrast the ways in which such people are treated in this world with the respect in which they will be held in the next life. Bontsye remains simple right to the end, even when he can see how important he is in the afterlife. He is regarded as the patient sufferer, humbly accepting every possible humiliation in this life, and just as humbly accepting his just reward in the next life. Now, it will not have escaped the reader's notice that Job is often regarded in much the same way. Zuckerman argues that for both Bontsye and Job this interpretation omits a vital aspect of the text, the fact that it is an exercise in parody. The story of Bontsye the Silent parodies the humble Jew, accepting every persecution and never losing trust in providence. The story of Job parodies the notion of the patient individual who responds to every turn of the screw by praising the owner of the castle in which the torture chamber is located. After all, the notion of Job the patient is very much later than the Book of Job itself, and resides in the New Testament Epistle of James. When we look at the Book of Job itself Job seems to be anything but patient, constantly arguing, complaining, challenging, moaning and so on – all activities which, given his circumstances, he is perfectly entitled to adopt.

The idea of comparing the Book of Job with a relatively modern and entirely different Yiddish text is an exciting one, and shows how revealing the interpretive tools of literary criticism can be when applied to religious texts. Other writers have attempted to deconstruct the Book of Job, which involves showing how it undermines the philosophy which at the same time it puts forward. David Clines is a representative of this approach, and he relates it to the Book of Job. He argues that the book deconstructs itself at least in two ways. The position of most of the book is that the doctrine of retribution is false (since Job is virtuous and does not therefore deserve to suffer) and yet the finale of the book claims that Job is rewarded for his piety, which is to assert that the doctrine of retribution is true. Secondly, the emphasis in the book on the uniqueness of Job's situation reduces drastically its point as a doctrinal work. The dissonances in the text make it possible for pious readers to identify themselves with Job by creatively reinterpreting the very uniqueness which makes it inappropriate for anyone to identify with him. Although the deconstructionist will insist that the book does not incorporate just one main message, but rather a variety of different and contrary messages, they accept that the beauty of the language makes it quite feasible for readers to identify with some passages and with some messages while not thinking seriously about others, those which would interfere with the reading which they want to extract. These readers do not go wrong, they just do not take on board at the same time the whole gamut of readings which are available to them in the text, since were they to do so they would regard the book as setting them a problem, not giving them a solution. It is not the role of the deconstructionist to legislate over the number of meanings which readers can find in a text, but rather to discuss the ways in which the available variety of meanings relate to each other and what they say about the structure of the text. It is worth noticing, though, that the grounds for our adherence to a particular reading of the text are not that they reveal the truth, since there is no access to any such product through reading texts, but they are rather aesthetic or quasi-aesthetic, depending upon what we find most fitting or moving. The scientific task of deconstructing the text is a very different activity from that involved in looking for spiritual guidance in it, and both activities are perfectly valid and can go on at the same time, and even by the same people, so long as they are all aware of the differing purposes for which their hermeneutic methods are designed.

It is important to be clear that the sorts of question which arise for the deconstructionist are often very different from those which arise for the philosopher. The latter is more concerned with the way in which religious texts work as arguments, although it is important to understand that arguments in religion may well have a different way of putting the points they make as compared with arguments in other areas of cultural life. The deconstructionist sees the religious text as rather akin to a novel or a painting, and countenances a whole range of possible readings which make sense or fit given the canons of literary or aesthetic criticism. Such an approach can be very revealing, and it can uncover forms of argument which were previously hidden, but it has its limitations as compared with the philosophical approach. For one thing, the rules of how to proceed are not common to all deconstructionists, and one often wonders what constraints there are on the subjectivity of the interpretation when one confronts a burgeoning variety of readings, all of which appear to be rather personal. Perhaps the biggest problem, though, is in the relation which philosophers seek between their arguments and some notion of objective truth. For deconstructionists this latter is a bit of a chimera, and gets in the way of a multiplicity of readings. We grow up, according to the deconstructionist, when we put away childish things like the belief in an objective standard of truth. In some ways this misrepresents what the believer is after when the Book of Job is consulted. The fact that this Book is in the canon tends to mean that it gains a degree of respect from the believer, since it is not in the canon for arbitrary reasons but due to the importance of what it has to say. What it has to say does not have to be obvious or simple – indeed, it might be argued that if it were obvious or simple it could not possibly be of religious interest. There must be a close relationship between what the book has to say and the truth, however that is interpreted, for the believer to be able to repose any trust in it. It is very different from considering a work of art, even a very moving work of art.

Now, it might be argued that works of art can have just as much significance for the lives of those who observe them as religious texts do for believers. Indeed, there is no need to separate them, since a believer might regard an aesthetic object as sharing in the glory of God. Works of art can help us grasp reality in just the same sort of way as religious works, in that they can be thought of as giving access to the way in which things are. There is going to be a difficulty in seeking to differentiate between them by looking at the authority which supports them, since both works of art and religious texts are based on authority, and the authority can be regarded as giving the object its status in both cases. There are important differences between them too. There is such a notion as truth in aesthetics, but it plays a different role from its place in the Bible. It is important for the sense of the Bible that the events which it describes are thought of as actually taking place. That is far from saying that all that we can say about those events is that they took place, since many commentators would argue that the events themselves have a much broader significance than being merely historical events – they represent very important aspects of human life and its contact with the divine. Job is taken to be a particular person, with a background and a future, and the Book is not supposed to be just a story. It is supposed to be a description of what took place a long time ago. Now, works of art are not quite the same. Although they can depict historical events, the actual existence of those events do not play an important part in the works of art themselves. They are not guides to what happened; rather, they are representations of what happened, on occasion, from the point of view of a creative artist. It would not be appropriate, for example, for God to criticise Blake's painting of Job for its inaccuracy compared with the original. What Blake tries to do is to sum up in the painting the experiences and feelings which beset Job, and the success or otherwise of the painting do not depend upon the accuracy which it has with respect to the historical individual himself.

Biblical texts should not, then, be seen as akin to works of art if this means that the issue of truth does not arise. The deconstructionist can be allowed to use that particular hermeneutic on the text since it does uncover a whole web of possible meanings, but as well as approaching the text in that way we must also insist that as a religious text the question of truth is paramount. The advantage of the deconstructionist technique with regard to the Book of Job is that it represents nicely the sorts of reaction to suffering which occur from a human point of view. When we suffer we often fail to be able to think clearly about what is happening to us. Both our body and our mind may be affected. If a major disaster affects us, perhaps involving the loss of close friends or relatives, a long mourning and bereavement process may be involved in which we are uncertain about how our feelings are moving and what is really happening to us. For example, there is some evidence to suggest that immediately after a death of someone close to an individual, that individual may not appreciate or feel the significance of the loss until some time later, when depression sets in for apparently no reason. We are no longer proximate to the death, and so there is confusion all round as to the cause of the depression. The individual is working through her feelings, and over a period acquires a whole range of different attitudes to the same event. This is far more like the attitudes which people may have towards works of art than it is to the attitudes which we have towards historical events, and the way in which the deconstructionist describes us as playing about with different readings of a text seems to apply nicely to the ways in which we may try a variety of interpretations of a particular disaster. One of the brilliant aspects of the Book of Job is its accurate representation of the confused and confusing way in which we both cast around for explanations of our suffering and hurl accusations at others for what is happening to us. This is something with which many people can identify, since it represents so well how we often react in such circumstances.

So it is a characteristic of suffering that there is a host of conflicting and pressing emotions in the mind of the sufferer. Some of these can be represented in terms of an argument, while others cannot. This suggests that we should be rather wary of the deconstructionist enterprise when it deals with aspects of suffering. To see the Book of Job as a parody, for example, and to see it producing doctrines which it then subverts is not difficult. After all, the Book replicates many of the contradictions implicit in suffering, and so does not present just one clear message. If it did present just one clear message, it would be of little interest for us. It is easy to find evidence of subversion in a text which describes someone in the grip of evil. The sufferer is floundering about in a sea of misfortune and tries to find a solution to his problems in a whole variety of contrary directions. It is not difficult, then, to look at these different directions and show that the Book subverts itself, since it advocates a variety of answers which cannot all be true together. As we have argued, it is the complexity of the Book of Job which gives it its point. If Job really was patient and just accepted quietly everything which happened to him, the Book would be anodyne and useless as compared with its reception over the last few millennia. It is not so much that the Book of Job subverts itself but that suffering subverts itself. Extreme suffering which strikes at every core of the existence of a person, the sort of suffering which afflicts Job, produces reactions which are often not well considered or weighed. That is why we get the effusion of ideas and accusations which we find in the Book.

It is important to appreciate that what Job wants is an answer to his leading question, namely, why is God permitting a virtuous person to suffer? He asks, indeed *demands* from God some explanation of this state of affairs. He is not asking for a reading of his situation which will help him to cope with it, although he does eventually receive such a reading. Job insists upon a response from God, and once he has it he is satisfied. God responds by emphasising his power as compared with the power of human beings. Yet this is not exactly new information for Job. He knew all this before, and in fact it is the interpretation of God as omniscient and omnipotent which makes the questions Job hurls at heaven meaningful. What is new is that God actually responds to Job, he shows that he is aware of Job's plight and is involved with his arguments. Job is concerned with the truth, and once God contacts him he knows that God is implicated in his life and is aware of his problems. Job concludes that he may not perceive the purpose of the sufferings which he undergoes, but he is consoled by the thought that there is a divine plan into which they fit. Whether or not we think this is a successful strategy for Job to adopt is not at issue now, but what is at issue is the nature of what he is seeking. He is seeking the truth about suffering. The truth about suffering is not to be found in the confused and ill-informed ramblings before the contact with God, since these are just an aspect of suffering, not an explanation of it. It is a mistake, then, to see Job as engaged upon finding an interpretation of his predicament which satisfies him. He wants to find an interpretation which is true.

Now, it might be thought that this is hardly fair on the hermeneuticists. Many commentators have remarked upon the fact that Job seems to resolve his queries in a suspiciously sudden manner, once he acknowledges the overwhelming power of God, and as a consequence he receives the generous reward of double his losses. This 'solution' has seemed to many not to be a solution at all, but instead a rather arbitrary refusal to carry on with the charges against the deity. That is, it looks as though the sort of answer which satisfies Job might not satisfy someone else, and so the analysis of the Book as a literary text might be enough to reveal its structure. The sort of answer which suits Job would not suit another sort of enquirer, and there is no point in asking which answer is 'true', since there is no objective standard of truth which stands over and against the variety of available answers. A different sufferer might have been satisfied only with an answer based on God's acceptance of his guilt, while yet another might have been satisfied with no reply at all. This does look very much as though we are confronting a work of art and asking for the different reactions which we have to it. This would undermine the argument that Job was looking for an objectively true answer to his problem, or at least that this is what he could get. All that he could hope for is an answer which would satisfy him.

In a celebrated prayer Rabbi Levi Yitzhak of Berdichev says 'Master of the Universe! I do not ask you to reveal to me the mysteries of your ways. I could not understand them. I do not want to know why I suffer, but I do want to know that I suffer for your sake.' This is not really what Job is after. He would agree with the modification of the prayer by Judah Magnes which runs 'I do not want to know why I suffer ... but only if you know that I suffer.' Job's God does not tell him that he suffers for *kiddush ha-shem*, but only that God is great and is aware of Job. Here we have a range of positions which different thinkers find acceptable to them, and they all differ from each other, albeit in rather subtle ways. Yet it is important to realise that behind each position lies an argument. Rabbi Levi implies that the sufferings of the Jews are acceptable only if they are for a purpose. If the Jews worship God, and if they are murdered because of their very Jewishness, then that state of affairs is acceptable only if that suffering has a purpose which God at least recognises. Magnes is unhappy with this position given the experience of the Holocaust, and he cannot think how the sufferings of the Jews in Europe could possibly be for the sake of God. He is looking for some evidence that God is at least present to observe the sufferings of his people, since were he to be unconcerned about those sufferings and unwilling to intervene on the side of the Jews we might seriously question the point of adherence to him. As we have argued throughout, Job too is more concerned to establish the presence of God than the precise nature of that presence.

What is behind these differences? No doubt the psychological constitution of the individuals concerned enters into the causal account of why they go in different directions on this issue, but there is far more to the story than this. There are good arguments available for each alternative, and such arguments have as their criteria of validity the perfectly objective standard of rationality. Magnes would argue that it is difficult to regard the death of patently innocent Jews as always for the sake of God, a point which is emphasised during an event such as the Holocaust, and that if we are to hold on to the notion of a God interested in the fate of his people he must at the very least be aware of that fate. If he is even abstracted from that fate he really is out of the picture as far as religion is concerned. Now, there are surely emotional reasons behind such an argument, and Rabbi Levi no doubt has personal reasons for proposing his prayer, but it is important to understand that what they are engaged upon is not the publicisation of a personal position. They are seeking to establish the truth of our relationship with God, with a God who is able to prevent the horrors which are inflicted upon his people and who nonetheless does nothing, or appears to do nothing, to save them. If we insist upon regarding their arguments as nothing more than rationalisations of emotional attitudes we do them a great disservice. For these thinkers, like Job, are immersed in suffering and they try to view that suffering calmly and objectively, so that they can draw some general conclusions about it which will be of value to those who are wondering how to combine their belief in God with their experience of the evil inflicted upon innocent people.

To say that we should respect the arguments of those Jewish thinkers who have sought to discuss suffering is not to say that we should treat everything they have produced as though they were arguments. This would be a great mistake. There is clearly much in the Book of Job and in the prayers we have just discussed which is very far from being just an argument. A whole range of tasks is supposed to be carried out by a piece of liturgy or a biblical text, and in this book we have concentrated upon those aspects of the works which can be characterised in terms of an argument. The deconstructionists make a very valuable point when they direct our attention to the effect which the disparate arguments of a text have on the reader. Reading the Book of Job may force a reader to challenge her fixed ideas about providence and examine the consistency of retribution with the early fate of Job. She may, on reading the conclusion, laugh at how ridiculous retribution seems when Job ends up with more than he started. Clearly the intermingling of the different arguments, poems, legal metaphors, quasi-historical accounts and so on has an effect upon the reader which is capable of making a considerable impact. The very different approaches in the text are likely to appeal to very different readers, and every reader is liable to be moved or persuaded by at least some part of the Book. The deconstructionist shows how the combination of different arguments and themes has a greater impact than is attainable merely through the arguments and themes separately considered. The whole is made up of the parts, but the parts do not explain precisely the character of the whole, since that character is formed by the playful manner in which we can relate the parts to each other to create a gamut of wholes.

The argument so far has been that it is important to distinguish between the arguments within a biblical text and the rest of that text, for while the arguments may play a role in the text which is not entirely dependent upon their demonstrative force, it is possible to separate out the rational and the emotional aspects of the text. An argument which purports to be rational is assessable in its own terms, in terms of rationality. It may help us understand the general issue of suffering, while not helping us actually to apply this understanding to our own situation. Let me give an example. Someone may discover that he or she has but a short time to live, and may be shocked by this since he or she is quite young. This particular individual may be a man with responsibilities to a growing family and on the threshold of an interesting career. There are a number of ways in which he can react to this news, and I give just two: he may resign himself to his fate, continue his adherence to God and await the end with a certain calmness; on the other hand, he may curse God, rail against his ill-fortune, and do everything he can to avert the evil hour of his death. Neither of these reactions is any more rational than the other. They both represent perfectly legitimate ways of coping with the drastic news which the victim has received. When we consider the different reactions which are represented here towards God we can say a bit more about the logical strength of the alternative attitudes. The person who puts his entire trust in God despite his sufferings is implying that the notion of God as a person who should prevent harm to the innocent is inappropriate. It does not matter at all what God allows to happen, this believer will continue to praise and worship him. The person who blames God for his sufferings implies that if God has brought about his pain then it is God who is to blame for it. This is even the case where God could have prevented it and chose not to do so. We can see why different people might come to different conclusions about the responsibility which God has for their sufferings, and we can understand why they might try to deal with their suffering in different ways. But the aspect of their reaction which is based upon a particular conception of God is not just a matter of their personal choice. It is based upon an argument for a particular view of the deity and of his relationship with life on this world, and that argument has to be assessed entirely in terms of the criteria of rationality.

One might doubt this. After all, when Judah Magnes extends and alters the prayer of Rabbi Levi he does not do this because he knows something which his predecessor did not know. Although the Holocaust is a particularly unpleasant kind of horror, the rabbi was also well acquainted with horrors in Eastern Europe during his own day, and in the past, and he certainly knew of many cases in which pious and virtuous Jews were slaughtered during pogroms merely on account of their Jewishness. The rabbi argues in his prayer that it is enough if we can know that these deaths play a part in God's plan. We cannot know what that plan is, since we are mortal and finite, but we can have confidence that whatever form the plan takes, we fit into it somewhere. For Magnes this is not sufficient. The notion of a plan into which so many innocent deaths could fit is nugatory. We need to know at least that God is aware of the deaths, that he knows and cares about them, and we can then reconcile ourselves to the fact that he does not do anything to prevent them. Why not? Perhaps we might think that God has a purpose here which we cannot fathom. Perhaps it is because he wants us to have the autonomy to make our own decisions and then suffer when some of those decisions go against us, thinking here in terms of the whole of humanity. What it is important to grasp about these different positions is that they are based upon arguments and are not just emotional reactions to the situations in which people find themselves. After all, when we think in terms of the discussions concerning the appropriate phrasing of the prayer, we are not talking about individual responses to suffering. On the contrary, a successful prayer has to encapsulate a response which has been universalised, and part of that process involves the underpinning by rational argument. It may be difficult to examine the argument apart from its ceremonial or historical baggage, but it is there, and it must be there if the response to the suffering is to be more than just emotional.

What aspects of a prayer are universal and general? It is true that part of a prayer may be a personal communication, or an attempt at such a communication, with God. Such prayers can even be entirely unique and individual in construction, and some believers feel that genuine prayers have to take such a form, since otherwise there is a tendency to repeat, parrot-fashion, familiar phrases without concentrating upon their meaning. What is important about all prayers, though, is that they are universalisable. Anyone standing in the position of the supplicant would be entitled to make the same request of the deity, or would be allowed to respond to God in the same sort of way. In so far as the statement in the prayer is universalisable it is also rational. To a certain extent we can use this criterion to assess the rationality of prayers. Someone who goes into a race and prays for victory might be criticised for that action. Is God really going to be interested in who wins the race? Is it reasonable to expect God to listen to our requests on such occasions? It is not, because the principle behind a race is that the best competitor wins, and divine intervention to work against that principle would damage the whole institution of sporting competition. In addition, any participant is entitled to pray to God for victory, and God cannot realise all such requests, however deserving the candidates. Of course, we could rationally pray before a race, but not for victory. We could pray for support in the ability to produce the best performance of which we are capable, and we could assert our understanding that the competition was part of the world which God created and in which we understand our role to be one as a created and dependent being. Every participant could quite rationally adhere to such a prayer. From an emotional point of view we might feel better if we undergo certain religious rituals before the race which we think will attract God's help. From a rational point of view we are able to work out which aspects of prayer can properly be put to God. We can then assess those aspects of prayer which call upon God to save us from evil and suffering apart from the emotional aspects which are designed to appeal to another feature of religion, the specifically arational and individual.

This comes out more clearly when we consider one of the most

famous incidents of martyrdom in Jewish history, the death of Rabbi
Akiva. He was burnt at the stake, and while reciting the *Shema*ᶜ before
death, as Jews are supposed to do, he is said to have reflected with joy
that for the first time he understood the part of the familiar prayer
which refers to loving God with all one's might. What we are supposed
to admire here is that Akiva was able to abstract himself from a very
unpleasant situation and use it to increase his understanding of his
relationship with God. A natural reaction to such a situation would be
to pray for rescue and to expect God to save one from such agonies of
incineration. Yet Akiva did not do this, he accepted that what was
happening to him was part of God's plan and used the experience in
what he took to be a positive way, to improve his grasp of his religion.
The angels who watched Akiva's suffering are said to have com-
plained that this seems to be a strange reward for upholding the
Torah, to which they received the rather dusty response from God
that the world would be turned to water if they said another word
(*Menaḥot* 29b). It is interesting to compare Job and Akiva, since both
were rewarded for their sufferings, although in different ways. Akiva
is supposed by Jewish tradition to have gone through life and the
afterlife in a particularly blissful manner, his rather gruesome death
notwithstanding. There is no doubt that if one examines his reported
comments upon important issues in religion a steadfast belief in the
justice of God manifests itself. Job is rewarded in a different way, by
coming into contact with God. Yet the interesting thing about the
comparison is that they both take up very different positions on
providence. The only parts of the Book of Job which Akiva thought
praiseworthy were the beginning and the end, the parts in which Job
does not question God's justice. Job was mistaken in questioning his
suffering, since others suffered much more (*Semachot* 8; *Midrash
Tehillim* 26: 2). He does not go quite as far as Raba in suggesting that
dust should be stuffed in Job's mouth (*Baba Bathra* 16a) for blaming
God for the evil in the world, but he certainly doubts the validity of
the way in which Job questions and challenges God. An appropriate
attitude to God is acceptance of what happens and a continuing
faithfulness to him despite everything which might happen to us.

It might seem strange that both Akiva and Job are rewarded, since
they are so different in their attitudes to their sufferings. Akiva is a
willing martyr, confident that he is dying for the sanctification of the
holy name, whereas Job is a most unwilling sufferer, complaining all
the time of the injustice and unfairness of his travails. On the one

hand, they are not as far apart as one might think. The martyrdom of Akiva might seem to be the epitome of supererogation, in that he goes further in the defence of his religion than one might expect the average believer to go. On the other hand, it might be thought that given his overriding belief in the justice of God, his sufferings could be put within a context which makes them understandable, albeit not immediately by him. However nasty the things which happen to him are, he can regard them as part of a rational and ultimately beneficial organisation of the world. This makes his adherence to a strong faith in God less praiseworthy, since he refuses to admit any evidence which runs counter to his view of reality. Job, by contrast, is not at all sure of the universality of divine providence, and yet he is not prepared to waver in his belief in the existence of God. Whatever happens to him, he is not going to challenge this very basic belief, despite his very real doubts about the role of justice in the world and his demand that God must come and answer his questions. When he insists on an appearance by God to answer the charge he is not asking for evidence that God exists, but only that God is concerned with the events in this world. Perhaps when we compare the attitudes of Job and Akiva in this way we can see why they might both be regarded as meritorious. The very patient Akiva displays perfect confidence and trust in the justice of God. The rather impatient Job displays complete trust in the existence of God but is confused by what God allows to happen in the world. Perhaps this is why it is said that had Job not questioned and rebelled against his sufferings, he would figure today in the *Amidah*. Jews would say, 'The God of Abraham, Isaac, Jacob and Job' (*Pesikta Rabati* 47).

When we consider the majority of the Jews who both today and in the past have suffered we are more likely to assimilate them to Job than to Akiva. Job is confused and angry during his sufferings, and so are most people. Most believers will start to question the basis of their faith in God if that God does not seem to do anything to help them when they are in peril. It is important to differentiate between the standpoint of Akiva on this issue and the normal orthodox position. The latter is quite simple. When there is suffering, it is for a purpose. The eventual purpose is *Geulah*, redemption, which can be achieved through *Teshuvah*, repentance, for the sins which led to the original expulsion from Israel. Through their sufferings the Jewish people purify themselves and bring nearer the time of the Messiah. Although Akiva has a deep personal belief in the ultimately beneficial organisation of the world, he does not tend to go in for such crude attempts at apologetics. The notion of God's goodness and its effect upon the world is not something one can perceive directly in the workings of the world. It is worth adding here that a world in which God's hand was as visible as it is to members of, say, the Lubavitch movement, would be a crass and banal place in which to live. The whole point of coming close to God and his organisation of the world is that both he and the organisation are far from obvious, and we have to work to get an appropriate idea of how they are. This working towards the idea is not just a theoretical process but also involves practical action, following the Torah, and continually trying to develop and refine our ideas about the nature of the deity and his world. Akiva's actions and words are impressive because they go against the appearance of the world. If they were in sympathy with a simple view of Jewish history according to which the hand of God in the world is easily visible then we should respect Akiva less.

Akiva and Job have different views on the nature of evil and suffering, and yet they are both rewarded. How can we explain this? It may well be because they both understand that what the issue of evil and suffering is really about is our relationship with God. This issue is in fact a misplaced metaphor. It seems to concern evil and suffering, but this can be very misleading. The development of this issue in Jewish philosophy throws light not so much on the nature of evil but more on the nature of God and on our relationship with him. What both Job and Akiva end up emphasising is the way in which we should relate to God as to someone who is the source of grace. The doctrine of retribution, with its basis on a balance between virtues and rewards, completely misunderstands the way in which God is to be understood. He need not have created the world at all; nothing made him do it. He need not now respond to our wishes or punish our faults. Akiva has a perfect belief in the divine grace and its impact upon the world. Job has to be shown that he has to accept what the nature of this grace is, and then he too comes to believe in it and in its role in our lives. Neither of them can be much more specific than this, though, and for an important reason. Since it is entirely up to the deity what he does and how he reacts to us, if he reacts at all, it is impossible to construct nice neat rules which encapsulate divine behaviour. The demand for such rules is a function of the confusion which many people have when talking about the deity as compared with talking about something contingent like a human being. We cannot describe

God in the same way that we can describe ourselves. We can see how we are to a degree responsible for evil in the world, and we can see how we can prevent it. We cannot legitimately move from this sort of language to language about God and his link with such evil. Although the relationship between these two levels of language might not be as equivocal as Maimonides argues, we are nonetheless confronted with two very different ways of talking, and we must beware assimilating them. They are distinct, and their distinctiveness must be preserved.

Associating God with our qualities is for many Jewish thinkers an exercise of idolatry. It is bringing God down to the level of his creatures and then wondering why he seems to exhibit imperfection. Yet 'whoever denies idolatry is as if he has fulfilled the whole Torah' (*Ḥullin* 5a) and 'anyone who repudiates idolatry is called a Jew' (*Megillah* 13a). Neither of these pronouncements is entirely true, of course, but they emphasise the significance of abandoning idolatry and all that goes with it for Judaism. The questions which have arisen with respect to evil and suffering are important not just in their own terms but also in the way in which they direct our minds towards trying to understand our relationship with God, If there is any common thread running through the discussion of evil and suffering in Jewish philosophy it is that a reorientation is necessary towards an improved and more accurate definition of our position *vis-à-vis* the deity. This might seem to be a terrible evasion. It is hard enough trying to solve the problem of evil within a Jewish context, and harder still trying to work out what our relationship with God is. The problem of evil is difficult and if its solution involves a grasp of the nature of God and our place in his creation then we seem to be seeking to throw light on the obscure by bringing into play the even more obscure. We seem to be trying to answer the question of the justification of evil and suffering by posing yet another question, namely, the nature of our relationship to God. We have seen how Jewish philosophers have addressed themselves to these two questions and if there is any result of the enquiry it is that we have a more complex understanding of the nature of these two questions. Yet is it satisfactory to set out to answer one question by posing another question, an even harder one? Perhaps the only thing we can say here is that it satisfied Job and so it might be good enough for us.

What we have to recall here is that Job was not satisfied with an answer, because Job did not get an answer. He got a response, which is entirely different, but it was after all a response to his question, in that he was insisting upon a reply by God to his question. The reply was not a solution to the problem contained in the question, but this is not what Job was pursuing. He was interested rather in establishing contact with God, so that he would no longer have to feel that he was entirely alone in his sufferings. To solve his questions about the existence of evil in the world and of innocent suffering he first of all had to establish the nature of the relationship he had with his creator. As we have seen, the subsequent discussion in Jewish philosophy takes Job's point seriously here and concentrates upon the nature of the relationship which he had in mind, albeit that different thinkers have different approaches to that topic. Once we realise that the problem of evil is connected with the problem of understanding our relationship with God, Job implies, we are on the right track. Where that track takes us is another question, and we have seen a variety of answers by different philosophers, but what Job thought was the most important thing of all was to set off on the right road. He might not manage to get to the end of the road, but his destination was actually to get to the right road, not to its end. Once one is on the right road one has established a certain relationship with God, and the next stage is to work out how what one can know about God explains the way things are in the world. The discussion in this book has looked at the treatment in Jewish philosophy of these two stages, and their link with the original formulation of the problem in the Book of Job. Since Job first described the problem it has been redefined and refined by his successors, yet this extended period of philosophical enquiry has not essentially changed the problem itself, so that we have been observing a continual interrogation of the logic of evil from the perspective of changing philosophical perspectives. These all represent phases of Jewish philosophy and make up a fascinating treatment of how to try to reconcile the existence of innocent suffering with a loving and powerful God.

Bibliography

Altmann, A., *Moses Mendelssohn: a Biographical Study* (London, Routledge Kegan and Paul, 1973)

Bennett, J., *A Study of Spinoza's Ethics* (Cambridge University Press, 1984)

Berkovits, E., *Faith after the Holocaust* (New York, Ktav, 1973)

Brookner, A., *Latecomers* (London, Grafton, 1989)

Buber, M., *I and Thou* (Edinburgh, T. & T. Clark, 1937)

The Prophetic Faith, trans. C.Witton-Davies (New York, Macmillan, 1949)

Between Man and Man (London, Routledge Kegan and Paul, 1949)

Good and Evil: Two Interpretations. Includes *Right and Wrong* and *Images of Good and Evil* (New York, Scribner's, 1953)

'Replies to my Critics', in *The Philosophy of Martin Buber*, ed. P. Schilpp and M. Friedman (La Salle, Illinois, Open Court, 1967)

Carroll, L., *Through the Looking-Glass and What Alice Found There* (London, Macmillan, 1904)

Clines, D., 'Deconstructing the Book of Job', in *The Bible as Rhetoric: Studies in Biblical Persuasion and Credibility*, ed. M. Warner (London, Routledge, 1990) pp. 65–80

Cohen, A., *The Tremendum: a Theological Interpretation of the Holocaust* (New York, Crossroad, 1981)

Cohen, H., *Religion of Reason out of the Sources of Judaism*, trans. S. Kaplan (New York, Frederick Ungar, 1972)

Delahunty, R., *Spinoza* (London, Routledge, 1985)

Fackenheim, E., *God's Presence in History* (New York, New York University Press, 1970)

Gersonides, *The Commentary of Levi ben Gerson (Gersonides) on the Book of Job*, trans. and intro. A. Lassen (New York, Bloch Press, 1946)

Goodman, L., *On Justice: an Essay in Jewish Philosophy* (New Haven, Yale University Press, 1991)

Halevi, Judah, *Book of Kuzari*, trans. H. Hirschfeld (New York, Pardes, 1946)

Leaman, O., *An Introduction to Medieval Islamic Philosophy* (Cambridge University Press, 1985)

Averroes and His Philosophy (Oxford University Press, 1988)

Moses Maimonides (London, Routledge, 1990)

Leibowitz, Y., *The Faith of Maimonides*, trans. J. Glucker (New York, Adama, 1987)

252   Bibliography

Levinas, E., *Difficile liberté* (Paris, Albin Michel, 1983). Part trans. S. Goodhart, '"One Isaac waiting to be slaughtered": Halpern Leivick, the Holocaust and Responsibility', *Philosophy and Literature*, 16 (1992) pp. 88–105; pp. 101–2

Levi of Berdichev, Rabbi Isaac, in Bergman, S., *Faith and Reason: an Introduction to Modern Jewish Thought*, trans. A. Jospe, (New York, Schocken, 1961) p. 149

Magnes, J., in Bergman, S., *Faith and Reason: an Introduction to Modern Jewish Thought*, trans. A. Jospe (New York, Schocken, 1961), pp. 142–51

Maimonides, M., *The Eight Chapters of Maimonides on Ethics*, trans. J. Gorfinkle (New York, Columbia University Press, 1912)

The Guide of the Perplexed (University of Chicago Press, 1963)

Maybaum, I., *The Face of God after Auschwitz* (Amsterdam, Polak and Van Gennep, 1965)

Mendelssohn, M., *Jerusalem or on Religious Power and Judaism*, trans. A. Arkush (Hanover, University Press of New England, 1983)

The Spinoza Conversations between Lessing and Jacobi, trans. G. Vallée (Lanham, University Press of America, 1988)

Nozick, R., *Anarchy, State and Utopia* (Oxford, Basil Blackwell, 1990)

Philo, *Works*, ed. and trans F. Colson, G. Whitacker and R. Marcus, 12 vols. Loeb Classical Library, (Cambridge, Mass., Harvard University Press, 1929–62)

Rosenzweig, F., *Gesammelte Schriften* (Dordrecht, 1976–84)

The Star of Redemption, trans. W. Hallo (London, Routledge, Kegan & Paul 1972)

Rubenstein, R., *After Auschwitz: Radical Theology and Contemporary Judaism* (New York, Bobbs-Merrill, 1966)

Saadya Gaon, *The Book of Beliefs and Opinions*, trans. S. Rosenblatt (New Haven, Yale University Press, 1951)

The Book of Theodicy: Translation and Commentary on the Book of Job, trans. L. Goodman (New Haven, Yale University Press, 1988)

Spinoza, B., *Short Treatise on God, Man and his Well-Being*, trans. A. Wolf (London, Black, 1910)

The Collected Works of Spinoza, vol. 1, (Princeton University Press, 1985)

Wiesel, Elie, *Night*, trans. S. Rodway (New York, Avon Books, 1969)

A Jew Today, trans. M. Wiesel (New York, Random House, 1978)

Zuckerman, B., *Job the Silent: a Study in Historical Counterpoint* (Oxford University Press, 1991)

Further reading

An excellent bibliography of works connected with the Book of Job can be found in David J. A. Clines, *Word Biblical Commentary*, vol. xvii, *Job 1–20* (Dallas, Word Books, 1989)

Bleich, J., 'Duran's View of Providence', *Jewish Quarterly Review* 69 (1979) pp. 208–25

Braude, W., *Pesikta Rabbati*, trans. Braude (New Haven, Yale University Press, 1968)

Burrell, D., 'Maimonides, Aquinas and Gersonides on Providence and Evil', *Religious Studies* 20 (1984), pp. 335–51

Dienstag, J., 'Maimonides' Epistle on Martyrdom', *Kiryat Sepher* 56 (1981), pp. 356–68

Fackenheim, E., *The Jewish Thought of Emil Fackenheim: a Reader*, ed. and int. M. Morgan (Detroit, Wayne State University Press, 1987)
To Mend the World (New York, Schocken, 1989)
The Jewish Bible after the Holocaust: a Re-reading (Manchester University Press, 1990)

Glatzer, N. (ed.), *The Dimensions of Job* (New York, Schocken, 1969)
Essays in Jewish Thought (University of Alabama Press, 1978)

Goodman, L., 'Maimonides' Responses to Saadya Gaon's Theodicy and Their Islamic Background', in Brinner, W. and Ricks, S. (eds.), *Studies in Islamic and Judaic Traditions II* (Atlanta, Scholars Press, 1989), pp. 3–22

Gutiérrez, G., *On Job: God-talk and the Suffering of the Innocent* (New York, Orbis, 1987)

Hick, J., *Evil and the God of Love* (New York, Harper and Row, 1966)

Katz, S., *The Holocaust in Historical Context. Vol. I: The Holocaust and Mass Death before the Modern Age* (Oxford University Press, 1994)

Kushner, H., *When Bad Things Happen to Good People* (New York, Schocken, 1981)

Laytner, A., *Arguing with God: a Jewish Tradition* (New Jersey, Jason Aronson, 1990)

MacIntyre, A., *After Virtue: a Study in Moral Theory* (London, Duckworth, 1981)

Pines, S., 'Spinoza's Tractatus Theologico-Politicus, Maimonides and Kant', *Scripta Hierosolymitana*, 20 (1968), pp. 3–45

Raffel, C., 'Providence as Consequent upon the Intellect: Maimonides' Theory of Providence', *American Jewish Studies Review*, 12 (1987), pp. 25–71

Reines, A., 'Maimonides' Concepts of Providence and Theodicy', *Hebrew Union College Annual* 43 (1972), pp. 169–206

Riemer, J. (ed.), *Jewish Reflections on Death* (New York, Schocken, 1974)

Rosenberg, S., *Tov ve Ra^c behagut hayehudit* (Good and Evil in Jewish Thought) (Tel Aviv, Ministry of Defence, 1987)

Rubenstein, R. and Roth, J., *Approaches to Auschwitz: the Legacy of the Holocaust* (London, SCM, 1987)

Sirat, C., *A History of Jewish Philosophy in the Middle Ages* (Cambridge University Press, 1985).

Steiner, G., 'The Long Life of Metaphor: an Approach to the Shoah', *Encounter* 48:2 (1987), pp. 55–61

Touati, C., 'Les deux théories de Maimonide sur la providence', in Stein, S. and Loewe, R. (eds.), *Studies in Jewish Religion and Intellectual History* (University of Alabama Press, 1979), pp. 331–43

Tzevat, M., 'The Meaning of the Book of Job', *Hebrew Union College Annual* 37 (1966), pp. 73–106

Wolfson, H., *The Philosophy of Spinoza* (Cambridge, Mass., Harvard University Press, 1934)

    Philo: Foundations of Religious Philosophy in Judaism, Christianity and Islam (Cambridge, Mass., Harvard University Press, 1948)

Index

Some terms are so ubiquitous that they have not been indexed, and these are Jews, Judaism, relationship with God, theodicy, suffering, Job, religion and God.

Abraham 28–9, 85, 233, 247
Adam 85, 129–30, 133, 168, 221
afterlife 20, 24, 36, 50, 53–5, 57, 61, 72–4, 77, 92, 132, 154, 163, 173, 224, 235–6, 246
akedah 233–4
Akiva 82, 246–8
anger 126–7
anthropomorphism, *see* language
antisemitism 163
Aristotle, Aristotelian 8, 14, 34, 51, 65–8, 72, 86, 90–9, 102–6, 123, 139, 190
Ashʿarism 49–52, 54, 59, 61–3, 72
Averroes 65, 87, 102–3, 110–11, 113–15, 117–18
Avicenna 87, 109–10

Bennett, J. 136
Berkovits, E. 191–2, 206–7
Bildad 19–21, 23, 105–6
Buber, M. 165–84, 216, 220

Cain 168, 173, 221
children 21, 25–6, 41, 55, 58–60, 72, 75, 80, 149, 152, 172, 186, 194–6, 199, 206–7, 216, 232, 234
Christianity 24, 47, 95, 122, 150, 194–9, 231
Chrysippus 39
churban 192, 207
Cohen, A. 189–90, 193, 205, 218–19
Cohen, H. 157–64, 220
conatus 123–5, 127, 132
contemplation 90
covenant 1, 179, 209, 213, 215, 221, 223

Day of Atonement 158, 162
death 36, 53–4, 74, 76, 107, 130, 132, 136–7, 148–9, 152, 154, 158, 161, 163, 172–4, 189, 203, 205–6, 208, 217, 230, 232, 239, 246

Egypt, Egyptian 64, 71, 213, 226
Elihu 21–2, 55, 107–8
Eliphaz 19–21, 23, 26, 28, 105–6
emanation 80, 87
Enlightenment 146–7, 150–3, 156, 163, 165, 177, 202
Epicurus 72
erfahrende Philosophie 13, 17–18
esoteric 80–1
evil 1, 3–6, 8–10, 13, 15, 19, 28–32, 35–40, 44–7, 56–9, 65–6, 70–2, 79–81, 90, 99–101, 103–9, 112–20, 122, 127–31, 133–42, 144–5, 147–9, 151–2, 157, 168–74, 176–7, 179–80, 182–5, 190, 200, 202, 204–5, 209, 219–21, 233, 240, 242, 244–6, 248–50
exoteric 79–81, 103

Fackenheim, E. 187–9, 191, 207, 211, 214–18, 224
faith 5, 14, 21, 28, 44, 46, 67–8, 73, 76, 96, 103, 117, 119, 146–7, 155–6, 162, 176, 188–9, 191, 204, 208, 211, 214, 222–4, 227–9, 232, 234, 247
Farabi 51, 87
father, God as 55, 58, 75, 91, 172, 178, 200, 213, 232
fear 137
finite, finitude 16, 114, 118–20, 128, 131–2, 136–7, 140, 144, 148, 154, 161, 163, 173, 197, 199–200, 244
free will: human 14, 37–8, 72, 79, 82, 85, 92, 97, 115–17, 125, 136, 140, 144, 148, 160, 164, 180, 190–1, 199, 205–7, 219, 226, 244
freedom: God's 78, 147, 214

Galen 51, 70
Germany, Jewish life in 65, 146–7, 157, 165
Gersonides 102–23, 121–3, 220–1

255

Ghazali 51, 78, 110
good 2, 15, 29, 36–40, 57, 74, 77, 79, 81,
   93, 104–7, 112, 127–30, 133–4, 136,
   139, 148, 168–9, 172–3, 204, 212, 221,
   232–3, 248
Goodman, L. 91–8
grace 37, 38, 52, 54, 56, 77–8, 221, 229,
   248
grief 75, 143–4

Halevi 3, 190, 229
happiness 35, 74, 80–1, 89, 93, 99, 109,
   116, 132–4, 147, 153, 222
Hasidism 171, 183
Hegel, G. 217–18
hester panim 24, 178, 191, 232–4
history: general 157, 162, 185, 192, 198,
   207, 213, 229–30, 238–9
   Jewish 2, 13, 24, 107, 157, 162, 191,
   203–4, 207–8, 213, 216, 220, 225, 232,
   248
Holocaust 4, 24, 185–220, 224–5, 227–9,
   231–3, 241–2, 244, 248
humility 26, 127–8, 229

idolatry 28, 70–1, 91, 157, 163, 249
I–It 166–8
imagination 71–2, 74, 87, 89–90, 105,
   125–6, 133, 135, 169–70, 173–4
inclination: evil 89–90, 173
   good 89, 173
innocence, innocent 1–2, 5, 10–15, 19–27,
   36, 42, 57–8, 60–1, 106, 128, 186, 190,
   192, 196, 198, 201, 204–7, 208, 213,
   222–4, 231, 242, 244, 250
Islam 47–50, 64, 95, 144, 150, 235
Islamic theology (*kalam*) 48, 51
Israel 1–2, 4, 71, 187–9, 191–2, 194,
   202–3, 205, 207–8, 216, 220, 225–9,
   231–2, 247
I–Thou 166–8, 170–1, 183

Jesus 24, 47, 194, 196, 231
Jewish philosophy, *see* philosophy, Jewish
Job: Christian commentators on the
   Book 24–5, 27, 29, 47, 194–6,
   199–200, 236
   deconstruction of the Book 235–43
   Septuagint version of the Book 23, 236
   talmudic and midrashic comments on the
   Book 28–30, 50,52
   tragic character of the Book 25–6
justice: human 26, 49, 51, 58–9, 61, 63, 77,
   79, 92, 107, 113, 115–16, 158, 160, 163,
   178, 205, 210, 232

God's 11–12, 27, 41, 49–51, 53–6, 58–9,
   61–3, 72, 76–7, 79, 92, 96–8, 100, 113,
   115, 182, 208, 222, 246–7

Kafka, F. 170
kalam, see Islamic theology
Kant, I. 157, 161, 166
Karaites 48, 50
kiddush ha-shem 188, 191, 230, 241, 246
knowledge: God's 2, 6, 11, 14, 22, 26,
   35–6, 43, 54, 73, 77, 79, 81–2, 104, 106,
   108–11, 113–15, 119–20, 148, 200,
   222–3, 240
   human 11, 15, 22, 43, 86–7, 89, 108–10,
   113, 119–20, 133–4, 148, 177, 199–200,
   226
   of God 29, 56, 76, 83, 85, 89, 133, 178,
   210, 240

language: of the Bible 34–5, 37, 49, 65, 89,
   130, 169, 220–2, 235, 238–9, 242–3
   religious 6–10, 12, 14–18, 29–32, 47, 76,
   80, 86–7, 89, 91, 96, 100–1, 103, 115,
   131, 139, 141, 164, 177–8, 193–4, 237–8
law: religious 7, 36, 66, 73, 76, 79, 83, 86, 139,
   162, 167–8, 181, 204–7, 225–7, 229, 249
Leibowitz, Y. 85
Lessing, G. 149–151, 153, 163
Levi Yitzhak of Berdichev 241–2, 244
Levinas, E. 232–3
light 83, 161
love 16, 58, 84–5, 100, 133–4, 170, 190,
   199, 205, 246, 250
Lubavitch movement 248

Magnes, J. 241–2, 244
Maimonides 7, 49, 64–104, 109–15, 117,
   121–3, 132–3, 140–1, 144, 148, 154,
   157, 159, 169, 174–5, 177–8, 190, 202,
   205, 207, 225–7, 229
martyrs, martyrdom 191, 194, 213, 226–7,
   230, 246–7
Marx, K. 169
matter 36–7, 53, 70, 74, 78–80, 82, 86–7,
   104, 111–14, 116, 120
Maybaum, I. 192, 206
Mendelssohn, M. 146–57, 163, 175–7, 202
miracles 112, 147, 149, 158, 212
monotheism 47, 158, 160, 162
Moses 47, 79, 85, 91, 174
Mu'tazilites 49–50, 52, 61–2, 72, 78

nature: laws of 36, 39–44, 51, 70–2, 78,
   82–5, 91–2, 96–7, 99–100, 104, 112–14,
   131–2, 135, 138–41, 148, 154, 175

Netherlands: Jewish life in the 121–2
New Thinking, the 181
Nozick, R. 56

passivity 123–5, 127, 138, 188, 209, 212
Philo 33–47, 122, 220
philosophy: Greek 30, 33–4, 48
  Peripatetic in Arabic 48, 51
  Jewish 1–10, 12–13, 27–32, 44, 47, 63–5, 67, 69–70, 99, 102, 139, 156, 165, 177, 185, 200–1, 202, 220, 249–50
Platonism 34, 36, 45–6, 51
plenitude 70, 139
poverty 75, 158, 161, 163, 235
power 2, 20–2, 24–6, 35, 37, 41, 43, 54, 58, 61, 73, 78, 80–2, 105, 114, 118–19, 127, 139–40, 144, 149, 168, 180, 182, 194–5, 203, 222–3, 229, 240–1, 250
praxis 183
prayer and worship 10, 28, 43, 76, 84–5, 106, 158, 176, 186–7, 190, 203, 205, 208, 223, 244–5
prophecy, prophets 8, 49, 52, 59, 85, 107, 138–9, 158–9, 181, 183, 221–2
Provence, Jewish life in 102–3
providence 15, 17–18, 29, 37–46, 52, 71–4, 76–91, 96–9, 101, 104–9, 111–16, 132–3, 135, 145, 147, 149–51, 152–6, 160, 175, 188, 192, 236, 240, 243–4, 246–7
punishment, and God 11, 20–1, 23, 26, 36–8, 50–1, 53, 56–9, 73, 75, 77, 80–1, 83, 85, 91–2, 97, 99, 105, 107–8, 110, 114, 129, 134–6, 151–2, 154, 158–60, 186, 188, 196, 204–7, 221–3, 248
  and schools 25–6
purity of heart 172

ratio 132
rationality, *see* reason
reason 7–8, 12, 16, 33–5, 38, 40, 43, 48–9, 51, 55, 58, 61, 66, 71, 75, 77–9, 87, 90–2, 104–5, 107–9, 111, 122, 125–6, 136, 139–41, 146, 149–53, 155–9, 163, 165, 176, 192, 212, 243–5, 247
redemption 1, 158–60, 162, 170–1, 209–11, 213, 221–2, 228, 231, 233
regret 57, 138, 140–4

repentance 22, 24, 36, 56–7, 141–4, 159, 162, 170
revelation 26, 35, 49, 66, 139, 153, 157, 165, 172, 176–7, 179, 181, 189
reward 11, 17, 20–1, 23, 27–8, 36, 38, 43, 50–1, 53, 55–8, 73–5, 77, 80–1, 85, 91–2, 97, 106, 110, 129, 132–6, 151–2, 154, 172, 205, 221, 223–4, 233, 236, 246, 248
Rosenzweig, F. 13, 165, 175–6, 178, 180–1, 220
Rubenstein, R. 186–8, 203–5

Saadya 48–63, 77–9
sadness 127, 137
salvation 122, 141, 159, 170–1, 195
Satan 26, 28, 89
scientia intuitiva 132
sin 19–22, 24–5, 50, 54–5, 60, 77, 105–8, 129, 154, 158–61, 169–70, 173, 186, 188, 192, 209, 221–2
soul 36–7, 88, 129, 131–2
Spain: Islamic 64–5
  Jewish life in 64–6
Spinoza, B. 34, 121–46, 150–1, 171, 174
Spinozism 50–2
stoicism 38–9, 42, 122, 138
sub specie aeternitatis 106, 114, 128, 131, 140, 143, 145, 229
sub specie boni 128, 143

Tautology, Great 174–83
tikkun 188, 207
tremendum 189, 207, 219

van Blijenbergh, W. 129, 133
via negativa 141, 174, 183

wickedness 20–1, 40, 56–7, 59, 76–7, 91, 104, 106–9, 129, 133–4, 169, 172–4, 198
Wiesel, E. 185–6, 194–5, 208–15, 231
will, God's 51, 55, 85, 187–8
wisdom, God's 15, 53, 72, 76, 103, 113, 152, 194
Wolfson, H. 34

Zionism 158, 189, 207, 225
Zophar 19–21, 23, 106
Zuckerman, B. 235–6

Printed in the United States
86317LV00004B/301-348/A